The Complete

ROSARIAN

6

1 821502

The Complete
ROSARIAN

*The development, cultivation and
reproduction of roses*

NORMAN YOUNG

edited by

L. A. WYATT

HODDER AND STOUGHTON
LONDON SYDNEY AUCKLAND TORONTO

Author's Preface

This is not a manual of instruction on How to Grow Roses. It is simply a book about roses. I should have liked to adopt that phrase as the title of my book, if it had not already been pre-empted by that great rose-lover, Dean Reynolds Hole. For the beginner who stands in need of elementary instruction, most of the catalogues issued by our leading professional rose growers contain brief notes comprising all that it is necessary to know—which is little enough, in all conscience. Growing roses is not a difficult task, but the simplest and most delightful of hobbies.

This book is intended primarily for those who already grow roses, who know roses, or who love roses, whether they grow them or not. It contains a great deal of information which is not in the least necessary, but which will, I hope, prove interesting. At the same time I have not forgotten the needs of the beginner, who will find nothing here which is beyond his grasp. In dealing with the technicalities of cultivation I have kept as far as possible to first principles, so that the reader may not only know what he ought to do, but why he should do it; so that he may be in a position to assess any advice he is given, and judge for himself whether it is sound. He will receive any amount of advice; rose growers, both professional and amateur, are among the the most kind and friendly of people; and he must not be either surprised or alarmed if much of it is contradictory. The rose is a very accommodating plant, and will grow and flourish in the widest range of conditions of soil, climate and treatment. Paul may plant, and Apollos water; but God alone giveth the increase.

It has been said, and with some degree of truth, that the literature of the rose comprises seventy-five per cent folklore, twenty per cent personal prejudice, and five per cent fact. That this book contains its fair share of prejudice I will not attempt to deny; I only hope that I may have succeeded in my endeavour to increase the proportion of fact.

Editor's Note

Over many years, Wing-Commander Norman Young contributed numerous articles and papers to specialist rose publications in Britain and abroad. His abilities as a historian, classical scholar, linguist and botanist were evident in all he wrote publicly and privately, coupled with a powerful style and an astringent wit.

An enquiring and severely practical mind with an insistence upon accuracy and honesty, he neither suffered fools gladly nor tolerated humbug. His writing was consequently often provocative and always original. The unconventional he applauded and the unorthodox was defended, invariably with an array of facts marshalled in a masterly manner—his evidence to the Committee on Plant Varieties and Seeds Rights (plant patents) was admirable in its presentation.

In his natural modesty, he never professed to be an authority on roses. He was, however, invited to serve as the European representative on the Revision Committee for the fifth (1958) edition of *Modern Roses*, the standard work of reference on rose nomenclature, and he was frequently consulted by rosarians in many parts of the world.

Norman Young died suddenly in September 1967, leaving the typescript of a book which he had completed some time previously. In it, he set down the results of many years' "ferreting" (as he preferred to term his researches) and the distillation of his wealth of knowledge on all aspects of roses. This, the most fascinating and popular of all plant genera, has attracted more literature than any other so that it has become increasingly difficult to add anything that is both new and true. Norman Young accepted that challenge and succeeded. Apart from meeting the due requirements of textual length and making such amendments as were dictated in the light of more recent developments, the following pages remain substantially as they were written. They stand as a worthy memorial to their author.   L. A. WYATT

Acknowledgments

One of the pleasantest parts of the task of writing a book comes at the end
—though it is customarily printed at the beginning; this is the rendering
of thanks to all those to whom thanks are due.

First, then, let me offer my heartfelt gratitude to my two tireless
correspondents, Mr. C. H. R. Morris, of Cardiff, and Mr. L. A. Wyatt,
of Teddington, whose information, criticism and advice has been a never-
failing source of pleasure and profit to me over many years. With theirs
should be coupled the name of Mr. Bertram Park, who has generously
placed various items of personal information at my disposal.

Next I must record my indebtedness to the officials of various learned
societies and institutions; to Lancaster Herald, of the College of Arms; to
the Directors of the Botanic Gardens at Kew, Dublin and Cambridge, and
of the Austrian National Library at Vienna and the Municipal Library of
Provins; to Dr. John Chadwick of Downing College, Cambridge; to Mr.
G. D. Rowley, formerly Keeper of the National Rose Species Collection
at Bayfordbury; to Miss Anne Wylie, of the University of Otago, New
Zealand, formerly of Manchester University; to Dr. Fred J. Nisbet,
formerly editor of the *American Rose Annual*; to the late Mr. H. Edland,
Secretary of our own Royal National Rose Society; to the authorities of
the Lindley Library of the Royal Horticultural Society; to Mr. Aubrey de
Sélincourt, the learned translator of the Penguin *Herodotus*; to Dr.
Dennison Morey, President of General Bionomics Inc., of Santa Rosa,
California; together with my apologies for any inadvertent omissions.

Finally, and collectively, I must thank all those, from Theophrastus to
Mr. Gordon Edwards, who have written about roses and added to my
knowledge of the subject.

NORMAN YOUNG

Contents

List of Illustrations

Figures in the Text

Part One

HISTORICAL

the word so translated is known today to stand for some sort of bulbous plant, which has been variously identified as a narcissus and an autumn crocus. If there is any mention of rose growing in the early history of India or China, it has escaped the notice of my predecessors, and I have been no more fortunate. The great Mesopotamian civilisation which has been traced back for more than five thousand years has yielded nothing more suggestive than some early jewellery and architectural ornaments whose forms are obviously based on leaves and flowers, but not recognisable ones. In ancient Egypt the rose seems to have been unknown—though Egypt has left us a record of the earliest known botanist and plant-hunter. In about the year 1450 B.C., King Thutmose III conducted a successful campaign into Syria and brought back as part of his spoils of war a collection of two hundred and seventy-five different plants. He recorded the fact with great pride in a bas-relief at Karnak which contains illustrations of every one of the plants, together with a hieroglyphic inscription conveying the King's personal assurance that the representations are all true to life—an assurance which modern botanists find it difficult to accept. That such a collection must have included roses seems certain, but as I have not myself seen the inscription and have been unable to find a detailed description of it, I cannot affirm or deny this. If roses there were they must have died out fairly quickly, as no trace of them can be found until over a thousand years later, when the Egyptian civilisation had been overlaid by the Greek.

Civilisation seems to have had its beginnings in what is known as the "fertile crescent", which stretches from Egypt, through Palestine, Syria and Iraq to Persia and western Pakistan. But some four thousand years ago, it began to spread, creeping westward along the Mediterranean basin. Its first European flowering was in the island of Crete, where, at about the same time that Pharaoh Thutmose was combining the practice of war with botany, the Minoans—named after their legendary King Minos—were living in conditions not strikingly different from those in this country under the Tudors; but with one very important exception. Writing they knew, but they had no literature; and as their language still defies all attempts at interpretation, the comparatively few inscriptions of theirs which have come down to us add nothing to our knowledge of them. On the other hand, the plastic arts flourished; and in one of the great painted murals which decorated the palace of Knossos—where Theseus met Ariadne and slew the Minotaur—we may see the representation of a flower which is undoubtedly meant for a rose. Its general character is unmistakable; but if it is an accurate portrait, it is a portrait of a species of rose unknown at the present day. It has a single flower, with six petals of an orange colour, and its leaves have only three leaflets. In all probability it is just a bit of artistic licence, since the flower has no important function in the composition, of which it is no more than a decorative detail. But there it is—a painting of a rose, perhaps three thousand five hundred years old.

To the north, on the mainland of what is now Greece, a different people held sway. They were not the Greeks of ancient history, but an earlier race who are known to us as the Mycenaeans, from the town of Mycenae, their chief centre. Their civilisation was not so highly developed as that of the Minoans—to whom, indeed, they were at one time bound to pay an annual tribute of youths and maidens, as we read in the story of Theseus. They, like their overlords of Crete, knew the art of writing, but like them too they employed it solely for "official purposes", mainly for the keeping of accounts. But thanks to an astonishing *tour de force* by the late Michael Ventris, their writings can be read, and their language—which bore much the same relation to classical Greek as Anglo-Saxon does to present-day English—can be understood. The earliest specimens of this Linear B script were found on tablets in Crete, which was apparently conquered by the Mycenaeans in about 1400 B.C., but from our point of view the most important find was the hoard of tablets which came to light in the palace of Nestor at Pylos, in the Peloponnese. These, which date from about 1200 B.C., are the "vouchers" recording transactions in and out of the royal oil stores; and no less than six of them make mention of "rose-scented oil". For example, tablet No. Fr 1223 reads:

> To Ti-no, oil, sage-scented, for anointing . . . LM 2.
> Also rose-scented, for anointing . . . LM 2.

The letters LM stand for some measure of capacity which is not precisely known, but which seems to have been about two and a half gallons.[1]

In about 1200 B.C. the palace of Nestor was overthrown and burnt, and the heat of its burning baked the clay tablets into brick, so allowing them to survive to bear witness to later ages. But it was not until some four hundred years later, when the Linear B script was replaced by the Phoenician alphabet (the Linear B symbols were not an alphabet as we

[1] I have to thank Dr. Chadwick of Cambridge, who collaborated with Ventris in the work of decipherment, for his kindness in furnishing me with these particulars.

know it; each sign represented a syllable) that the greater flexibility of this system of writing ushered in an age of literature. The old tales of the doings of gods and heroes, handed down by word of mouth from generation to generation, were finally reduced to writing, and the *Iliad* and the *Odyssey* came into being in the form in which we know them. And in Book XXIII of the *Iliad* we may read how Aphrodite anointed the body of the dead Hector with rose-scented oil. Thereafter the mention of rose oil becomes a commonplace. It was widely used as an adjunct to the toilet, and remained so for two thousand years. We know how the oil was produced, by steeping rose petals in oil of sesame, olives or almonds—a simple process, calling for no great technical skill; but to produce it in quantities measurable in gallons did call for large quantities of rose petals, far larger than could be gathered from the single flowers of wild roses growing by the wayside. One thing is certain: that the Greeks of Homer's day, and the Mycenaeans before them, must have cultivated roses for the purpose, and double roses at that. What sort of roses they were we have no means of telling.

Sappho, the Greek poetess who lived about 600 B.C., seems to have been the first to celebrate the rose in verse, and it was she who first bestowed on it the title of Queen of Flowers. But her works have almost totally disappeared, and we are dependent upon quotations in later writers for our knowledge of them. In the poetry of her successors, Anacreon, Lycophron, Bion, Nicander, Theocritus, roses play much the same part as they do in the works of our own lyric poets; but the Greeks tell us no more about the flowers themselves than that some were white and some were red, and that their fragrance was greatly esteemed.

A hundred and fifty years after Sappho we come to the historian Herodotus, who gives us the earliest description of a particular rose. In his account of Perdiccas of Macedon he tells how he and his two brothers escaped from the king of Lebaea, who was seeking to kill them, and then "settled near the place called the Gardens of Midas, where roses with sixty petals, and sweeter smelling than any others in the world, grow wild". The roses have nothing to do with the story he is telling; this is simply one of the chatty "asides" with which Herodotus was wont to interlard his discourse. Although this is, in fact, the first written record we have of the existence of double roses, Herodotus, who was a much-travelled and observant man, must have been perfectly familiar with them in cultivation. It is clear that what made him take note of these particular specimens was their exceptional quality and the fact that they grew wild. Dr. C. C. Hurst's suggestion that they were damask roses which had been imported into Macedonia by Midas from his native Phrygia, which was in Asia Minor, cannot possibly be taken seriously. The description is obviously insufficient to allow of any identification of the roses. The Midas of legend was a myth; and "the gardens of Midas" was no more than a nickname, perhaps inspired by the richness of the roses which grew there, but more probably, one would think, from the prevalence of golden-yellow flowers— perhaps buttercups.

After Herodotus—about another hundred and fifty years after, towards the end of the fourth century B.C.—we come to Theophrastus, the favourite pupil and successor of Aristotle, who has, rather unfairly, been styled the Father of Botany. I say unfairly because it is tolerably certain that much of his botanical knowledge was derived from his great predecessor; moreover, he was not specifically a botanist but like his master took all knowledge for his province; but his *Enquiry into Plants* is one of the few works of his which survive. His account of the rose is worth quoting in its entirety:

> Among roses, there are many differences, in the number of petals, in rough-
> ness, in beauty of colour, and in sweetness of scent. Most have five petals, but
> some have twelve or twenty, and some a great many more than these; for there
> are some, they say, which are even called "hundred-petalled". Most of such
> roses grow near Philippi; for the people of that place get them on Mt.
> Pangaeus, where they are abundant, and plant them. However, the inner
> petals are very small (the way in which they are produced being such that some
> are outside, some inside). Some kinds are not fragrant, nor of large size. Among
> those which have large flowers those in which the part below the flower is
> rough are the more fragrant. In general, as has been said, good colour and scent
> depend upon locality; for even bushes which are growing in the same soil show
> some variation in the presence or absence of a sweet scent. Sweetest scented of
> all are the roses of Cyrene, wherefore the perfume made from these is the
> sweetest. (Indeed, it may be said generally that the scents of the gilliflowers
> also, and of the other flowers of that place, are the purest, and especially the
> scent of the saffron crocus, a plant which seems to vary in this respect more
> than any other.) Roses can be grown from seed, which is to be found below
> the flower in the "apple", and it is like that of safflower or pine-thistle, but
> it has a sort of fluff, so that it is not unlike the seeds that have a pappus. As
> however the plant comes slowly from seed, they make cuttings of the stem, as
> has been said, and plant them. If the bush is burnt or cut over, it bears better
> flowers; for if left to itself, it grows luxuriantly and makes too much wood.

Also it has to be often transplanted; for then, they say, the roses are improved. The wild kinds are rougher, both in stem and leaf, and have also smaller flowers of a duller colour.

The rose comes last of these [mountain flowers] and is the first of the spring flowers to come to an end, for its time of blooming is short.

A rose-bush lives five years, after which its prime is past, unless it is pruned by burning; with this plant too the flowers become inferior as it ages. Position and a suitable climate contribute most to the fragrance of roses, gilliflowers and other flowers. Thus in Egypt, while all other flowers and sweet herbs are scentless, the myrtles are marvellously fragrant. In that country it is said that the roses, gilliflowers and other flowers are as much as two months ahead of those in our country, and also that they last a longer, or at least not a shorter, time than those of our country. And, as has been said, the particular season according to its character, makes a great difference to the fragrance, not only by reason of rains and droughts, but also according as rain, wind, and in general the changes of climate occur or do not occur at the fitting moment. Also it appears that in general roses, gilliflowers and the rest bloom well on the mountains, but many of them have there an inferior scent.

There is little in this account that one can criticise in the light of modern knowledge; indeed, it probably contains as much factual and useful information as one would find in the same number of words in a modern book. In his remarks about the variability of scent he is ahead of most modern writers, who usually rest content with affirming or denying that such and such a rose is fragrant, forgetting those possibilities of variation that were clearly recognised over two thousand years ago. Elsewhere in his treatise Theophrastus mentions both grafting and budding as means of propagation, so that there was little, apart from the practice and possibilities of hybridising, that he was not familiar with. It is plain from his remarks that there were no perpetual flowering roses in ancient Greece. This is confirmed by another passage in the *Enquiry into Plants*, where Theophrastus says: "If there is a late Autumn, we might expect even roses and other similar plants to come out, just as is said to have happened near Dium in Macedonia." (The same thing happened in my own garden in the autumn of 1960, when *R. gallica* flowered again in September, and *R. spinosissima lutea* in November!)

Theophrastus makes no mention here of the pests and diseases to which roses are subject. In all probability the practice of burning the plants to the ground every few years contributed greatly to garden hygiene and kept most of them in check. But we know that the Greeks were not entirely free from them; the word *thrips* has come down to us unchanged through two thousand years.

Curiously enough, the *Enquiry into Plants* was not only the first botanical work to appear, it was also the last for many hundreds of years—with the exception of Pliny's *Natural History*, which was largely based on Theophrastus. This was owing to the rise of the art of medicine, which switched attention from plants as objects of study in themselves to plants as curative herbs. At the end of the second century B.C., one Crataevas, physician to King Mithridates of Pontus, produced a *Herbal* which has not survived, but which we know on the testimony of Pliny to have been copiously illustrated with paintings. We know, too, that much of this work was incorporated in the *Materia Medica* of Dioscorides, which was written in the first century A.D. and remained the standard textbook on the medicinal properties of plants for about fifteen hundred years. There is reason to believe, too, that Dioscorides also adopted the paintings of Crataevas to illustrate his own work. These paintings were copied from one manuscript to another down to the fifteenth century; with the arrival of printing as a means of reproduction, they formed the basis of the woodcuts used to illustrate the first printed herbals. The *Grete Herball* of 1525 has a woodcut of *The Rose* which plainly derives from the painting in the earliest manuscript of Dioscorides which survives, dating from early in the sixth century; but this particular illustration does not seem to be one of those copied from the work of the painter-physician of Pontus. Unhappily, as I have said, these physicians were not interested in the various garden varieties of roses, and the single illustration is so conventionalised that identification is out of the question.

Another early picture deserves mention here, and that is the representation of a rose which appeared on the early coins of the island of Rhodes. I must confess that I have never seen one; so many experts in that field have already decided that the flower in question is not a rose at all but a pomegranate flower that it is plain that there is no hope of gaining useful information from this source. Rhodes, by the way, was not the only place to take its name from the rose. (The Greek for a rose is *rhodon*.) The town of Rosas in Spain was originally called Rhodopolis—"Rose City"—when it was founded by Greek colonists. Nor was the Battle of Minden, whose memory is still celebrated today by the wearing of roses by men of those regiments which took part, the only engagement to be celebrated in this way. At Minden the troops passed through a rose garden on their way to the battle, and stuck the flowers in their caps and button-holes as they passed. In the year 202 B.C. when Scipio Africanus defeated the Carthaginians at the battle of Zama, he decreed that the men of the VIIIth Legion, who were the first to break the enemy's line, should carry roses in their hands at the subsequent triumph, and bear the image of a rose on their shields forever after. (One Lucius Fluvius, a Roman banker, who was so ill-advised as to wear a wreath of roses in public at the celebrations, was promptly arrested and held in gaol for the rest of the war for usurping the soldiers' privileges.) Much well-intentioned effort has been wasted in the attempt to identify the original "rose of Minden"; since the battle was fought in August the choice should not be wide, but the researchers overlook the fact that a garden big enough to furnish decoration to an army was likely to contain many different kinds of roses. But I have jumped too far ahead, and must go back to classical times.

Caius Plinius Secundus, "Pliny the Elder", was not a botanist, or even a creative philosopher in the Greek sense. He was a man of varied talents; the intimate friend of Vespasian, he had served his Emperor both by land and sea; at the time of his death he was admiral of a fleet of ships, and in true naval tradition he lost his life in going ashore to help the refugees fleeing from the eruption of Vesuvius which destroyed Pompeii and Herculaneum in A.D. 79. His *Natural History*, if not a great original work, was at least a monumental compilation. For his knowledge of plants he was largely indebted to Theophrastus, but he added a good deal of information culled from other sources as well. But we still cannot place a finger on a single one of his roses and identify it with certainty.

When reading the old accounts one has always to bear in mind that the ancients had no conception of plant species as we understand them today. They regarded plants as a sort of extension or exhalation of the soil that they grew in; the nature of the soil not only determined the health and vigour of the plant, but to a large extent its very form also. Thus Pliny could say that the soil of Philippi was incapable of producing hundred-petalled roses, though they flourished in it when transplanted there. Hence, too, the practice of describing roses by the names of the places where they grew; they were regarded as a natural manifestation of the soil of the place. It was an unfortunate practice for us, since it is inevitably ambiguous. We can never be sure whether the "Rose of Cyrene", for instance, means a particular sort of rose which could only be produced by the soil of Cyrene, or whether it means any sort of rose which happens to be grown at

Cyrene. Even in one particular soil the forms of plants were not regarded as permanent; as late as the thirteenth century Albertus Magnus could cheerfully say that if you cut down an oak wood the trees would grow again in the form of poplars.

Pliny referred to the forcing of roses by heat. The practice seems to have been widespread in his day; his contemporary Seneca—the brother of that Gallio who "cared for none of these things"—disapproved of the practice as contrary to Nature. Not many years later, Martial sneered at the Egyptians for sending roses to Rome in winter when the Romans were perfectly capable of raising their own winter roses. We do not know who invented it or when it began, but there are some grounds for believing that it was first—or most extensively—adopted at Paestum, a town on the borders of the rose-growing district of Campania. Paestum was evidently an important rose-growing centre. A century before Pliny, both Horace and Ovid mentioned the roses of Paestum, Horace suggesting that they came originally from Persia. And that the merchants of Paestum dealt in forced roses we may gather from the poet Virgil (who died in 19 B.C.) who referred to *biferi rosaria Paesti*[1]—literally, "the rose gardens of twice-bearing Paestum". "Twice-bearing" here is obviously a transferred epithet, which really refers to the rose gardens and not to the town; but the commentator Servius, in the fifth century, thought it sufficiently ambiguous to warrant the gloss: "Paestum, a city of Calabria where roses blow twice in a year." The fact that Virgil thought it worthy of mention perhaps suggests that the practice was new in his day.

In Rome under the Caesars the love of roses developed into a positive mania. The feast of the "Rosalia", celebrated in Rome on the 23rd of

---

[1] It is this passage which has given rise to the legend of the perpetual-flowering Rose of Paestum which has been current for so long. It is very doubtful if any such rose ever existed. If it did, we have to account for the fact that a rose with such desirable qualities was well-known in the first century B.C., quite unknown to the great natural historian of the first century A.D., familiar again to the obscure writer Servius in the fifteen century, and then disappeared once more until it reappeared in the form of the Autumn Damask in the seventeenth century. It may be significant that neither Virgil nor Servius states specifically that "the Rose of Paestum" flowers twice; they only say that roses flower twice at Paestum. Morus Cambrensis suggests that Virgil's "*bifer*" may mean no more than "bearing two-fold", i.e., "plenteously", which is eminently reasonable. But since we know for a fact that in Imperial Rome the rose gardens *were* capable of yielding two successive crops of flowers, one forced and one natural, we are under no obligation to fall back on this interpretation.

May in each year, was no doubt observed with "all the accessories of a high-class profligacy", to quote a strictly non-classical writer; but roses were not only honoured—or dishonoured—on one day of the year. The Roman powdered his body after the bath with dried rose petals, and anointed himself with rose oil; he reclined on a couch strewn with rose petals to drink rose-flavoured wine, with a garland of roses on his brow, and a rose suspended from the ceiling to show that all that passed was *sub rosa*—"under the rose", and off the record. (Julius Caesar was accused of introducing the fashion for rose garlands as headwear in order to hide his premature baldness.)

The custom of hanging a rose from the ceiling was said to commemorate the gift of a rose by Cupid to Harpocrates, the God of Silence, in return for a promise that nothing should become known of some misconduct by his mother Venus. I have forgotten (if I ever knew; perhaps Harpocrates kept his promise) what the particular trouble was, but judging from the normal goings-on on Olympus it must have been something particularly flagitious if it was thought worth hushing up. The Emperor Nero was held up to contempt for spending four million sesterces (perhaps £150,000 of our money today) on roses for a single banquet; but it must be admitted that in the late Mr. Vanderbilt, who spent $50,000 for roses to decorate a ballroom in 1885, he had a very promising pupil. But the Emperor Heliogabalus, or Elagabalus, set an all-time high in this direction by showering so many rose petals on his guests at an entertainment that several of them died from suffocation. On the other hand, roses could also be associated with shrinking modesty. When Nero announced his determination to see the famous beauty Poppaea, a respectable married woman—well, a married woman, anyway—in her bath, she defeated his lewd designs by floating quantities of rose petals on the surface of the water. However, as she shortly after became his mistress, and he eventually killed her by kicking her in the stomach, the Emperor may be said to have had the last laugh.

But the rose was not exclusively associated with junketing and debauchery. It was also the favourite flower for strewing on the graves of the dead. Many ancient tomb inscriptions have survived ,which record how the occupant built the tomb for himself in his lifetime and bequeathed a sum of money or a plot of land—it might be an actual rose garden—to some institution on condition that the tomb should be regularly strewn with roses in perpetuity. And under the Romans as well as the Greeks roses were used for the preparation of medicines to ward off death.

Chapter Two

INTERLUDE ON CLASSIFICATION: SPECIES

The herb yielding seed, and the fruit tree yielding fruit, after his kind . . .

Genesis 1:11

The systematic classification of the vegetable kingdom was first achieved in the middle of the eighteenth century by the great Swedish naturalist Carl von Linné—better known, perhaps, under the latinised form of his name, Linnaeus. We need not trouble ourselves with the details of his system, which was fundamentally the same as that in use today; it is enough to note that he divided the whole kingdom into a dozen or so main divisions, of which one comprised all the flowering plants, and that these divisions were subdivided and then divided again, so as to produce, as one proceeds downwards from the top, an arrangement of groups at successive levels, the groups at any one level being more numerous, but smaller in content, than those at the previous level. Let us confine our attention to the last three levels.

The first of these, reckoning downwards, consists of a number of fairly large groups which are known as families; and the family that we are concerned with bears the Latin name of the *Rosaceae*—the "Rose-like plants". This is a specially important family from the economic standpoint, since it contains beside the roses themselves a large proportion of our ordinary fruits: apples, pears, plums, cherries, peaches, almonds, strawberries, blackberries and raspberries are all members of the family *Rosaceae*. At the next lower level the families are divided into smaller groups, each of which is called a genus (plural, genera). Each genus does not necessarily correspond with a sort of plants which we normally lump together under the same name; for instance, both Blackberries and Raspberries fall into the same genus, *Rubus*. However, this is not the case with the genus *Rosa*, which includes all those and only those plants which we call roses; those which have obviously usurped the name, like the Rock Roses, Christmas Roses, etc., which no-one supposes to be true roses, are of course excluded.

The genera are further divided into the last and lowest category, the species. In theory, all the members of a species are alike, so that no further subdivision is possible. In practice, no two plants that ever grew were exactly alike in every possible respect, so that the taxonomists (as those who deal in classification are called) have to decide what particular characteristics must be taken into account in determining a species, and what characteristics may be ignored.

Each of the species has a botanical name consisting of two words, of which the first is always *Rosa*. This is part of the Linnean system. Every species has a "binomial" or name of two words, of which the first is a Latin noun—being in fact the name of the genus to which it belongs—and the second a Latin adjective, called the "specific epithet", which serves to distinguish the separate species within the genus. Many of these specific epithets are descriptive; *arvensis*, for example, means "of the fields", and *spinosissima* means "most spiny". The name of the Dog Rose has come down to us from the earliest times; it does not, as in the case of the Dog Violet, imply that it is an inferior kind, which it certainly is not, but its true implication is not known with any certainty. In ancient Greece and Rome it was believed that the roots of the Dog Rose were a specific against the bite of a mad dog, but it is just as likely that the belief arose from the name as that the name was given on account of the belief—which is quite mistaken, alas. The epithet *eglanteria* reminds us of the old name "Eglantine" by which the Sweet Brier was known in Shakespeare's day. However, it is obvious that a single word cannot possibly convey enough meaning to distinguish one species from all others—many other species beside *arvensis* grow in fields, and *spinosissima* is not the only rose to possess a multitude of spines—so that in course of time the specific epithet has become a purely arbitrary label, whose actual meaning, if any, may well be misleading; *Rosa damascena*, for example, does not come from Damascus, and *Rosa praelucens* certainly does not, as its name would imply, "shed light upon" anything, except perhaps the queer state of mind of its sponsor. Of more recent years it has become the general habit to manufacture specific epithets out of the names of the discoverers of a new species, or of someone it is desired to honour; hence, for example, the meaningless and unpronounceable *Rosa ecae*, whose name is dervied from E. C. A., the initials of the discoverer's wife. But it doesn't matter, so long as the name is universally recognised.

It has not infrequently happened that the same species has been discovered independently by two different men in different places and at different times, and that they have proceeded to give it two different names. This is an awkward state of affairs, which clearly calls for some action by the international conferences on nomenclature which are convened from time to time. Unfortunately, the rule which at present governs such questions seems to be in many ways the worst that could have been adopted. This is, that the name which was first validly published (we need not bother about what constitutes "valid publication") shall be adopted and all others be rejected. It is not merely that this means, as a great modern authority has pointed out, that we are forced to accept the description of the species given by the man who knew less about it than anyone; nor does it greatly matter that this rule sometimes demands the rejection of a good name in favour of a bad one, as for instance in the case of the Austrian Brier, which for many years was known indifferently as *Rosa foetida* and *Rosa lutea*, of which the first name is now the only approved one, although this lovely rose is *not* fetid (*foetida*) and *is* yellow (*lutea*). But the most serious effect of this rule is to deprive every species name of permanency, since no man can say when a previously unknown "valid publication" may come to light. However, there it is, and we are stuck with it, at least until the next international conference. Superfluous names which are rejected under this or some other rule are known as "synonyms", which gives rise to the paradox that in the botanical world, A can be a synonym of B although B is not a synonym of A—a state of affairs which would astonish the student of philology.

It must be borne in mind that this business of sorting out the roses and putting them into pigeonholes labelled "species" is an arbitrary affair; man-made, for man's own convenience. True, it is based on real differences which are found in nature, but it is the taxonomist who decides which differences to take into account and which to ignore. Hence there has arisen the long-drawn-out war between the Lumpers and the Splitters. The Splitters (according to the Lumpers) are those fussy pedants who grasp at every opportunity to divide up recognised species into two or more new ones, on the basis of trivial variations of no importance; the uncrowned king of the Splitters must surely have been that botanist—was it Wolley-Dod?—who claimed to recognise over a hundred different species among our native wild roses; so that (according to the Lumpers) it was often possible to find two or even three of his species growing on the same bush. The Lumpers (according to the Splitters) are those lazy and unobservant slovens who are content to lump together half a dozen clearly distinguished sorts into one species, just to save themselves trouble. All that the authority can do is to adopt what he considers a reasonable basis for a classification, and stick to it. At one time it was hoped that the question could be settled once for all by appeal to the laws of nature as revealed in the breeding habits of plants. If two plants could be crossed with the production of fertile offspring, it was argued, they must be of the same species; if they produced sterile offspring, they must be different species of the same genus; and if they refused to interbreed at all, they must belong to different genera. It would have been an admirable solution if it had been true, but alas, it wasn't. Cases are now known where plants of two different genera can not only be crossed successfully, but produce fertile offspring which have been crossed successfully with a third genus. Of course, in such an artificial business as this, it would always have been possible to revise our classification so that this rule *would* hold good, but this would have entailed such a radical revision of the present system that it simply would not be worth the trouble. It is really a very remarkable thing that the Linnean system, which was devised at a time when it was firmly believed that every single species had been created once for all on Tuesday, the 25th of October, 4004 B.C., should survive with so little alteration in an age when the evolution of species is universally accepted; when it is known that the whole living world is in a constant state of flux, old species dying out and new ones evolving to take their place.

The reader may well have noticed that so far I have only spoken of wild roses, and he may be forgiven if he falls into the common error of supposing that a "species rose" is the same thing as a wild rose. It usually is, but it is not necessarily so. Hybrids—that is, the offspring of a cross between roses of two different species—may appear in the wild; and such hybrids may display "hybrid vigour" (the technical term for it is *xenia*, in case you should come across it anywhere) and prove stronger in growth than either of their parents. But this hybrid vigour dies out in subsequent generations, and hybrids, however strong-growing they may be, are usually less effective as parents than the true species, if they are not actually sterile, so that such wild hybrids must often succumb to the competition of their more pure-bred competitors. If they do manage to survive, they will in course of time—a thousand years, or a million, who can say?—settle down and behave exactly like species, and may be legitimately counted as such. *R. foetida*, the Austrian Brier (it is an accepted convention that when one is discussing one genus only its name may be abbreviated to the initial letter when using the botanical names) is an example of a true wild species which is almost certainly of hybrid origin; *R. damascena* and *R. centifolia* are others, although in their cases the wild originals have been lost, if they ever existed, so that these two species are not wild roses in any sense today.

This brings us to the definition of a species, which was first propounded by the great English naturalist, John Ray, in 1686, before Linnaeus was born. He laid it down that a species comprised a group of plants whose offspring, when raised from seed, grew into plants exactly like their parents, within accepted limits of variation. As we say nowadays, a species breeds true from seed.

For the reasons that I have already mentioned it is not possible to say precisely how many different species there are in the genus *Rosa*. However, there are about 150 species over which the majority of modern authorities would not quarrel unduly; but at least two-thirds of these are of small interest or importance to the ordinary rose grower.

I said above that a species breeds true from seed "within accepted limits of variation". Down to the seventeenth century the only known method of obtaining new varieties of garden plants was by sowing seed in large quantities, picking out and cherishing any variety of special merit which appeared among the seedlings so raised.

Originally a variety was given a botanical name by adding a third Latin word to the specific name, preceded by the abbreviation *v.* or *var.* (for *varietas*=variety), thus: *R. spinosissima var. lutea*, the yellow variety of *R. spinosissima*. (In practice the *v.* or *var.* is often omitted.) Today, however, the Powers that Be have ruled that for all "cultivars" (a horrid word, intended to denote varieties arising in cultivation as distinct from those that arise in the wild—a distinction without a difference) shall be given varietal names in a vernacular language and not in Latin or anything resembling it; they have further decreed that the Latin part of the name shall be printed in italics and the vernacular part in roman type, distinguished by single inverted commas, thus: *R. moyesii* 'Geranium'. They have also ruled that the specific epithet shall always be spelled with a small initial letter, whether or not it is derived from a proper name. The colour of the ink to be used, and the quality of the paper are still left to the discretion of the printer. Seriously though, this sort of pedantry does no good and only brings the authorities into ridicule; however, few have read the latest edition of the code, fewer have understood it, and fewer still take any notice of it.

Unhappily, although the current code of nomenclature is so overscrupulous in attention to trivial and unnecessary details, it is deplorably lax in some other respects. In particular, it permits the giving of specific names to known hybrids "when it seems necessary or useful", whatever that may imply, merely demanding that such names must be distinguished by the addition of the sign " × " in front of the specific epithet, thus *Rosa × borboniana*, the Bourbon Roses. This strikes at the root of the whole species concept, which is based on the assumption that all members of one species are alike. Where a group of roses, such as *R. alba*, does breed true and display all the other hall-marks of a species, it would be quite wrong to distinguish it by the hybrid mark " × ", merely because some taxonomists have speculated on its probable hybrid origin untold ages ago. It is a true species now, whatever it may have been in the distant past. On the other hand, where a rose is known to be a hybrid, being the result of a cross between two known species at a comparatively late date, it is ridiculous to give it a pseudo-specific name when it does not display the properties of a species. No doubt the devisers of the code would extricate themselves from this dilemma by saying that such cases as the latter are those in which it is not "necessary or useful" to bestow a specific name; from which we might conclude that the only cases in which it is necessary are those in which the rose's hybrid status is doubtful; that is, that a specific name should only include the sign denoting that it is a hybrid if there is a possibility that it is not. Lewis Carroll would have appreciated that reasoning.

Let me sum up briefly. All the roses in the world together constitute the genus *Rosa*, which comprises some 150 different groups known as species, together with many others which are hybrids, the result of inter-breeding between two species or more. What the gardener calls a "species rose" is a member of some particular species, and not a hybrid. All the members of one species are alike in possessing certain characteristics which, taken in conjunction, distinguish them from all other species. They all breed true from seed, so that their offspring are all alike in possessing the distinguishing characteristics of the species, a fact which enables a species to survive unchanged in the wild over many generations; which is not true of hybrids. Hence it follows that the great majority of species roses are, in fact, wild roses, and the great majority of wild roses are species roses, though there are known exceptions to both statements.

An important contributor to rose development, Rosa moschata, the **Musk Rose.** *European introduction* circa 1540. *Small* ($1\frac{1}{2}$–2 in.) *blooms in corymbs 7–9 per stem in creamy-white. Very sweet fragrance. Free flowering from August onwards. Slender growth from 8 to 12 ft. Somewhat tender, requiring protection of a wall. Western Asiatic origin, but widely distributed in Southern Europe and North Africa. Photograph: Max Stutz.*

The earliest known striped rose, Rosa gallica versicolor, syn. **Rosa Mundi.** *Occurred as a sport from* R. gallica officinalis, *The Apothecary's Rose, possibly between 1535 and 1581. Medium-sized (2–3 in.), semi-double blooms in small clusters of flesh-pink, splashed and striped with the bright carmine of the parent to which it has a tendency to revert. Good fragrance. Upright, well-branched shrub to 4 ft. with dark green, plentiful foliage and few thorns. Very free summer flowering, not recurrent. Remains one of the most spectacular of the parti-coloured roses.*

Chapter Three

THE AGE OF SPECIES

Wee hold none other flower in sic dainty
As the fresh rose, in colour red and white.
William Dunbar (1465?–1539?)

We do not know what roses the Romans found in cultivation in Britain when they arrived here; but if they found none we may be sure that they wasted no time before importing them. In their day, the rose was not only used for purposes of display or for the preparation of perfumes and ointments which could be imported ready-made; it was employed in medicinal plasters and eye-salves; a dusting-powder of dried rose petals was used after the bath; and it was extensively used as a flavouring agent. (It is even recorded that a Roman legion on active service once mutinied because the troops were issued with wine lacking the customary rose flavour.) The Roman soldier or administrator on colonial service would have felt it a hardship indeed to be deprived of his roses, and in this country at least there was no reason why he should lack them. Tacitus had some hard things to say of our climate, which he, like many others, thought too damp and foggy; but he admitted that the cold was not extreme, and that most plants flourished well in our soil, excepting only the olive and the vine.

We cannot identify the garden roses with any certainty before the end of the sixteenth century, by which time five main species had become established in cultivation; these were the White Rose, *R. alba*, the French Rose or (as it was then called) the Red Rose, *R. gallica*, the Cabbage Rose, *R. centifolia* (no connexion with the "Rosa centifolia" of Theophrastus), the Damask Rose, *R. damascena*, and the Musk Rose, *R. moschata*. The Cabbage,

C

Damask and Musk Roses were recognised as recent introductions; the Red and White Roses had been grown in Britain from time immemorial—an expression which, in Law, means not later than the 6th of July, 1189, but which for us goes back to Saxon times; and since neither of them is indigenous to these islands, it is reasonable to suppose that they were introduced by the Romans, if they were not here already.

The Romans departed from Britain at the beginning of the fifth century, yielding place to the Saxon and Danish invaders from over the North Sea. I do not know of any British rose records of this period—though the word "rose" itself has come down unchanged from Saxon times—but King Childebert I of the Franks (511–588) and his Queen Ultrogoth grew roses in the royal gardens, where the King did not disdain to graft them with his own hands. (The Franks were another German tribe, who chose to conquer Gaul instead of Britain.) Gregory of Tours tells us this; he also records that in the year 584, roses came into flower in January, which was considered a very bad omen; a superstition which still persisted in France fifty years ago, and perhaps persists at the present day, though the introduction of perpetual roses has greatly reduced the rarity of such an event.

In its earliest days, the Church had frowned on the rose, too closely associated with the worst pagan excesses; Clement of Alexandria expressly forbade the wearing of rose garlands by Christians. But only nine years after the death of Alban in about the year 303, the Emperor himself was converted and Christianity became the official religion of the Roman Empire, and the Church was enabled to set about its task of adapting the old pagan festivals and customs to its own beliefs—which included the adoption of the rose as a symbol of this, that and the other, as circumstances dictated. Down to the present day, I believe, a red rose is the accepted symbol of martyrdom in the Roman Church.

We need take no account of the Norman Conquest in this outline of rose history. It had little effect on the way of life of the common Englishman; little more than is caused by a change of government today. Some would have exchanged good overlords for bad, some the reverse, and the monks continued to grow their red and white roses, no matter who sat on the throne of England.

The two hundred years which followed the Conquest, however, saw a series of events which are commonly believed to have had an influence on our rose gardens. These were the Crusades—those aggressive wars waged by the Christians of Europe against the Muslims of the Levant, in painful contrast to the tolerance which the Muslims had previously extended to all religions, Buddhism, Christianity and Zoroastrianism, within their own empire, which at this time extended from India to Spain. It is frequently said that the Damask Rose takes its name from the city of Damascus—which is perfectly true—having been brought back from Damascus by a returning crusader—which is very doubtful indeed. It seems to be a fairly modern belief in this form; the only really old tradition that I have been able to find is that which relates how the Rose of Provins was brought back to France from the Holy Land by Thibaut VI. But unhappily the Rose of Provins, at the present day at least, is not a Damask but a Red Rose. The town of Provins, in Champagne, has been famed since the fourteenth century for its *conserve de roses*, which was originally made by the apothecaries, of which the town contained a great number. The rose grown for this purpose was a variety of *R. gallica*, called *R. gallica officinalis* or the Apothecary's Rose, also known today as the Rose de Provins. It is doubtful if this existing variety is identical with the original rose of Provins, since it cannot even be identified in the pages of Gerard or Parkinson, in the early seventeenth century; but there are good grounds for believing that the roses of Provins were always red, while the Damask is typically neither red nor white but a soft pink. Bartholomaeus Anglicus, "Bartholomew the Englishman", who was a professor of theology at Paris in about 1240, says that garden roses were of two sorts, red and white; Albertus Magnus, who expounded the doctrines of Aristotle in Paris and Cologne and died in 1280, recognised four sorts of roses, of which two, the "Tribulus" and the "Bedegard", had only five petals and grew wild (the latter was distinguished by the fragrance of its leaves and so can be identified as the Sweet Brier; the former may have been more than one other wild rose). Albertus seems to have been uncertain whether these two were really roses at all, though he noted the resemblance between their hips and those of the cultivated roses, which he too divided into two kinds, "Rosa alba", the white rose, and "Rosa rubra", the red rose. He knew nothing of any pink rose of Damascus. Finally we know that the Damask Rose was not introduced into England until the beginning of the sixteenth century, from Italy; while Mattioli, an Italian, speaks of it in 1544 as a comparatively new introduction.

While I am in the vein for debunking old wives' tales I might as well deal with two others which are often trotted out as facts, even today. The first is the legend that the striped form of the Rose de Provins, *R. gallica versicolor*, known as Rosa Mundi ("Rose of the World"), derived the latter name from its association with Fair Rosamund, the mistress of Henry II. The story goes that Henry installed the frail daughter of Walter de Clifford in a bower all set about with roses and surrounded by a maze; which did not prevent the jealous Queen Eleanor from finding her way in and offering the lady her choice of dagger or poison. The roses, of course, were all of the variety Rosa Mundi. Dr. Hurst even goes so far as to suggest that "an earlier Crusader found the striped form in a Syrian garden and on his return presented it to her, after giving it her name". Any school textbook would have told him that the Second Crusade ended in 1149, some years before Fair Rosamund was born, while the Third Crusade did not begin until 1189, twelve years after her death. It is true that in betweenwhiles there was always some traffic of pilgrims, would-be palmers and knights doing penance for their sins, travelling to—and, if they were lucky, from— Palestine. But they did not go to the Holy Land to pick flowers, and they would have been extremely ill-advised to offer surreptitious gifts to the King's so-jealously-guarded mistress. The first we hear of her is in the *Polychronicon* of Ranulf Higden, written nearly two hundred years later, and he makes no mention of any roses, striped or plain; later accounts seem to be mere imaginative embroidery on Higden's story. The only way a rose enters into her story is in the epitaph carved over her tomb in God-stow nunnery, which ran:

> *Hic jacet in tumba,*
> *Rosa mundi, non rosa munda.*
> *Non redolet, sed olet,*
> *Quae redolere solet.*

Which may be freely translated into English:

> A Rose lies here, within this tomb,
> More chased than chaste, methinks;
> She once exhaled a sweet perfume,
> But now, alas, she stinks!

As a matter of fact, her name was not Rosamund. As Dryden wrote:

> Jane Clifford was her name, as books aver;
> Fair Rosamund was but her *nom de guerre!*

In any case, the name Rosamund has no connexion with roses; it is derived from Teutonic roots and means "horse guard" or "protector of horses". And just to clinch the argument, we may read in *The Garden Book of Sir Thomas Hanmer*, written in 1659, that the variety Rosa Mundi was "first found in Norfolk a few years since upon a branch of the common Red Rose and from thence multiplied". L'Obel's description of 1581 could also be applied to this rose, but his statement is not so specific as Hanmer's.

The second baseless fable is the story that the Red or French Rose and the White Rose were the "originals" of the rose badges of the houses of Lancaster and York. If the badges had been chosen in the way described in the first part of *King Henry the Sixth* there might have been some excuse for this belief, but this famous scene is pure fiction. The white rose was adopted as a badge by the first Duke of York nearly fifty years before, and the red rose of Lancaster was a hundred years older still. The founder of the House of Lancaster was Edmund of Langley, called "Crouchback", the younger son of Henry III and Eleanor of Provence, who was born in 1245. His mother, one of the four famous daughters of Count Raymond of Provence, who all became queens, used a rose as her badge; probably a red rose, since according to Queen Elizabeth I it was derived from the rose in the crest of the noble Italian family of Orsino, which was red. Both her sons in due course adopted roses as badges, the elder, King Edward I, a gold rose, and the younger, Edmund first Earl of Lancaster, a red one. Edmund's great-grandson Henry was raised from the rank of Earl to Duke of Lancaster, but the male line expired with him; his only child, a daughter, Blanche of Lancaster, married John of Gaunt, who thus acquired the dukedom. John's younger brother Edmund, also curiously enough "of Langley", was created Duke of York by his father Edward III, and took a white rose for his badge. He was the grandfather of that Richard who features in the Temple Garden scene in *King Henry the Sixth*.

The first rose badge to be used by a sovereign of England was the gold, or yellow, rose of Edward I, although no yellow roses were in cultivation in Europe at the time. Those who insist that the roses of Lancaster and York must have been inspired by the red and white roses of the garden are invited to identify the originals of the rose badges of the families of Relongue, Macé de Gastines and Selmnitz, which were purple, blue and black respectively.

The expression "Wars of the Roses" was no more than a nickname which was first coined some twenty-five years after the conflict was over and the usurper Henry VII had (in defiance of the strict laws of heraldry) superimposed one rose on the other to make his own badge with ten petals. It is significant that in a letter written in March 1471 from one James Gresham to Sir John Paston, conveying the news of "false fleeting, perjur'd Clarence's" latest treachery, the writer says simply; "It is told me by the Under Sheriff, that my Lord of Clarence is gone to his brother, late King; insomuch as his men have the Gorget on their breasts, and the Rose over it." He doesn't trouble to mention the colour of the rose (the gorget was another of the badges used by Edward IV). Indeed, Edward's opponent in this campaign was not the poor, mad King Henry VI of the red rose, but Warwick the Kingmaker, whose badge was the "Ragged Staff".

The "identification" of the red rose of Lancaster with the Rose of Provins depends upon the word of one M. Opoix, who wrote a history of Provins in the early years of the last century. He tells us there how Edmund Crouchback, who was "acting" Count of Champagne on behalf of his infant stepdaughter, Joan of Navarre, was sent to Provins by his titular overlord, the King of France, to avenge the murder of William Pentecost, the mayor, and to punish his murderers. "When he returned to England," says Opoix, "he took as his device the rose of Provins—the Red Rose. He was the head of the family of Lancaster, which still retains this Red Rose. The House of York, its rival family, took, in opposition, a White Rose for its badge."

Reference to more serious historians shows that M. Opoix is stronger in local patriotism than in history. Lancaster did not go to Provins to hunt out and punish a handful of murderers, but to execute the King's dreadful vengeance on the whole town, which had risen in revolt against excessive taxation. He had little to do there beyond publishing the King's punitive decrees and seeing that they were obeyed; he had no opportunity for any display of personal prowess, and next to the King he must have been the best-hated man in Provins, so why he should have chosen to take its "trade mark" as a personal memento is a mystery. As he was then thirty-four years of age, it is plain that he must have been using his red rose badge for many years before his descent on Provins; there is no historical basis for any belief that he formerly used a different badge and changed it in 1279. Opoix's remarks about the "rival House of York" are of course ludicrous; it did not come into existence until a hundred years later, and even then Lancaster and York were in no sense rivals; they were the fourth and fifth of the seven sons of Edward III, and at that time neither of them had a shadow of a claim to the throne. Opoix has simply seized upon the coincidence between Lancaster's badge and the staple trade of the town and twisted it into a pretty story.

A few writers have even gone so far as to identify the pink-and-white particoloured Damask rose, York and Lancaster, with the bush from which the rival parties plucked their roses during the quarrel in the Temple Garden described in Shakespeare's *King Henry the Sixth,* Part One. This is not a very profitable exercise, seeing that the whole scene is pure fiction; but the identification is all nonsense, anyway. The play was first performed in 1592. Gerard, in 1597, had never even heard of the rose York and Lancaster (which is first mentioned in England by Parkinson in 1629) —and Gerard, beside having a well-stocked garden of his own, was also superintendent of Lord Burghley's gardens, and so better placed than most men in England to encounter any important new introductions. In any case, one has only to read the scene in question to see that there is not a word in it which suggests that the red and white roses were both plucked from the same bush. Indeed, Shakespeare goes out of his way to emphasise that two different plants were concerned by calling one a "thorn" and the other a "briar". But there is no limit to human perversity, and the tale still crops up in modern literature.

But in hunting down these chimaeras I have got far ahead of my period, and must retrace my steps.

In the thirteenth century, one Ibn el-Awam, an Arabian authority on plants, published a list of roses which included a yellow rose, for the first time in the western world. This rose may have been either *R. foetida* or *R. hemisphaerica,* both of which are natives of the Near East, so that it is only our knowledge of them which is new. Since the all-wise Greeks had said that all roses were either red or white, one must suppose that these yellow flowers had not previously been counted as roses. Ibn el-Awam's list also included a blue rose, which has given rise to some speculation, but it need not detain us. More than one member of the Mallow family has masqueraded as a rose in popular belief from time to time and since *Hibiscus Syriacus,* for one, has a form with blue flowers we need not ascribe this Arabian blue rose to the magical powers of the djinns and afreets. I cannot discuss el-Awam's list in detail, much as I should like to, since I only know of it from quotations in other works, and experience has taught me that if I cannot verify a quotation for myself I had better leave it alone.

To return from Islam to the Christian Church, two associations with the rose had their origin in mediaeval times. The first of these is the rosary, the string of beads representing fifteen paternosters, fifteen doxologies and 150 aves, which is used in the Roman Church. The origin of the name is uncertain, but it is probable that it is derived from an early collection of prayers to the Virgin which went by the name of *Our Lady's Rose Garden*. The literal meaning of rosary is, of course, a rose garden ("*biferi rosaria Paesti*"), so that the transference of the name from the book to the beads is easily understood. The use of the rosary apparently goes back at least to the year 1100, and it is interesting to note that it has given us the word "bead" in common speech; the original meaning of bead was "prayer".

The second is the "Holy Rose" or "Golden Rose" which is blessed by the Pope on Laetare Sunday, the fourth Sunday in Lent. The origin of the custom is lost, but it seems to be nearly as old as the rosary, with which it may perhaps be connected. The Holy Rose is an artificial flower of gold-smiths' work which has taken various forms over the years; occasionally in the past it has been made to represent a complete rose bush, copiously studded with precious stones, and of immense value. From time to time the Pope has bestowed it on such foreign rulers as have been thought to deserve well of the Church. The Emperor Sigismund received two in his lifetime, one from the Schismatic Pope John XXIII in 1415 and another from Martin V in 1418; the only other monarch to earn the twofold honour was, ironically enough, our own Henry VIII, "while yet he went to shrift, and long before he stamped and swore and cut the Pope adrift". He received his from Julius II and Leo X.

In the middle of the fifteenth century, when the Dark Ages were al-ready yielding to the light of the Renaissance, the invention of printing from moveable type gave an immense impetus to the dissemination of knowledge, and from then onwards the black-and-white evidence for the state of our rose gardens multiplied exceedingly. The first printed botanical works were no more than versions in type of works that had existed in manuscript form for centuries, such as those of Dioscorides and Apuleius. Original works quickly followed, though the earliest of them add little to our knowledge of the rose. The first printed herbal in English seems to have been Banckes's *Herbal* of 1525, whose author is unknown (Banckes was the publisher), though in later editions his initials appear as W.C.—perhaps Walter Cary, perhaps not. This book contains no illustration of the rose, and its account of "Rofa" consists of the opening statement: "This is the reed Rofe", followed by details of its healing qualities. The mention of "grene Rofes" is a little startling until one realises that they were no more than the opposite of dried ones.

The first helpful work for us is the herbal of William Turner, of which the first part was published in 1551. This, however, contained nothing to our purpose but a description of the "Eglentine, or swete brere", which he regarded as the same thing as the plant which the Latins called "rosa canina". (He may of course have been right.) The woodcut of eglentine is hopelessly inaccurate and quite unrecognisable. Turner, however, was a parson and something of a stormy petrel in theology, who was frequently compelled to interrupt his herbalising to go abroad to avoid prosecution for heresy, treason and the like, so that the second part of his book did not appear until 1562, having been printed at Cologne. It is in this part that his account of the rose appears, illustrated by a single woodcut which is still quite unidentifiable, though it is rather more accurate than the earlier effort. He only devotes two and a half pages to the rose, most of which is taken up with quotations from the standard authorities on the medical properties of the plant; but his introductory paragraph contains the following sentence: "Dioscorides maketh mention of but one kinde of roses, but Mesue maketh two kindes, that is of the whyt and rede: but sence Mesues tyme, there are found divers other kindes, as Damaske rosens, incarnation roses, muske roses, with certayn other kindes, whereof is no mention in any olde writer." The old monopoly of the red and white roses has been broken at last.

The Norfolk parson, Richard Hakluyt, that indefatigable chronicler who devoted his life to the collection of evidence of the benefits that England had derived from the daring and enterprise of her seamen, writing in 1582, says: "In time of memory many things have been brought in that were not here before, as the Damaske Rose by Doctour Linaker, King Henry the Seventh and King Henrie the Eight's Physician." The learned Linacre gained his M.D. at Padua in 1496 and then went to Vicenza for further studies; he is known to have been back in England in 1499, so that if he brought the Damask Rose back with him its introduction can be dated very closely. However, he may have imported it at any later date up to his death in 1524; if we say that it first came into England in the first quarter of the sixteenth century it will be near enough. Dr. Johnson tells us that Linacre brought it from Italy, and there is no doubt that it was known in that country in the sixteenth century; but Mattioli, who wrote a commentary on Dioscorides in 1544, says that it was a comparative newcomer in his day.

How it came into existence is another mystery. It bears an obvious affinity with R. *gallica*, but differs from it in too many points to be regarded as a simple variety of that species. Hurst, as a result of careful analysis, declared that those of its features which were not characteristic of R. *gallica* were derived from R. *phoenicea*, another Near Eastern species; but it is one thing to accept this as a fact, and quite another to explain how it came about. By all the laws of genetics, a cross between these two species should produce a rambler, not a bush rose, and one moreover which was so sterile as to have a negligible chance of survival in the wild. But the one chance in a million does come off sometimes, and it is by no means impossible that the Damask Rose we know may be the outcome of such a cross, or rather, of one of the innumerable different forms which must have appeared in the next generation—supposing that a second generation could have been produced.

For information on the introduction of the Musk Rose we are also indebted to Hakluyt, who wrote: "Of later times was procured out of Italy the Muske Rose plant, the Plumme called the Perdigwena, and two kindes more, by the Lord Cromwell after his travel." I do not know when the Lord Cromwell (this was Thomas Cromwell, Wolsey's one-time secretary and successor, and not the Lord Protector) travelled in Italy; but he finished his earthly travels on the block in 1540, so the Musk Rose cannot have arrived much later than the Damask. It was described by Dodonaeus, a native of the Low Countries, in his *Cruydtboek* of 1554, of which an English translation by Lyte appeared in 1578; but the description is hopelessly inaccurate and was plainly derived from hearsay, perhaps mixed up with the description of some other rose. From Gerard (1597) onwards the descriptions are perfectly consistent down to the end of the eighteenth century; they reveal a rose of the sort that today we should call a "rambler"—it was the first climbing rose to be cultivated in this country. The flowers were small and creamy-white, with a distinctive scent said to resemble Musk; though as the same thing was said of the clove carnations, the resemblance cannot have been close.

John Gerard was a member—and sometime Master—of the Barber-Surgeons Company, and also superintendent of Lord Burghley's gardens. In 1596 he published the first English garden catalogue, a list of all the plants growing in his own garden in Holborn, which included quite a number of different roses; but as they were merely listed by their Latin names we need not bother with them here, as they were all described in

English in his *Herball, or Generall Historie of Plantes,* which was published in the following year. It is a strange thing that Gerard and his *Herball* are better known to the general public than any of his predecessors or successors. In its first edition it was an unreliable work—while Gerard himself was nothing less than an unscrupulous rogue. He had got possession in some way of a translation by one Price of a later work, the *Pemptades* of Dodonaeus, the Flemish herbalist. Price died before his work was published; and Gerard, having appropriated it, proceeded to tear it to pieces and rearrange it in a different way. For illustrations he obtained from Germany the woodcuts which had been prepared for a picture-book of plants by Dietrich of Bergzabern—better known under his Latin pen-name of Tabernaemontanus (this borrowing of illustrations was common form in those days, and need not be considered an aggravation of Gerard's crimes); these he proceeded to fit to his stolen text to the best of his ability, which was only slight. At first he had the assistance of a much greater botanist than himself, de l'Obel (who gave his name to the lobelia), but he soon grew impatient of the numerous corrections that de l'Obel was compelled to suggest and cut adrift, finishing the work by himself—with the result that many of the cuts were annexed to the wrong plants. He then added an entirely original section dealing with the "Barnacle-Tree", in which he gave his personal assurance that he himself had seen live geese hatched out of the barnacles which grew on the tree. This hotch-potch he then published as his own work—with great popular success, sad to say. In 1633 a new edition appeared, after Gerard's death, corrected and revised by Thomas Johnson, who added a preface which completely blew the gaff on Gerard's dishonesty; yet his reputation still stands above all the rest in public estimation.

Happily for us, however, his section on the rose is free from any serious blunders or blemishes. The following is the complete list of roses that he mentions:

The White Rose.
The Red Rose.
The common Damask Rose.
The lesser Damask Rose.
The Rose without prickles.
The Holland or Province Rose.
The single Musk Rose.

The double Musk Rose.
The Blush Rose.
The Velvet Rose.
The Yellow Rose.
The Canell or Cinnamon Rose.
The single Cinnamon Rose.
The Eglantine or Sweet Brier.
The Brier Bush or Hep Tree (Dog Rose).
The Pimpernel or Burnet Rose, also called the Rose bearing Apples.

The illustrations are in general too conventionalised to be of much help in identifying the roses. Unhappily, where they do display recognisable features these are often in conflict with the text.

We have already discussed the Red, the White and the Damask Roses; of the "Rose without prickles" I can say little. To judge from Gerard's enthusiastic description, one would imagine that it was (save in the absence of thorns) a climbing form of the red Cabbage Rose; but since this is contradicted in almost every respect by Parkinson thirty years later, it is perhaps wiser to pass it over in silence.

The Holland or Province Rose seems beyond all doubt to have been the earliest known form of the Cabbage Rose, *R. centifolia*. The origin of this species is as completely unknown as that of the Damask Rose—or of the White Rose, for that matter. In the quite recent past it was widely assumed that this was the *Rosa centifolia* of Pliny, an identification which was based on nothing more substantial than the name—which, being applicable to any very double rose, tells us virtually nothing. It may well have been cultivated two thousand—or ten thousand—years ago, but we have no good evidence for the fact. Gerard identifies it with Pliny's Roses of Philippi and of Campania; but later he says: ". . . The Great Rose, which is generally called the great Province Rose, which the Dutch men cannot endure; for say they it came first out of Holland, and therefore to be called the Holland Rose: but by all likelihood it came from the Damaske Rose, as a kind thereof, made better and fairer by art, which seemeth to agree with truth."

One thing at least is certain—that the theory which has become popular in recent years, that *R. centifolia* was "created" by Dutch rose breeders in the sixteenth to seventeenth century, is quite untenable. There were no plant breeders—in the sense of hybridists—in Holland or anywhere else at that time. It was not until the end of the seventeenth century that even the possibility of producing deliberately plant hybrids was discovered; the practice did not become widespread until a hundred years later, and it was not generally adopted by rose growers until a hundred years later still. When confronted with these facts the pro-Dutch enthusiast protests indignantly that of course he wasn't talking about hybridising; he meant that the "breeders" raised huge numbers from seed, and by selecting the best forms which appeared in each generation effected a gradual improvement in the quality of their flowers. The Dutch tulip growers were in fact doing just this with immense enthusiasm at this time, and in the "Tulip Mania" of the seventeenth century bulbs changed hands for enormous sums. But the rose growers were not doing the same thing with *R. centifolia*, for the very good reason that down to the end of the eighteenth century every known form of this rose was completely sterile and never set seed at all. One can only bracket the Cabbage Rose with the Damask, as probably a very old species in cultivation which had taken a long time to find its way to western Europe. Like the Damask, it has a close affinity with *R. gallica*, while remaining sufficiently distinct to be accepted as a species in its own right; and like the Damask, it has never been found in the wild.

Before going on with the rest of Gerard's roses I think I should stop here to tackle a task which has been looming ahead for some time, namely, to clear up the confusion which has grown up around that word "province" as applied to roses. Firstly I must point out that it has nothing whatever to do with the town of Provins. "Province" is the translation of the Latin word *provincia*—a province—which the Romans applied to that part of Gaul surrounding Marseilles, and which today is called Provence. The Provence rose today is *R. centifolia*, the Cabbage Rose. The Province Rose or *"Rosa provincialis"* of the sixteenth and seventeenth centuries was *R. damascena*, the Damask Rose; while the town of Provins (whose name was not derived from the Latin *provincia* but from the name of the Emperor Probus) has no connexion with either. But one must be on one's guard against the name "Red Damask" which was frequently but incorrectly given to the Rose of Provins in this country. The "provincial roses" on Hamlet's shoes, however, were not flowers but rosettes.

To return to Gerard's list of the roses which were grown in his day, the Musk Roses have already been discussed. The Velvet Rose, which according to the illustration had some fifteen to twenty petals, was "of a deepe and blacke red colour, resembling red crimson velvet"; in other respects it resembled the Red Rose, and we need have no hesitation in identifying it with the variety of *R. gallica* which goes today under the name of Tuscany. The Yellow Rose, which was single, was almost certainly *R. foetida*, commonly called today the Austrian Brier, although it originated in what is today Northern Persia.

The Blush Rose (which I ought to have mentioned before) is more uncertain than these last. Gerard included it with the Musk Roses, from which he distinguished it by the larger size of its single flowers and its colour, which was white "dasht over with a light wash of carnation, which maketh that colour, which we call a blush colour". It seems to correspond to what Parkinson thirty years later called the "Spanish Musk", and which from his description must have been very similar to the shrub rose grown today under the name of *R. dupontii*. The latter first appeared under that name in 1825 or thereabouts, and took its name from Dupont, gardener to the Empress Josephine, though it was not raised by him. It is supposed to have originated in a cross between *R. gallica* and the Musk Rose, whose scent it retains; but as it hasn't inherited the laciniate stipules of the latter, some other member of the *Synstylae* may have taken its place, perhaps *R. sempervirens*, which occurs wild in southern Europe.

The Canell or Cinnamon Rose ("Canell" is an old name for Cinnamon) is another natural species which grows wild over a large part of Europe and Asia, and which takes its name from the resemblance of its scent to the smell of cinnamon. The form grown in sixteenth-century gardens had double flowers; Gerard mentions having a single form in his garden as though it were something of a rarity; evidently he was unaware that this is the normal wild form. The double form seems to have disappeared from English gardens, though it is still recorded as in cultivation.

The Sweet Brier and the Dog Rose call for no comment. The Pimpernel Rose is our native Burnet Rose, *R. spinosissima*; a variety of this species, *R. spinosissima pimpinellifolia*, is sometimes distinguished as a separate species, *R. pimpinellifolia*. The "pimpernel" in question is not the Scarlet Pimpernel of our fields, but the wild Burnet—hence the name.

The "Rose bearing apples" is *R. pomifera*, also sometimes called *R. villosa*, a European wild rose which has dark red globular hips up to an inch in diameter. The double form is sometimes met with in cultivation under the name of Wolley-Dod's Rose. Gerard says that his Pimpernel Rose "groweth in a pasture as you go from a village hard by London called Knightsbridge, unto Fulham, a village thereby". It would be hard to find it there today.

After John Gerard, John Parkinson, who published his *Paradisi in Sole Paradisus Terrestris* ("The Park on Earth of Park-in-Sun") in the year 1629. Parkinson was an apothecary, but he was less concerned with plants as medicines than as garden ornaments; his rose descriptions are more detailed (and more accurate) than Gerard's, and he wastes little space on their "virtues". He mentions twenty-nine different roses in all, counting single and double forms of the same rose as different, but none of his additions to Gerard's list is of great importance.

Perhaps the most important of all the new roses he listed was a new variety of the Holland Rose, which he calls the Red Province Rose. (He had also heard rumours of a white one, but he dismissed them as probably mistaken references to a form of *R. alba*—in which he was no doubt right. The first authentic white Cabbage Rose did not arrive until many years later.) The red Cabbage Rose was inferior in most respects to its pink forerunner; the remarkable thing about it was the fact that it existed at all, since the usual source of new varieties, new roses raised from seed, was closed in this case, the Cabbage Roses being sterile. Happily, however, they proved to be greatly given to "sporting", that is, to the spontaneous production of new forms, which could be cut off the parent plant and perpetuated by grafting or budding. It was, in fact, in this way that all the different forms of *R. centifolia* arose, down to the end of the eighteenth century, when a single variety, with its full complement of stamens, appeared. (In double flowers the extra petals are usually formed at the expense of stamens, and the Cabbage Roses were so double that they possessed no stamens at all.) This for the first time permitted breeding from the species; but very little was ever done in this direction and no important "Hybrid Centifolias" have ever appeared. *R. gallica* is also given to sporting, but being fertile and liable to cross with other species and varieties, the gallicas are a more mixed lot than the centifolias today.

Thirty years after Parkinson's book was published, one Sir Thomas Hanmer, a Cheshire squire and a noted horticultural authority of his day, wrote his *Garden Book*; but it never achieved print, and the manuscript disappeared from sight for nearly three hundred years, until it came to light in a sale room in the 1930s. Fortunately its importance was at once realised, and *The Garden Book of Sir Thomas Hanmer* appeared in print at last. Sir Thomas was a great tulip enthusiast, at a time when the world was going mad over new tulips; but he grew roses, too, and has left us brief descriptions of the varieties in his garden. He starts off by saying, "none of the single roses are much valued by us except the Sweet Brier, for the scent of its leaves, and the Scarlet Rose, which is yellow within and scarlet on the outside". This last is clearly our Austrian Copper, the bi-coloured sport from the Austrian Brier known as *R. foetida bicolor*, although Sir Thomas has got his "inside" and "outside" crossed. Whether it was imported in this form, or whether the sport arose in some English garden, we do not know.

Sir Thomas recognised the "Province" roses as a class, though he spells the name "Provins" throughout; this may be an early instance of the confusion I have already referred to, but since he nowhere makes mention of the town of Provins in connexion with the Red Roses, it may be no more than a coincidence arising out of his unconventional spelling. He grew both the red and the "damask" Province Roses (he says that the latter has a "damask" colour, and just by way of being cussed he says that the Damask Roses are "carnation" in colour), and also what he calls the "White Provins", though this, as Parkinson suspected, was more probably *R. alba*. The "Purple Rose" seems to have been a new variety of *R. gallica*—there are several purple varieties in cultivation today—as was also the "Purple striped with White", which he said came from about Norwich, and was very rare; it has disappeared from our gardens. The "Marbled Rose" is given by Parkinson as an alternative name for his thornless rose, but Sir Thomas grew both; the former was probably another gallica variety. He also grew "Rosa Mundi", or the "Christmas Rose", which he said was first found in Norfolk "a few years since" on a branch of the common Red Rose, and thence multiplied. This is the earliest use of the name "Rosa Mundi" that I have come across; earlier descriptions of a similar rose can be ascribed to some other striped variety (such as Parkinson's "Chrystall Rose") in the light of Sir Thomas's circumstantial account of the origin of this one. He also includes the Hungarian Rose in his list, but as he says that it was "of an ill, faded red, and fit only for stocks" we can understand why it has disappeared from cultivation.

His most exciting newcomer was undoubtedly what he called the "Monthly Rose", "a very Damask in leaves and flower and scent, but it bears two or three moneths more in the year than the ordinary Damask, and very plentifully if it stand warm". This was the first mention of the Autumn Damask in England; his statement that it was often called "Rosa Italica" gives a very broad hint where it came from. Modern

A modern rose in the old floral style, **Colonial White** *(Climber). Raiser: Melvin E. Wyant, Mentor, Ohio, U.S.A. Introduced 1959. Parentage: New Dawn × Madame Hardy (Damask). Medium-sized (3–3½ in.), very full blooms in pure white with creamy centre, opening flat, solitary and in small clusters of 2–3 on short stems. Very sweet Damask fragrance. Small, very deep bluish foliage. Free, repeated bloom into late autumn. Slender, moderately vigorous growth from 8–10 ft. Photograph: J. L. Norton, A.R.P.S.*

Two famous Moss Roses. **Communis,** *syn.* **Common Moss, Old Pink Moss.** *Occurred as a mutation of Rosa centifolia in Carcasonne, France, about 1696. Medium-sized ($2\frac{1}{2}$ in.), very full blooms in mid-pink with fine green "moss" on sepals, calyx and pedicel, borne singly and in small clusters. Very fragrant. A lax-growing, prickly shrub to 4 ft. with plentiful light green foliage.* **Nuits de Young,** *syn. Old Black, Hermann Kegel. Raiser: M. Laffay, Bellevue, near Paris, France. Introduced 1845. Small ($1\frac{1}{2}$–2 in.), full blooms in deep reddish-purple, shaded violet. Very fragrant. Elongated bluish-green foliage with coppery overtones. Neat, upright, prickly growth to 4 ft. The "moss' is short and dark brown. Both roses flower very freely at midsummer only. Photograph: J. L. Norton, A.R.P.S.*

writers are all agreed, no doubt from personal experience, that the Autumn Damasks today give only a very small second crop of flowers, which suggests that the type has deteriorated—or else, perhaps, that they are not giving it enough warmth. Cheshire is not a particularly warm county, and Sir Thomas had no more luck with the double yellow *R. hemisphaerica* than his predecessors; he says that it was "as big as a reasonable Provins when it blows well, which it seldome does, either in England or other countries, being commonly eaten up with wormes in the bud".

At the end of his own list Sir Thomas adds a note. "In Italy," he says, "there hath been above twenty years a fine Rose, the seed whereof came thither from the East Indyes. It is called in Latin commonly Rosa Sinensis, and by the Indians Fuyo." This sounds most promising; unfortunately the next words let us down: "It grows to a high tree for a rose, hath a leaf like a figg or the Ivyes, . . . etc." Plainly it was not a rose at all; there is no known member of the genus *Rosa* which has leaves like a fig. It may have been the plant now known as *Hibiscus rosa-sinensis,* a member of the mallow family. On the matter of raising roses from seeds, what he actually says is this: "In old tyme the seed was ordinarily sowne, but now 'tis left off, it being so long before it comes to beare, and the other wayes of multiplication soe easy; but the sowing of the seed in great quantities certainly produces some new differences."

But tempting though it is, I must not allow myself to go on quoting from one old authority after another. We have now reached the point where the four basic species, *R. alba,* the White Rose, *R. gallica,* the Red or French Rose, *R. damascena,* the Damask Rose (including the sub-species *R. damascena semperflorens,* the Autumn Damask) and *R. centifolia,* the Cabbage or Provence Rose, are all firmly established in English gardens, where they remained unchallenged until the end of the eighteenth century. When people speak of the "old-fashioned" roses, these are the ones they mean, and a very good name it is, too. Most of the old-fashioned roses listed in modern catalogues are not particularly old in years. Relatively few of them were in existence a hundred and fifty years ago; but they are true descendants of the roses of the Elizabethan and Jacobean ages, and they differ markedly from the Hybrid Teas which mark the peak of the present fashion in roses. Large and, it must be admitted, straggling and untidy bushes, with small flowers by present-day standards, either formless and untidy, or else flat and with a multitude of small petals. Many of them have a scent which has rarely been equalled, and never surpassed;

D

and if their flowering season is limited to a single burst, this is not always brief. The gallicas, in particular, are capable of keeping up a show for the best part of two months, from the middle of June until well into August, and during that time they produce more flowers than the best of our perpetual roses are capable of yielding in six months. It is a significant fact that the perfume industry is virtually dependent upon once-flowering roses; no perpetual variety has ever been produced which could rival the yield of essence from the Damask and Cabbage Roses.

One more historical event remains to be chronicled in this chapter which—like so many in the history of the rose—cannot be exactly dated; but at some time, either at the end of the seventeenth century or the beginning of the eighteenth, the Cabbage Rose produced a sport of a new kind, in which the sepals and flower-stalks were covered with a growth of glands resembling moss. This Moss Rose was not a new species; in every other respect it was identical with its centifolia parents. In due course it sported again and again and produced a number of different coloured forms paralleling the different forms of the un-mossed Cabbage Roses; they are known collectively as the sub-species *R. centifolia muscosa*. Attempts have been made in the present century to breed this attractive moss into our modern garden roses, but with negligible success.

Where the Moss Rose first appeared is equally uncertain, both Holland and Provence laying claim to it, thus repeating the history of the Cabbage Rose over again. We know that it was grown in Leyden in 1720; Miller tells us that its first appearance in England was in the Kensington nursery of Robert Furber, who included it in his catalogue for 1724. It seems to have become especially popular in England, so that by 1824, when Vibert wrote his *Essai sur les roses* he could say: "Almost all our moss roses come from England." This was not, unhappily, because English growers were exceptionally enterprising in raising new varieties of roses; on the contrary, the abandonment of the old practice of obtaining new varieties by growing roses from seed, which Hanmer noted in 1659, persisted for the best part of two hundred years, so that in 1848 William Paul could still complain, "Why seedling roses should not be raised in England is a question I could never yet determine." But the Moss and Cabbage Roses could not be raised from seed anyway, the new varieties coming into existence as sports. At least we may claim that these spontaneous variations were eagerly looked for and cherished in this country.

Not only have the attempts to reproduce the mossy growth on other roses by interbreeding failed to achieve any useful results, but the moss has never appeared spontaneously on any other species but *R. centifolia*—with one exception. Early in the nineteenth century a new moss variety, the Rosier de Thionville or Perpetual White Moss, was put on the market. White forms of *R. centifolia* have always been uncommon—indeed, the first one, discovered in a Norfolk garden in 1775, was named "Unique"—but this one differed further from the majority in that it gave a second crop of flowers after the first one was over. This habit is known among a few of the surviving varieties of moss roses, and is usually attributed to a strain of Autumn Damask in their (quite unknown) parentage; but what several generations of experts failed to notice was that the Perpetual White Moss was, in fact, a pure Damask and not a centifolia at all. This has been proved on several occasions in recent years by its having reverted to its (presumed) original form, an Autumn Damask, and a pink one at that.

From the arrival of the Moss Roses, the story is one of increasing variety, but all within the species already described. Thory, who wrote the text for Redouté's *Les Roses*, tells us that in 1724 the Duchess of Beaufort, a notable gardener, was only able to assemble sixteen different varieties for her collection at Badminton—which suggests that Her Grace was not as enterprising as Thory supposed, since Parkinson was able to muster twice this number a hundred years earlier. But during the eighteenth century the Dutch rose growers took a hand in the multiplication of varieties, chiefly of what Vibert calls "Provins", by which he as a Frenchman meant gallicas; the Autumn Damasks seem to have become a Belgian speciality; the Cabbage Roses were apparently favoured in Provence. By 1828, it was estimated that not less than 2,500 varieties were known, of which 1,200 were gallicas. Vibert in 1824 claimed to possess "more than seventy alba varieties, and about the same each of damasks and centifolias". Prévost's great catalogue of 1829 describes fifty-four albas, fourteen "Belgicas" (presumably Autumn Damasks), fifty-eight centifolias, forty-four damasks, 305 gallicas, fourteen moss roses, eighteen provincialis (how these were distinguished from the centifolias I cannot say), twenty-three sweet briers and thirty-six burnet roses, in a grand total of 880 varieties grown in his nursery at Rouen.

In England, the interest in roses was no less great. The 1826 catalogue of Conrad Loddiges and Sons, whose nursery was in the now inner London suburb of Hackney, listed 1,452 species and varieties. At about the same time, at Hammersmith on the opposite side of London on the site now occupied by Olympia, Lee and Kennedy were offering nearly as many. With the exception of the burnet roses, nearly all those listed in the English catalogues had been raised by French growers who had established their country as the unquestioned leader in the rose world. This supremacy was maintained without any major competition for over a century—roughly, the period 1800 until the outbreak of the First World War.

But the rise of the French growers was paralleled by a gradual decline of the "old-fashioned" and generally once-flowering kinds. This fall from favour can be traced most conveniently through William Paul's *The Rose Garden*, the first edition of which appeared in 1848 and the last in 1903. It was Paul's practice to list (as he put it) "in natural groups the most esteemed varieties of roses recognised and cultivated in various rose gardens, English and foreign". The following table (Fig. 1) has been compiled from Paul's book:

Class	1st Edn. 1848	2nd Edn. 1860	9th Edn. 1888	10th Edn. 1903
Alba or White Rose	61	16	15	8
Centifolia, Provence or Cabbage Rose	76	17	9	9
Centifolia muscosa, or Moss Rose	84	76	62	44
Damascena, The Damask Rose	87	17	8	8
Gallica, The French or Provins Rose	471	68	26	18
Total	779	194	120	87

Fig. 1   Table showing the decline of the "old-fashioned" roses.
(Source: William Paul, *The Rose Garden*, various editions.)

Paul died in 1905 at the age of eighty-three. Had he lived another ten years, it is a safe assumption that his list would have shrunk to even smaller proportions. Sanders' *List of Cultivated Roses* which the author stated was compiled from the up-to-date lists of English and Continental nurseries published in 1912, described nearly 1,900 varieties of which only thirty-six were "old-fashioned" roses; Moss Roses accounted for just over half, a proportion similar to that of Paul's in 1888 and 1903. They were, in fact, the only group to retain any semblance of popularity, but in ever-reducing numbers.

Following the Second World War, thanks to the efforts of a few enthusiasts, there was a revival of interest in the Old Roses and the accounts of finding and identifying them make fascinating reading. Today, many rose nurserymen catalogue a few and several firms make them a speciality. Such was the assiduity of Mr. Graham Thomas and his success in publicising them that by 1960, Sunningdale Nurseries, in Surrey, were offering almost as many varieties as Paul had listed a hundred years earlier. More recently, there has been a tendency towards rationalisation and those varieties now most usually listed represent the best of the reintroductions.

As I said earlier, the majority of "old-fashioned" roses make large, rather ungainly shrubs, a factor which militates against their use in all except large gardens. Anyone with a real feeling for roses should, however, find room for a few of these survivors. They have much to offer in colours, shapes and scents not found in any other classes.

It is not my intention in this book to set out exhaustive (and exhausting!) lists of varieties. Popularity, and therefore availability, is ephemeral, and choice highly personal. To anyone contemplating growing a small, representative collection, I offer the following for consideration. All are in some way distinctive and unless otherwise stated, are of relatively restricted growth suitable for small gardens.

Feeding and pruning are dealt with elsewhere, but personal experience has shown that all these varieties need a high potash intake, certainly more than those of modern derivation. A dressing of sulphate of potash at the rate of three oz. per square yard in March when the bush is starting into growth and a further dressing at the same rate after flowering has finished is not too much, particularly on light soils.

ALBAS

Most of these are in delicate shades of pink, not white as the class name suggests. Their height and density make them better suited for informal hedging than garden subjects. Happily, one of the shorter, bushier varieties happens to be one of the best: Félicité Parmentier (Parmentier, 1836). The creamy-yellow buds open to medium-sized, flat blooms in palest pink, margined white, with a sweet scent; the foliage is large and grey-green and healthy. William Paul, who used his superlatives sparingly, stated throughout all editions of his book: "A most abundant bloomer and indispensable even in a small collection." I see no reason to dissent from that opinion.

CENTIFOLIAS

Petite de Hollande (in cultivation prior to 1796); most centifolias are of loose, arching habit of growth. This is a scaled-down, more compact plant to about three feet with small, sweetly scented pink blooms held more upright than in most of the larger flowered, taller growing varieties whose flower heads tend to droop. There is some tendency to mildew but there are many worse offenders and the systemic fungicides now being developed will probably eliminate this problem.

Robert le Diable (raiser unknown. As a clue to its probable date of introduction, Eugène Scribe wrote the libretto and Meyerbeer the music for an opera of this name, first performed in Paris in 1831), included for its unusual colouring; purple and violet predominate with splashes of cerise and scarlet and occasional touches of grey. The foliage is dark green. An untidy grower needing some staking, but worth that extra bit of care.

DAMASKS

Most, but not all, of the Old Roses are fragrant, but there is no question about this quality in any of the Damasks. Those who describe some modern roses as having "Damask scent" suggests that either their sense of smell or knowledge of these roses is faulty, for no roses in any other class possess the fragrance so characteristic of them. They are in general stalwart shrubs but tend to flop with the weight of bloom they bear, particularly in a wet season.

Marie Louise (Hardy, about 1810); the above remarks apply especially to this variety which has some of the largest blooms to be found among the old-fashioned roses. They are bright pink with a mauve cast on ageing and the fragrance is intense. It is best grown at the back of a border and trained along nylon trellis or netting. When associated with a short growing white or lavender clematis, the effect is most agreeable. The rose was named for the Austrian princess who supplanted Josephine in Napoleon's affections and became his wife in 1810.

Madame Hardy (Hardy, 1832); everyone who has written about roses since the introduction of this variety considers it to be one of the most beautiful ever raised. I make no apology for joining them. The medium-sized blooms form a shallow cup filled with pure white petals, occasionally with a hint of yellow at their base, in a formation that is almost geometric in its regularity. A green carpel surrounded by a ring of petaloids heightens the effect. A repeat-flowering climber, Colonial White, was raised from Madame Hardy in the United States a few years ago. It has much of its parent's beauty and fragrance and deserves to be better known.

R. *damascena versicolor*, the York and Lancaster Rose, despite its pseudo-historical association, cannot be recommended. It is neither a good grower nor a free bloomer and its choice could well lead to disappointment; it lacks all the good qualities of Marie Louise and Madame Hardy.

MOSS ROSES

So many of the Moss varieties have survived that selection becomes difficult, and it would be better to visit a specialist nursery before making a choice. Some grow no more than two feet while others can be treated as pillar roses. My list is, therefore, simply those which performed well for me.

Communis (syn. Common Moss, Old Pink Moss), the original mutation from R. *centifolia* which occurred about the end of the seventeenth century. By general consent, it is still one of the best and is a little less vigorous than the parent. The light green "moss" is always in evidence, acting as a perfect foil to the pale pink flowers which are inclined to nod. Very free-flowering and excellent in dry weather but impatient of rain.

Alfred de Dalmas (Portemer, 1855); several of the moss roses have a second period of bloom. In Victorian times, they were assigned to a separate group as 'Perpetual Moss'. This is a compact grower, flowering reliably a second time. Blooms are small, cupped and creamy blush and the moss short and bristly, showing relationship to the Damasks. In 1881, another Moss was sent out as 'Mousseline' but modern specialists agree that it is synonymous—probably a reintroduction of the older rose. Nineteenth-century records were not precise and the rose men of that time were not over-scrupulous when they felt that a good, old rose and their own order books needed a boost. Several British catalogues list it as 'Mousseline'; the older, original name should take precedence.

Henri Martin (Laffay, 1863). This variety, named for the eminent French historian, makes a tall, wiry bush to five feet and produces in its season a multitude of rather small blooms, little more than semi-double but of attractive form in light crimson. They stand rain and have a pleasing scent. It is the best moss of its colour.

Nuits de Young (Laffay, 1845). Also known as Old Black Moss and Hermann Kegel. The deepest coloured of the several maroon-purple moss roses, forming a neat, upright bush to three feet or so, covered with small, rosette-shaped blooms. The deep blue-green foliage with a coppery sheen is in keeping with the overall nocturnal effect. The name is appropriate, being the French translation of the long poem written in 1744 by the Reverend Edward Young entitled "Night Thoughts" which enjoyed considerable popularity in France in the early nineteenth century.

There are several white Moss Roses in cultivation; but as they are all highly susceptible to rain damage, they are best avoided.

GALLICAS

There are more survivors of this class than in any other of the Old Roses, and I venture three reasons. The first is statistical—there were very many more of them raised. The second is their characteristic tendency to send out suckers (shared with some of the Moss Roses) and thereby to exist independently of any understock on which they might have been budded originally and, thirdly, their wide distribution from their ancient origins and extreme hardiness.

Of all the old-fashioned roses, they are the most compact growers, rarely exceeding four feet, usually less, in height with their width in proportion. They present no accommodation problems in the garden, large or small.

There are some points about the gallicas which so far have never been satisfactorily explained. It is the only class of roses, old or modern, which contains no white varieties. Some of the sub-class of agathe were described as flesh and one or two which were styled by Paul as "Hybrid French" were creamy-white, but Paul felt they were closer to the centifolias than the gallicas.

Another matter which has, at least, intrigued me is the complete disappearance of three varieties which were highly esteemed by the professional nurserymen and many of the amateurs who wrote throughout the nineteenth century. Two of them, Boule de Nanteuil and Ohl, were sufficiently good to form part of Ben Cant's prize-winning box of seventy-two distinct varieties at the first National Rose Show held in London on the 1st of July, 1858. The third, named Kean, described as "brilliant crimson and of perfect shape" was in almost everybody's recommended list. They may, of course, be masquerading under some other names—very many old roses were known under several synonyms making positive identification difficult—but none that I have seen fits their descriptions. Of the forty or so commercially available—the list was rather longer a few years ago—the following can be recommended:

Belle Isis (Parmentier, 1845); pale pink with a hint of peach is contained in the sweet-scented, smallish blooms which are of perfect form produced in great quantities on a fairly short bush. It is a distinct and charming plant.

Belle de Crécy (Roeser, between 1830–1836); alas for modern legends, this variety has no connexion with Madame Pompadour as has been suggested. That lady lived for a brief time at Crécy some eighty years before this variety was raised in one of the many rose nurseries for which Crécy-en-Brie was famous. A more plausible explanation is that Roeser merely wished to indicate the provenance of his rose, as other raisers had done before and since. The blooms are carmine on opening and change quickly to mauve and slate grey—colours found in several others in the class—and very fragrant.

Charles de Mills (syn. Bizarre Triomphante) (Desportes, active 1800–1835) is one of the most vigorous of the class and has more thorny growth than many. The half-open bloom resembles a sliced-off sphere crammed with petals in deep crimson clouded with maroon and purple. Friends in this country and abroad who collect old roses regard it as one of the best of all.

Rosa Mundi (*R. gallica versicolor*) was discussed earlier. I mention it again as it is one of the most effective of the several striped roses and a garden shrub of a high order. Not more than semi-double, it is profuse and spectacular, especially if several plants are massed together, an effect it will produce naturally, as it will soon get down on its own roots and sucker even when budded on an understock. As with many striped sports, flowering shoots often revert to its red parent. *R. gallica officinalis*.

Tricolore de Flandre (Van Houtte, 1846); the gallica class produced many striped sports—fifty-four have been recorded—far more than in any other group, old or modern. This tendency is doubtless derived from their common ancestor, *R. gallica officinalis*, mentioned above. In this variety, the carmine stripes on a blush background change to deep purple and grey. Rather fuller, but smaller blooms than Rosa Mundi, of the several tri-coloured gallicas I have grown, this proved to be the best. There have been several reports of its reversion to its parent, the carmine and purple Gloire des Jardins, raised by Descemet prior to 1817.

Tuscany and Tuscany Superb, most probably Gerard's Velvet Rose and its seedling, which was called Royal Velvet. The two are similar, deep crimson to maroon with a velvety sheen, set off with a boss of yellow stamens, less conspicuous in Tuscany Superb which is more double. The latter is also slightly taller, to about four feet—Tuscany is one foot or so shorter. A pair of highly satisfactory roses which played no small part in later developments to be discussed in the next chapter. Indeed, their usefulness in this direction is by no means finished; Tuscany Superb is one of the parents of the new, deep purple floribunda, News (Le Grice, 1969).

Chapter Four

FURTHER INTERLUDE ON CLASSIFICATION: HYBRIDS

Ye happy mixtures of more happy days
Byron—*Beppo*

The botanists of the past hundred and fifty years have done some very deplorable things to the English and Latin languages, but they may claim credit for one thing at least: they have brought the word "hybrid" into a degree of respectability. Its original Latin form, *ibrida* or *hibrida*, (the "y" is due to mistaken association with the Greek *hybris* meaning arrogance) meant a pig which had been begotten on a domestic sow by a wild boar. In course of time, the pig being a universal symbol of contempt, it was transferred to the human race, denoting the child of a Roman father and a "barbarian" (i.e. non-Roman) mother. But apart from its contemptuous connotation its basic meaning has always been the same, the offspring of two different parents.

Hence it was not until the end of the seventeenth century, when Nehemiah Grew announced to the assembled members of the Royal Society that sex reared its head in the vegetable kingdom no less than in the animal, that the possibility of plant hybrids could even be contemplated. Men had dreamed before this of combining the virtues of two plants in one, but lacking this essential clue, the way to achieve such a result remained hidden. One might have expected that when Grew provided the key to the door which had been closed for so long, a flood of new hybrids would have poured through it; yet nothing of the sort happened.

Not only was the hybrid surrounded by an aura of disreputability; to many, the whole subject was tabu. To suggest that the author of Genesis had been mistaken in ascribing sexual differences to animals only was shocking; while to suggest that Man could bring into existence new plants which were not to be found among those divinely created on the third day was nothing less than blasphemy. It would not be true to say that Grew's announcement caused any widespread commotion, because at first it was known to comparatively few; but the knowledge spread very slowly. Nearly twenty years elapsed before Camerarius, in Germany, published the results of his experiments which proved the truth of Grew's contention, and he was content to show that plants did reproduce by sexual means; he made no attempt to discover what happened when two different plants were mated. A few rather trivial and amateurish experiments on the same lines as those of Camerarius were made in this country. Botanists of many countries (including the great Linnaeus) published learned treatises on hybrids or supposed hybrids which added remarkably little to the world's store of knowledge. But the first man to make a deliberate cross between two plant species (*Nicotiana paniculata* and *N. rustica*) was another German, Joseph Gottlieb Kölreuter, who published the results of his researches between the years 1761 and 1766, nearly a hundred years after Grew had shown the way. Kölreuter's results divided the botanical world into two schools. One of them vigorously denied the truth of everything he said; the other contented itself with ignoring it. As late as 1849, von Gärtner could write of Kölreuter: "Hybridisation in its scientific significance was so little thought of, and at the most regarded merely as a proof of the sexuality of plants, that the many important suggestions and actual data which this diligent and exact observer recorded in various treatises have found but little acceptance in plant physiological papers up to the most recent time. On the other hand, even as regards the sexuality of plants, they were attacked to such a degree that their genuineness was doubted." We have no need to follow the history of hybridisation beyond Kölreuter, since it was he who established the two basic principles that concern us here, namely, (i) that it does not matter which way round a cross is made, as the result is normally the same in either case, and (ii) that while the offspring of a true species are uniform, those of a hybrid display wide variation.

Except in the regrettable cases where pseudo-specific names are bestowed, hybrids are described in botanical terms as, for example, *R. multi-flora* × *R. foetida*, which can be read quite literally as "a cross between *R. multiflora* and *R. foetida*". Hitherto it has been the accepted practice that the species first named is the one which acted as seed-parent—i.e., which yielded the actual seeds sown—while the second was the pollen-parent—furnished the pollen which was applied to the stigma of the seed-parent. Unhappily the international code now rules that the names of the species ought to be given in alphabetical order (which must be very confusing to members of those nations which do not use our alphabet), the two parents being distinguished by the conventional signs ♀ (female) for the seed-parent and ♂ (male) for the pollen-parent. At present this is widely disregarded. The reader may well protest that if the first principle quoted above is correct there is no need to distinguish the parents, since *R. multiflora* × *R. foetida* ought to yield the same results as *R. foetida* × *R. multiflora*. That is true enough, but there are practical questions to be considered also. If the reader is anxious to try the quoted cross, he would be well advised to adopt the first mode, using *R. multiflora* as seed-parent, because this rose is fully fertile and sets seed readily, whereas *R. foetida* is practically sterile and seldom sets seed at all. All roses produce pollen-grains in vastly greater numbers than seeds, so that where the chance of fertility is small, it is always better to use the pollen of the doubtful rose. What is more important, there are a number of plants, including the whole of the *Caninae* section of the genus *Rosa*, whose mode of reproduction is abnormal, so that with such species it does matter considerably which way round the cross is made.

When the scientific world as a whole shut its eyes to the importance of Kölreuter's discoveries, it is not surprising that the practical gardeners followed suit. It was not until the last quarter of the nineteenth century that rose growers began to adopt the practice of deliberate hybridisation widely. The existence of hybrid roses had been recognised for the best part of a hundred years, and in fact the great majority of the roses raised in the nineteenth century were hybrids, though not always known to be such. But not one practical rose grower had the enterprise to hunt through the records to find out the facts that Kölreuter had established for him, and which had been repeatedly confirmed by the small but devoted band of investigators who followed in his footsteps—often without knowing it. Then as now, rose growers were a conservative lot, who worshipped the great god Modas. "My Old Dad Always Said . . ." was the ultimate authority. And what My Old Dad said in this connexion was, firstly, that no roses ever bred true from seed, and secondly, that the character of a hybrid was predominantly due to its seed-parent, the pollen-parent only introducing superficial changes. The first misconception arose from the fact that so many of the important new introductions of the period, the China Rose, the Tea Rose, the Bourbon Rose, the Noisette Rose, etc., were automatically assumed to be species although, in fact, they were hybrids. The second really arose from the first, since when it was firmly believed that almost any rose could give rise to any other among its seed-lings, there was no incentive to look closely and discover the truth.

What our forebears may have thought and what mistakes they may have made a hundred and fifty years ago do not particularly matter. What does matter is that the system of classification of the garden roses that we grow today is still based on the ideas that were current at that time. The observant reader will have no doubt spotted that Dad's two rulings were contradictory. If any rose could come from any other, then clearly nothing could determine the form of the offspring, whether hybrid or species; but our fathers of old were not to be put off by trifles like that. Since there was no apparent limit to the variability of rose seedlings, there was little incentive to try crossing two together; it was sufficient to collect the seeds that were set in the course of nature, and these were sown, sometimes by hundreds of thousands at a time, the desirable new varieties being selected as they appeared. And in the light of Dad's second ruling, every new rose raised in this way was classed with the rose whose seed had given it birth. If it came from the seed of a Bourbon Rose then it was itself a Bourbon Rose. Only if it differed markedly from its seed-parent, it was assumed to be a hybrid and was then called a Hybrid Bourbon. Certainty on the point was rarely possible. Many of the nineteenth-century writers on roses paid lip-service to the possibilities of hybridising, but their descriptions of the process showed only too clearly that in their hands it can rarely have succeeded. The commonest and easiest way of setting about it was simply to plant the two proposed parents side by side and hope that nature would achieve what the gardener usually failed to do. Successes were achieved in this way; Rivers, for example, managed to raise a cross between the Ayr-shire Rose, which was a cultivated form of our native *R. arvensis,* and the deep red gallica Tuscany, and in this case the differences between the two parents were so extreme that the assumed parentage of the seedling which showed characteristics of both must almost certainly have been correct.

But in the majority of cases, the parentage of hybrids was an assumption; and as the importance of the pollen-parent was always underrated, it was scarcely ever recorded, even where it could be guessed. It was never considered worth incorporating into the name of the class; a Hybrid Bourbon was a Hybrid Bourbon and nothing more, whether its pollen-parent was a white rambler like the Musk Rose or a red bush like *R. gallica*.

Kölreuter's second principle, that hybrid plants do not breed true from seed, was no less important—and true—than the first; and taken in conjunction with Ray's definition of a species it provided an almost infallible test to distinguish a species from a hybrid. What he did not know, and what nobody could know until the work of Gregor Mendel was uncovered at the beginning of the twentieth century, was that if one continued to breed from a hybrid by selfing for enough generations, certain characteristics would become stabilised and the variations would eventually die out, so that ultimately one would be left with plants which bred just as true as any species, although an examination of their external features would show that many, if not most of them, were derived from the two species which contributed to the original cross. Such plants *are* species for all practical purposes; and since the whole system of classifying plants into species is only adopted for practical purposes, there is no point in distinguishing them from others which do not show signs of a hybrid origin. This point was unfortunately overlooked by Hurst in his well-known paper on the history of garden roses, so that when he declared, for instance, that *RR. alba, damascena,* etc., had been derived from crosses between *R. gallica* and other species, he omitted to make it clear whether he intended to say that they were hybrids which did not breed true, or whether they were no more than species of hybrid origin. It seems likely that the latter is the case. I have myself tried to raise seedlings from *R. chinensis*, which Hurst described as an undoubted hybrid between the true wild *R. chinensis spontanea* and *R. gigantea*, but its seeds do not ripen easily in our climate, and I have never yet succeeded in persuading one of them to germinate. In California, however, Moore has raised a miniature in a lilac shade, Mr. Bluebird, which is stated to have been obtained from selfing of *R. chinensis*, Old Blush.

Thanks to these complexities and misunderstandings, the nineteenth century has bequeathed to us a system of classifying our garden roses which purports to be based upon botanical principles, but which in fact violates those principles at every turn. There was no Salic Law in the rose world; each class consisted of the descendants, by maternal inheritance, of one particular rose which originated and gave its name to the class. Roses secrete little or no nectar and are not dependent upon insects for their pollination. When left to their own devices—or "open-pollinated", as we say—they normally fertilise themselves with their own pollen, and thus give rise to what are called "self-seedlings". If the originals of all the nineteenth-century classes had actually been the species that they were believed to be, all the members of each class would have been identical, except for such variations as arose accidentally by chance hybridisation or sporting. As it was, the great majority of the classes were founded by hybrids, whose natural tendency to variation provided some ten thousand new rose varieties for nineteenth-century gardens. But the classes in which they were arranged had little or no meaning. The original "Bourbon Rose", for example, was a chance hybrid arising in the Île de Bourbon between *R. chinensis* and *R. damascena,* and thus would have been classed as either a "Hybrid China" or a "Hybrid Damask" (depending upon which parent supplied the seeds) if it had come into existence in this country. As it was no-one in Europe ever saw it at all; the first Bourbon Roses raised by the Duc d'Orléans came from seeds which had been sent to France, and how closely they resembled their parent we have now no means of knowing. As the remontant offspring of a (presumably) once-flowering hybrid, they had as much right to the title of Hybrid Perpetual as any other rose. The so-called Hybrid Bourbons were mostly once-flowering—this being the chief factor which revealed their hybrid origin. Perpetual Roses which arose amongst their self-seedlings were frequently described as Bourbon Perpetuals, although many were indistinguishable in any way from the Hybrid Perpetuals, with which many of them were actually classed. It cannot be denied that there was a family resemblance between all or most of the members of one class, since the variation exhibited by hybrid seedlings does not normally extend beyond the range delimited by the characters of its two parents. Moreover, it must be borne in mind that for every new variety which is sent out, perhaps a thousand inferior ones have been rejected, so that in course of time, the typical form of a class tends to become fixed, not from natural causes, but from the selective breeding which is imposed upon the raisers by public taste and the views of the show judges. In general, the breeders select for their parent roses those varieties which have won approval in the past; and from the heterogeneous

An outstanding white climber, **Madame Alfred Carrière** *(Noisette). Raiser: Joseph Schwartz, Lyons, France. Introduced in* 1879. *Parentage not known. Large, full flowers, loosely formed, in ivory-white with flesh centre, solitary and in small clusters on long, firm stems. Strongly fragrant. Pale green, graceful foliage on very vigorous growth to* 20 *ft. Profuse summer flowering and intermittently thereafter until late autumn. Very hardy for its class and much less susceptible to rain damage than most roses of its colour. Photograph: J. L. Norton, A.R.P.S.*

An influential rose of world renown, **Souvenir de la Malmaison,** *syn.*
Queen of Beauty *and* **Fragrance.** *(Usually accepted as a Bourbon, but
classification doubtful.) Raiser: Jean Béluze, Lyons, France. Introduced* 1843.
*Parentage: Madame Desprez (Bourbon) × unknown Tea. Very large (4–5 in.),
full blooms in blush "Malmaison" pink usually solitary on long, firm stems.
Sweet, highly individual fragrance. Free, recurrent bloom. Dwarf, branching
habit from* 2½ *to 4 ft., well-furnished with particularly fine foliage. The climbing
sport (1893) performs well only in a dry climate. Photograph: J. L. Norton,
A.R.P.S.*

crowd of seedlings which results they naturally tend to pick out those which conform most closely to the approved type and are therefore most likely to win approval in the future. This is most noticeable among the Hybrid Teas today, whose "typical" shape is due far more to selection than to hereditary factors.

Chapter Five

THE AGE OF HYBRIDS

The Nineteenth Century

Ask me no more; where Jove bestows
When June is past, the fading rose.
Thomas Carew

The age of hybrids was ushered in by the arrival in Europe of the ever-blooming China Roses. But it was not ushered in with any flourish of trumpets; the date of their first arrival is very uncertain. Some have even held that they were known in Italy from an early date in the sixteenth century, basing the belief on the fact that in a painting by Bronzino in the National Gallery dating from about 1530, Cupid is represented with a handful of what look like pink China Roses. I agree that they do look like China Roses, but I do not for one moment believe that that is what they are. Nor is the evidence of Montaigne any more convincing, when he records that in November 1678 he saw a rose in the monastery at Ferrara which was said to flower all the year round. The Autumn Damasks were well known by that time, and there is no need to look beyond them for an explanation.

There is in the British Museum, in the herbarium of the Dutch botanist Gronovius, a pressed and dried specimen of an undoubted China Rose, bearing the date 1733. But no-one seems to know how it got there, or where it grew when it was alive; there is always the possibility that it was sent to Holland as a dried specimen. On the other hand, we do know that living specimens of what was then known as *Rosa indica* were brought back to Sweden from Canton in 1752, and several dried examples of these may still be seen in the herbarium of Linnaeus, at the Linnean Society in London. In 1759, Philip Miller grew one variety at least of the China Rose at Chelsea. Thereafter there were numerous reports of arrivals at various places and at various dates, many of them contradictory. It is enough to say that by the turn of the century, both the Pink China (now known as *R. chinensis*) and the Crimson (*R. c. semperflorens*) were established in the more important rose gardens of Europe.

They do not seem to have caused any very great sensation. Remontancy in roses was not entirely new; it had been known in the Autumn Damasks for a hundred and fifty years; and so long as it was confined to only one or two varieties—and those, in the Chinas, rather small and unimpressive plants compared with the "old-fashioned" roses, and with little or no scent—it was not greatly esteemed. By mid-August the rose season was over; the fact that a few bushes might continue in flower merely helped to emphasise the bareness of the rose garden as a whole—even though a specimen of the Pink China did inspire the poet Thomas Moore (on a visit to Jenkinstown House, Kilkenny, in the autumn of 1815) to write 'The Last Rose of Summer'.

No doubt many of the varieties of the old-fashioned species, which numbered several hundreds by the end of the eighteenth century, were actually hybrids, but they gained nothing from their hybrid nature; such inter-crossing as did occur gave rise to no striking novelties. But with the arrival of the Chinas, chance hybrids could not escape notice as they had often done hitherto. Not that they inherited the perpetual-flowering habit of the China parent; this is what is called a "recessive" quality and disappears in the first generation of offspring, to reappear in the second; but the difference in habit of growth and in the style of the flowers—the Chinas were little more than semi-double, but did not open flat like the semi-double gallicas—were enough to single them out. In fact, a glorious opportunity offered itself to any rose grower who would take the trouble to acquaint himself with the works of those authorities, from Kölreuter onwards, who had made a serious study of hybrids and hybridising. To our shame it must be said that no-one availed himself of it. Hybrids with the China Roses did arise, but all those of which we have any detailed knowledge arose by an accident of Nature.

The first one to come to light seems to have been the mysterious Portland Rose, of whose origin we know practically nothing. It is generally believed to have first seen the light in Italy, and it may have been a cross between the crimson China and an Autumn Damask; at all events, it presented many of the characteristics of the Damasks, combined with a true red flower such as was never seen in any Damask rose, and some degree of remontancy. From Italy it found its way to England before the end of the eighteenth century, where it was known as Rosa Paestana, after the mythical Rose of Paestum; and from England it crossed the Channel again into France, where Dupont re-named it for the Duchess of Portland, a noted rosarian of the day. Being a first-generation hybrid it did not inherit the full remontancy of the Chinas, but was capable of passing it on to its own offspring. In 1816, Souchet, gardener to the king of France, raised the lucky seedling which combined the bright red colour of the Portland Rose with the remontancy of the Chinas, and named it the Rose du Roi. Others followed, to constitute a class of Portland Roses or Damask Perpetuals, as they were also called. Its purple coloured sport, Rose du Roi à fleurs pourpres, is one of the few survivors at the present day. But the Portlands were soon overtaken in the race for bigger and better remontant roses.

Meanwhile, a pink form of the China Rose had been put on sale about 1795 by Colvill under the name of the Pale China Rose—also known, for no very good reason, as Parsons' Pink China, and today as the Old Blush China or Monthly Rose, the latter a title stolen from the Autumn Damask. It found its way across the Atlantic and into the garden of one John Champney, a rice-planter of Charleston, South Carolina. In the first few years of the nineteenth century it formed a liaison with the Musk Rose and produced a seedling which became very popular in America under the name of Champney's Pink Cluster, or the Champney Rose. This was a rambler which did not differ much from its Musk parent, except for the colour of its flowers, which was pink. But like the Portland Rose, it bore within itself the seeds of future greatness. A year or two later, Philippe Noisette, a French nurseryman of Charleston, raised a second generation from the Champney Rose, which included one variety with pale blush double flowers, which did not climb but formed a tall, compact bush and produced its flowers in large clusters without a break from early June to autumn. In 1814 he sent a specimen of this rose to his brother Louis in Paris, who marketed it a year or two later as the Noisette Rose. This very fine rose was generally known in England as the Blush Noisette; it can still be found in a few English catalogues under the name of Champney's Pink Cluster.

As in Italy and America, so also in France the China Rose formed an irregular union, with a wild rose from Southern Europe, the Alpine Rose, *R. pendulina*. This time, however, the result was not so successful. The offspring were known as Boursault Roses (and also as *R. l'héritierana* after a famous French botanist, L'Héritier de Brutelle) but they never made a great impression on the rose world. They were very sterile, and no remontant member of a second generation ever appeared. Of the two or three survivors, the best is the variety Mme. Sancy de Parabère, introduced by Bonnet of Nantes as late as 1874. It is devoid of thorns.

The pink China Rose was a great traveller. Not only did it cross the Atlantic to America in its early days, but it also found its way to the Île de Bourbon (now Réunion) in the Indian Ocean, where it was extensively grown, often side by side with Damask Roses. In 1817 the French botanist Bréon, then visiting the island, discovered a natural hybrid between the two, and took it into cultivation. By rights this hybrid should have been just as sterile as the Boursault Roses (for reasons which will be explained later); however, by one of those lucky chances, it proved to be fertile; it set seed the following year, and Bréon sent some back to France, to Jacques, a gardener to the Duc d'Orléans at Neuilly, who has left us the following account.

"The seeds of this plant," he wrote, "were sent to me by my friend M. Bréon, who sent them direct from the Île de Bourbon. I received the seed in October 1819. I sowed them at once, and four or five seedlings came up in the spring of 1820. The variety which I have described [under the astonishing name of *Rosa canina borbonica*] has always been the most vigorous and it is quite certainly from this one that the many varieties since obtained were raised." These four or five seedlings were the first Bourbon Roses, and gave rise to a relatively large class of 428 varieties, of which more than a score of first-class roses are still grown today, though the purity of their descent may be open to question in some cases.

Meanwhile, other China Roses had arrived in England from the Far East. (Their then common name of Bengal Roses, and the botanical name of *R. indica*, was due to the fact that they usually travelled in the ships of the Bengal trade.) In 1809, Sir Abraham Hume imported Hume's Blush Tea-scented China Rose, the first of the Chinas to possess a really adequate fragrance. This was the first of the Tea Roses (the name is an abbreviation of Tea-scented Rose), but being the first of its kind it was reckoned with the rest of the Chinas; it was not until some years later that the Tea Roses were recognised as a class of their own. Although the Napoleonic war was at its height, it is related that the next year, 1810, a special truce was negotiated in the Channel to permit the free passage of a ship carrying specimens of this desirable rose as a gift to the most illustrious of contemporary rosarians, the Empress Joséphine. This is such a charming story that I have not had the heart to investigate it to find out if it is really true.[1] There is no reason why it should not be; war was a gentlemanly affair in those days.

Not many years passed before Hume's Blush also joined in the race to produce hybrids. In 1815, Brown of Slough produced a rose from the seed of Hume's Blush which was supposed to have been pollinated by a gallica variety, under the name of Brown's Superb Blush. It was at first classed as a "Hybrid China", but it was unquestionably a Hybrid Tea, and it is interesting to note that it was in commerce before any of the Noisettes, Bourbons or Hybrid Perpetuals that are generally regarded as the forerunners of the class. It was almost certainly sterile (and quite certainly once-flowering), and it gave rise to no known progeny.

In 1824 came the last important new arrival, in the shape of Parks' Yellow Tea-scented China Rose, brought back from China by John Dampier Parks on behalf of the Royal Horticultural Society. This was generally similar to Hume's importation of fifteen years before, save for its clear yellow colour. Both Hume's Blush and Parks' Yellow have unfortunately disappeared from cultivation, but (in theory, at least) the whole class of true Tea Roses is descended from one or the other—or both—of these. The variety Adam, sent out by the French nurseryman of that name in 1833, is generally credited with being the first Tea Rose to have been bred in Europe; but nothing is known of its provenance. The origin of the name of the class is equally uncertain. Some have claimed that the scent of these roses resembles the scent of the fresh leaves of the tea plant when crushed; others say that the plants themselves smelled of tea through having been imported in tea chests. The fact that both these explanations have gained currency shows that many people do not share the commonest belief, that the scent of the roses is the same as that exhaled by the family teapot. It is worth remembering that the scent of tea is perhaps even more variable than the scent of roses. I can detect no noticeable resemblance between the two; but while I know that my sense of smell is not defective, it may be that my imagination is.

Although it founded no hybrid line of its own, Parks' Yellow Tea Rose had an important effect on another line, the Noisettes. The original Blush

[1] The story has been checked and found to be correct.—Ed.

Noisette produced few if any direct descendants, but in 1830 two "Hybrid Noisettes" appeared, both of which owed their existence to the pollen of the Yellow Tea. These were Lamarque, sent out by Maréchal of Angers, whose flowers were white with yellow centres, and Desprez à fleurs jaunes (or Jaune Desprez), by Desprez of Yèbles, a pinkish yellow. It is these two, rather than the original Noisette Rose, which were the true founders of the Noisette line. One cannot help wondering if their reputed parentage is correct, since both of them were vigorous climbers, which is more than either parent was. Be that as it may, most of the Noisette Roses still in cultivation trace their descent from one or other of the two, which accounts for the predominant yellow colour of the class. As the direct line petered out, these yellow climbers and their descendants soon dropped the epithet "hybrid" and usurped the name of Noisette.

For the last important cross with the China Roses we have to jump forward to about 1860, when Sisley of Lyons raised a number of plants of the true wild *R. multiflora* (then more commonly known as *R. polyantha*) from seeds that he had received from Japan. This is another member of the *Synstylae* group, a white rambler rose; other, cultivated, forms of the species had been imported many years before, but these were mostly pink and more or less double, whereas Sisley's plants had single white flowers. In February 1869, Guillot *fils*, also of Lyons, sowed a number of seeds from these plants and raised a second generation which exhibited wide variation, most of them being sterile. One of them, however, with ten-petalled white flowers, produced a number of hips. The seeds were sown in February 1872, and among the resulting seedlings Guillot found several plants which were not ramblers but perpetual-flowering dwarfs. One of these which had double white flowers he sent out in December 1875 under the name of Pâquerette; a second, much like the first but pink in colour, was marketed in November 1880 as Mignonette. These were the first of the dwarf polyantha roses. One curious thing about this story is that Guillot insisted that for his first sowing he employed "a large number" of seeds, and that their seedlings displayed "total variation"—which seems to imply that all his plants of the first generation were hybrids. The need for accuracy was not then appreciated, and the evidence is too scanty and unreliable to bear very close scrutiny. The identity of the unknown pollen parent in this case can only be guessed, but there is little doubt that it was one of the China Roses, in all probability the Old Blush. The suggestion that it was the miniature form, *R. chinensis minima*, is not borne out by an

examination of the resulting hybrids, which display none of the characteristics of the miniature form.

                    ✳   ✳   ✳

With so many different lines to follow through the ensuing hundred and
fifty years a purely chronological survey would be hopelessly confusing, so
from now on I shall deal with each class separately.

THE CHINA AND TEA ROSES

In the province of Hupeh in central China, near the city of Ichang on
the upper Yangtse river, there grows a wild rose which has been given the
name of *R. chinensis spontanea*—the true wild China Rose. At least, we
suppose it to be; very few people have ever seen it, and no specimen has
ever been cultivated in Europe, so far as we know. From such descriptions
as we have, it seems to be a vigorous brier, with single flowers of a deep
pink or red colour, and like the vast majority of wild roses, it produces
them at one season only. At some time in the distant past, this rose
sported and produced a new form which yielded flowers continuously
throughout the growing season. Such a change would be of no benefit to
the plant from the point of view of survival, since it necessarily meant that
a large proportion of its seeds were produced too late in the season to ripen
properly, and in course of time it would no doubt have succumbed to the
competition of its more conventional rivals; but some enterprising
Chinese gardener must have found it and taken it into cultivation. No
trace of this sported form can be found at the present day, but in Miss
Lowe's Variety, which apparently came into existence as a sport from a
variety of the crimson China, we have something which must be very
similar, if not identical. The flowers of Miss Lowe's Variety have the
remarkable property of reversing the usual fading habit of the rose; they
open pink and deepen to crimson as they age. Whether this is also characteristic of the wild brier does not seem to have been recorded, but the same
habit appears in several of the China Roses and in a few of their later
descendants, so it very likely was.

In the course of hundreds, perhaps thousands, of years of cultivation the
perpetual flowering China Rose gave rise to other forms, both by sporting
and also, perhaps, by crossing with *R. gigantea*, a closely related but very
different species, being a rampant climber with huge five-inch white
flowers. As the native habitats of these two species are many hundreds of

miles apart, the crossing probably took place in cultivation, though certainly by accident; when and where we have no idea, but the Old Blush China, which is said to be one of the descendants of this cross, can be recognised in Chinese paintings of a thousand years ago. One of the mysteries presented by the history of the China Roses is, what became of all the climbing forms which must have resulted from such a cross? Since the climbing habit is dominant over the dwarf, they must have been in a majority; and although the perpetual habit is recessive, still some of them must have been perpetual, and one would have thought that these at least would have been treasured. But since the original cross is itself hardly more than a matter of speculation, there is little hope of further enlightenment.

The China Roses are not good breeders in this country. They produce good pollen, for the most part, and so are capable of fertilising other roses, but many of them are reluctant to set seed, and when set, it often fails to ripen out of doors. As a result of this they have not really established any "line" of their own, many of the named varieties being comparatively modern hybrids mostly of French origin. There are, however, some varieties which may be regarded as of pure descent. If the Old Blush is a hybrid, at least some forms of the Crimson China apparently are not. *R. chinensis mutabilis*, a single-flowered form whose three-inch flowers open yellow, but change through orange to crimson as they age, seems to be of true China blood. *R. c. viridiflora* is a very double form whose petals have been transformed into leaves, or nearly so; but the appearance of these green "flowers" is usually spoilt by the presence of a crimson pigment which partly suffuses the green "petals", giving them a brownish, withered look, though they have the compensating advantage of remaining open for weeks, if not months, on end. *R. c. minima*, the miniature rose, has never been accused of possessing any taint of *R. gigantea* in its ancestry; it has recently attracted the attention of hybridists who have produced new varieties by crossing with other roses. The true miniature China is, as its name implies, an almost perfect miniature of an ordinary bush rose, the plant itself and its leaves and flowers all being reduced in size in perfect proportion. The oldest named variety, Pompon de Paris, seems to have disappeared from the catalogues, except in its climbing form, which is exquisitely dainty, but the later introduction, named *R. rouletii*, is probably the same plant, and is widely offered.

The Tea Roses are genetically identical with the Chinas, with which

they were originally classed, being also allegedly the descendants of a cross
between *R. chinensis spontanea* and *R. gigantea*. There is no need to look
beyond the two original importations of Hume and Parks for their
ancestry. Their colour range was not wide, being generally restricted to
white, pink, yellow and intermediate pastel shades. The few crimson
varieties which appeared may have been due to the natural tendency of the
China ancestor to produce flowers of this colour, or to accidental hybridising, which probably occurred far more frequently than our records show.
This would also account for the fact that a few of the later varieties to
appear proved on examination to be triploids. They did not differ strikingly
from their descendants, the Hybrid Teas of today, but they possessed
two unfortunate weaknesses; their flowers had a characteristic tendency to
droop on their stems, and they were not completely hardy in our climate.
They were thus par excellence the roses for growing in pots in a conservatory, and when conservatories disappeared with the Edwardian era, the
Tea Roses disappeared too—although they are still grown under the
warmer skies of southern France and California. About the only variety
still to be found in English catalogues is Lady Hillingdon, which exists
in both dwarf and climbing forms. It is perfectly hardy, a rich apricot in
colour, with a lovely scent, and in its climbing form (I am not familiar
with the dwarf) it repeats well. Although a typical Tea in appearance,
it is a triploid, which suggests that its unusual hardiness is due to one
parent not being a Tea. It not infrequently set seed for me, but the
enormous size of the seeds—as big as peas—suggested that there was
something abnormal about them, which was confirmed by the fact that I
never persuaded any of them to germinate. Devoniensis, the first Tea
Rose to be raised in England, by Foster of Devonport in about 1840, also
survives as a climber, which safely passed through three winters outdoors
in east Norfolk with me; and there seems no doubt that it would flourish
in a warm position in normal years. The flowers are cream in colour, very
double and rather untidy, though a warm flush of pink or orange at the
heart makes them most attractive; and the scent pervades all that corner
of the garden when they are open.

Mention should be made here of two roses which fall into no particular
class, though they resemble the Chinas more closely than any other. These
are Cécile Brunner and Perle d'Or, which appeared in 1880 and 1884
respectively. They were said at the time to be the offspring of two Tea
Roses, the pink Mme. de Tartas and the yellow Mme. Falcot, crossed with

R. multiflora. This is impossible; such a cross would inevitably have produced a once-flowering rambler. Today it is more usual to say that the unnamed parent was "a polyantha", which is certainly more plausible, though one should bear in mind that at this time there were only two polyanthas, Pâquerette and Mignonette, in existence. But as a matter of fact, these two roses show little sign of multiflora influence anywhere; in everything but bloom they closely resemble the pink China, but the flowers which are more double but much smaller, come in widely-spaced clusters. There is very little difference between them; Cécile Brunner is pale pink, and Perle d'Or is not gold, but a pinkish apricot. They are very dainty and attractive, sweetly scented and just as perpetual as the Chinas, and a lot more graceful than the modern floribunda roses—with the honourable exception of Jenny Wren, raised in 1957 by Mrs. Ratcliffe from Cécile Brunner × Fashion, which is very like its predecessors. There is an opportunity here for an enterprising hybridist to build up a new class of bedding roses.

THE NOISETTE ROSES

As the earliest authenticated hybrids with the new China roses, the Noisettes may claim to be considered first. The true line, however, did not extend very far. The original "Rosier de Philippe Noisette" is still available (under the name of Champney's Pink Cluster) but all its direct descendants have disappeared. Two of them are illustrated in the 1835 edition of Redouté, the Purple Noisette, raised by one M. Ternaux, and Isabelle d'Orléans, raised by Laffay "who has also raised many others". Aimée Vibert, raised by Vibert in 1828, is still to be found, but is not a true Noisette; it is said to have resulted from a cross with *R. sempervirens*, but its actual pedigree is quite unknown.

A plant which produces such an immense quantity of flowers over so long a period as the original Blush Noisette has little energy left for climbing. The two hybrids with Parks' Yellow Tea which appeared in 1830 or thereabouts, however, reverted to the climbing habit, at the cost of quantity of flowers, though they were both remontant. They were, in fact, the first true remontant climbers, which no doubt accounted in part for their popularity. Jaune Desprez was actually marketed by Sisley Vandael, who paid the raiser 3,000 francs for his rights in the variety—a substantial sum in those days. But it was the other one, Lamarque, which really founded the new Noisette line, through its two self-seedlings Mme.

Schultz and Chromatella. The former yielded Rêve d'Or in 1869, which sported with Veuve Ducher of Lyons in 1878 to give William Allen Richardson. The bearer of the name in life was a rosarian in Kentucky who had corresponded with Madame Ducher. Chromatella (also known as Cloth of Gold) became the parent in 1864 of Maréchal Niel which was the most esteemed of all yellow roses until well into this century. All these varieties were repeat-flowering climbers, some more reliable in this respect than others, all sweetly scented, the fragrance from a few blooms of Maréchal Niel will, for example, quickly pervade a room. They are all in varying shades of yellow. Mme. Schultz has disappeared, but the rest are still in cultivation, though they inherited some of the tenderness of the Tea side of the family and prefer the shelter of a south-facing wall, or better still, a greenhouse or conservatory as they are also susceptible to damage by rain.

Claire Jacquier and Mme. Alfred Carrière are often included among the Noisettes, but they are not typical. The latter, sent out by Schwartz of Lyons in 1879, is a white triploid usually with a flesh pink, but occasionally lemon centre. Its parentage is unknown, but it remains one of the best white climbers we possess as it is extremely vigorous, hardy and freeflowering from June until frost and its loose, but charming petal formation is remarkably tolerant of rain. Its scent is far nearer the Damasks than the Noisettes. This factor and a hardiness not found in other Noisettes put its classification in doubt.

Two other roses whose classification is arguable are often listed as Noisettes. The old favourite, Gloire de Dijon, quite easily might be; it differs from them only in its considerably greater hardiness. There is, however, a tradition that its raiser, Jacotot of Dijon, obtained it from seed of a yellow Tea pollinated by Souvenir de la Malmaison. In its long history, it produced a number of colour mutations, one of the best being Belle Lyonnaise, in canary yellow, which is still in cultivation. It was also the parent of a number of seedlings, all climbers of similar persuasion, which were separately classed as Dijon Teas. Being hardier than the Climbing Teas and Noisettes, they enjoyed considerable vogue during the last quarter of the nineteenth century. The second, Mme. Plantier, is now thought to be more correctly placed with the albas. It is pure white with fully double, sweetly scented, small blooms and forms a once-flowering vigorous shrub rather than a true climber.

The Noisette line came to an end with the nineteenth century. No new developments have appeared in the past seventy years, and none are to be looked for in the near future now that we have an almost unlimited choice of remontant climbers derived mainly from the Hybrid Teas. In the original Blush Noisette, however, we have a type which is almost unique and a number of variations on this theme would be very welcome. So far, no breeder has attempted to go back to it.

THE BOURBON ROSES

This is another class which has survived to the present day, although all of Jacques' original seedlings have disappeared from cultivation, along with the great majority of the 428 varieties that have been recorded.

There have been very few instances where the varietal parentage has been stated, and of the handful still grown, it is tolerably certain that many of them are not true Bourbons, but Hybrid Bourbons and Hybrid Chinas.

In order to understand the difference, it is necessary to look at the position in the second quarter of the nineteenth century when interest in hybrids was increasing. At that time, it was natural that in raising them priority should be given to the crossing of the repeat-flowering Bourbons and Chinas on the one side with the best of the older, once-flowering kinds on the other, in the hope that the repeat-blooming characteristic would be passed on to the seedlings.

It must not be supposed that "raising hybrids" at this time implied artificial pollination. This was occasionally practised, but so unskilfully that it can rarely have succeeded. Hybrids were usually raised by planting the proposed parents side by side—one French writer of the period actually recommended planting in the same hole—in the hope that cross-fertilisation would occur. It sometimes did, but there was no guarantee that the strange pollen came from the next-door neighbour.

What the raisers did not know and did not suspect was that when a repeat-flowering rose is crossed with a once-flowering kind, the repeat-flowering character is completely submerged in the first (f_1) generation and will reappear only in a small proportion of seedlings in the second (f_2) generation. Thus if a seedling arose from a cross between a remontant Bourbon and a rose of another class and displayed the general character of the Bourbon parent but missed out on the repeat-flowering habit, then it was classed as a Hybrid Bourbon. The same working principle applied to the Chinas. Any seedlings which showed affinities to the Chinas but failed to repeat were regarded as Hybrids and like the Hybrid Bourbons, were assigned to a separate class.

Modern literature and catalogues make no distinction, but all the writers in England and France of a century ago indicate quite clearly the existence of three separate classes, with only the Bourbons grouped with the Autumnal roses. The following varieties now offered as Bourbons are not strictly members of that class, but are Hybrid Bourbons and Hybrid Chinas since they have only one annual flowering, although there may be an odd bloom or two later.

Bourbon Queen (1835), an enduring old rose in carmine-pink with a sweet scent. It strikes well from cuttings which probably accounts for its wide distribution in old gardens, although its name is often unknown to the owner.

Charles Lawson (1853), soft pink with a deeper reverse, rather large, but loosely formed; Commandant Beaurepaire (1874), an interesting striped variety with smallish, cupped blooms; Blairii No. 2, the sole survivor of three seedlings raised by Blair, an amateur, first sent out in 1845. The blooms are pink with a deeper veining and highly scented. Others are Coupe d'Hébé (1840), Great Western (1840), Mme. Lauriol de Barny (1868), Vivid (1853) and a purplish coloured variety sold under the name Prince Charles, although the identification is doubtful. With the exception of the latter, all the others are of climbing habit and are best treated as pillar roses.

Of the existing true Bourbons, the oldest is the famous Souvenir de la Malmaison, sent out by Béluze of Lyons in 1843. By happy chance, it is also one of the few where the parentage has been recorded, the seed parent being Mme. Desprez pollinated by an unnamed yellow Tea. Mme. Desprez is no longer in cultivation, but was described as a lilac-pink, full petalled Bourbon of vigorous growth introduced in 1831. Souvenir de la Malmaison makes a small but vigorous shrub whose pale flesh-coloured blooms are produced with great freedom throughout the season. It is often confused in this country with the climbing sport, which occurred in 1890 with Henry Bennett and was sent out three years later. It is less satisfactory than the bush and intending purchasers should make quite sure which form they are getting. No other Bourbon has ever been recorded as having produced a climbing mutation, although as we have seen, the Teas, with their *R. gigantea* ancestry, frequently did so. Three colour variants are also known to have occurred. The deep pink and red forms seem to have been lost, but the third and last to appear is still with us. Sent out in 1888 as Kronprinzessin Viktoria, its French synonym, Malmaison jaune, gives a clue to its coloration which is white with a sulphur-yellow centre and in the folds of the petals—a colour combination found in no other Bourbon and which could only have come in from the Tea parent. It is, therefore, a nice point to decide whether or not Souvenir de la Malmaison and Kronprinzessin Viktoria (and the other colour sports if they should ever recur) ought to be classed as Hybrid Teas.

In 1851, Margottin in Bourg-la-Reine, near Paris, sent out Louise Odier. It was first seen in England in 1855 when the reporter for *The Florist, Fruitist and Garden Miscellany* observed that it "was most distinctive and should be in every collection". A century later, an American enthusiast was saying the same thing. The lilac-pink, shallow-cupped flowers form a near-perfect geometrical circle and they appear in good numbers through-out the season on a shapely bush to five feet. The same perfection of form is found in Reine Victoria (1872) with a deeper cup in a deeper pink. Its blush-to-white sport, Mme. Pierre Oger, which occurred in 1878, is gener-ally more popular. Both are highly acceptable plants of slender growth and good health. A striped pink and white sport of Louise Odier is recorded as having occurred in 1882 and was distributed as Mme. Olympe Terest-chenko. It seems to have been lost to cultivation, but I take the liberty of mentioning it here in case it should occur again.

There is another striped Bourbon still in commerce named Honorine de Brabant with lilac-pink blooms striped and mottled deep crimson which changes to violet. It forms a big shrub to six feet, flowers freely in the first flush and then sparingly for the remainder of the season; its provenance and date of occurrence are unknown, although it is obviously a sport.

Three other Bourbons were sent out when the popularity of the class was already waning (see Fig. 3), but held their place in the post-war revival. When Garçon of Rouen raised a seedling, it was his intention to send it out as "Le Bienheureux de la Salle", and had actually cata-logued it under that name. His "Blessing of the Bower" was seen by Margottin, mentioned earlier, who acquired it and having secured the patronage of Mme. Isaac Pereire, wife of a well-known Parisian banker, distributed it under her name in 1881. It has the largest blooms of any in the class; they are deep pink clouded magenta and wonderfully fragrant. I have never seen it grown in a rose-bower, but can imagine the effect, especially if it were coupled with its paler pink sport, Mme. Ernest Calvat, which arose in 1888. The third of this handsome trio, Mrs. Paul, a seed-ling from Mme. Isaac Pereire raised by George Paul in 1891, is several shades lighter still—almost white with pearly pink, but otherwise very similar to the parent. All three flower reliably a second time.

The best known and perhaps the best loved of all the Bourbons is Zéphirine Drouhin, the so-called thornless rose. (It is not absolutely free from thorns—a fact which ruins the plot of one of Miss Agatha Christie's early books!) As a climber it can be trained up to ten feet or so, but its canes are sufficiently sturdy to allow it to stand by itself as a large shrub. It was sent out by Bizot in 1868 and is the sole variety with which he is credited. Its parentage is unknown. Its semi-double, vivid pink blooms are produced in enormous quantities at the first flush, and thereafter with hardly a break except for a short rest at the end of July or beginning of August. Like all the Bourbons, it is very fragrant. For those who find its colour too shocking, there are two paler sports, Martha (1912) in medium pink and Kathleen Harrop (1919), a pretty shell-pink. They are a little less vigorous than the original.

A few so-called Bourbons have appeared in the present century, but their authenticity is generally dubious. Variegata di Bologna occurred in 1909 and is characterised by white blooms irregularly striped with purple. Its parentage has not been revealed, but it occasionally reverts to an all-purple flower which has not been identified, but a Bourbon in this colour named Victor Emmanuel was long popular in Italy. Adam Messerich, which came from Lambert of Trier, Germany, is a complete mongrel whose only connexion with the Bourbons is through its great-grandparent, Louise Odier; while Zigeunerknabe (Gipsy Boy), also from Lambert, is stated to be a seedling from Ruselliana, an old purple rambler rose. It has only one period of bloom and makes a grand display; the other two have some repeat.

As with the Noisettes, the Bourbons have died out because they have nothing more to offer us. The best of them make fine, sturdy shrubs, most have a powerful scent and some have flower formations not found elsewhere in the genus. They deserve the niche they have made for themselves in the fascinating history of rose development, but our modern resources permit us to produce shrub and climbing roses in far greater variety and range of colours than the Bourbons can ever display.

THE PORTLANDS AND HYBRID PERPETUALS

The Portland Roses, as we have seen, were a flash in the pan. They had their brief period of popularity in the early years of the nineteenth century,

A pair of Bourbons **Reine Victoria.** *Raiser: Joseph Schwartz, Lyons, France. Introduced 1872. Parentage unknown. Medium-sized (3 in.), very full, symmetrically cupped blooms in deep lilac-pink, solitary and in small clusters on long, firm stems. Very fragrant. Tall, slender growth to 6 ft. and over, with good, mid-green foliage and characteristically pointed leaflets. Very free, recurrent bloom into late autumn.* **Madame Pierre Oger,** *cream to flesh sport of the above, occurred with Arthur Oger, Caen, France. Introduced 1878. A bloom here shows a partial reversal to the parent. Photograph: J. L. Norton, A.R.P.S.*

A foundation crimson, **Général Jacqueminot** *(Hybrid Perpetual). Raiser: A. Roussel, Montpellier, France, who died prior to its introduction in* 1853. *Parentage unknown, but generally considered to be a natural seedling from Gloire des Rosamanes. Large, high-centred blooms with 30–35 light crimson petals ageing to Tyrian purple. Strongly scented. Profuse, repeated bloom. Mid-green, plentiful foliage on very vigorous, tall, thorny growth to 7 ft. Best grown pegged down. Much favoured as a florist's forcing rose for over half a century on account of its high bloom yield. Photograph: J. L. Norton, A.R.P.S.*

but we really know very little about them—where they came from, how they originated, what they looked like. Only one, the Rose du Roi, achieved any sort of fame, and that one was so superior to the rest of the class that it is often spoken of as the first of the Hybrid Perpetuals. There can be no serious objection to this. The Hybrid Perpetuals—the name is a mistranslation of the French *hybrides remontants*, "remontant hybrids", and is a description rather than a title—were not a precisely-defined class, but rather something of an omnium-gatherum. As a result of the disappointing experience with the early Hybrid Chinas and Hybrid Bourbons, the idea soon gained currency that hybrid roses were not remontant, and as most of these early hybrids were not only once-flowering but also highly sterile, some time elapsed before the perpetual-flowering habit reappeared in plants of the second generation. When it did appear, they naturally attracted attention.

This is not the place to go deeply into the Mendelian rules of inheritance, but it may help the reader to understand what was happening if I give a little table of the possibilities. In what follows, O stands for a once-flowering rose, P for a perpetual rose, and O(p) for a rose which while itself once-flowering, is capable of passing on the perpetual habit to some of its offspring. We find that:

O selfed, or O x O, yields O.
P selfed, or P x P, yields P.
O x P, or P x O, yields O(p).
O(p) selfed, or O(p) x O(p), yields some P.
O(p) x O, or O x O(p), yields some O(p).
O(p) x P, or P x O(p), yields some P.

Perpetual hybrids were, therefore, liable to arise among the self-seedlings of a Hybrid Bourbon or a Hybrid China (no class of Hybrid Portlands seems ever to have been recognised), or as the result of crossing any two of these classes, or of crossing any one of them with a Bourbon, China, Tea or Portland Rose. Under the then system of classification no name could be found for the result of a cross between, say, a Hybrid China and a Hybrid Bourbon, and so the noncommittal expression "remontant hybrid" came into use. Generally speaking, any rose was a remontant hybrid—or Hybrid Perpetual in England—if it was a hybrid, was remontant, and did not fit into any other accepted class.

The father of the Hybrid Perpetuals was the Frenchman Laffay of

F

Auteuil, who confided to his friend, William Paul, that he raised many of his best roses from crosses between the Hybrid Bourbons Athalin and Céline and the freer-flowering varieties of the Damask Perpetuals (or Portlands). Thus in the beginning, these roses combined the features of the China, Damask and Gallica. Sisley, writing forty years later, does not credit Laffay with having employed artificial pollination; indeed, if he had, he would have had no need to raise the enormous numbers of up to 200,000 seedlings annually that Paul describes. Laffay sent out several good roses of this type from 1837 onwards, but his first great success came with the Rose de la Reine, which appeared in 1842 or 1843. Baronne Prévost was sent out by Desprez at about the same time. Both these roses were lilac-pink in colour, but in 1845 Nérard produced a crimson variety, Géant des Batailles. The parentage of these roses is not known, but each of them produced a line of self-seedlings (or supposed self-seedlings). According to Ellwanger (1882), the first two lines were all fully perpetual, with plenty of autumn bloom, though the third were less free in this respect. These three important varieties have been preserved in cultivation.

Ellwanger, a nurseryman of Rochester, N.Y., whose intelligent and common-sense views on rose breeding were in refreshing contrast with those of most of his contemporaries, investigated the parentage of 968 varieties of roses known to him, but in only thirty-eight cases was he able to establish the names of both parents with any certainty, and only nine of these were Hybrid Perpetuals. All the rest were produced by open pollination, and so were, for the most part, self-seedlings. Among the H.P.s he traced eleven separate lines of direct descent and the more influential of these deserve a word of description.

Three of them, Rose de la Reine (now commonly shortened to La Reine), Baronne Prévost and Géant des Batailles, have already been mentioned. The fourth was the famous Général Jacqueminot, raised by an amateur, a certain Monsieur Roussel of Montpellier who had raised hundreds of seedlings without obtaining anything worthwhile. On his death, his last batch of seedlings were taken over by his gardener, who was rather confusingly named Rousselet. The latter doubtless had assisted his late employer in his hobby, recognised the value of this seedling and arranged for its distribution in 1852. This magnificent rose, which can still be bought, has suffered the quite unjustified accusation that it is not fully perpetual. This calumny has apparently arisen because there was another rose, a Hybrid China, of the same name raised a few years earlier which did not repeat. The true 'General Jack' produces its bright crimson, highly fragrant blooms with great freedom in autumn as well as in early summer. The fact that it was a favourite forcing rose for the cut-flower trade until well into the present century is sufficient evidence of its freedom of bloom and reliability of cropping. Allow it plenty of space, for it has lost none of its vigour and ensure that it is obtained from a reliable source.

The next was Victor Verdier, raised by Lacharme of Lyons and introduced in 1859, a bright pink rose with a deeper centre. This variety is of special interest, since it is recorded that its pollen parent was the equally famous yellow Tea Rose, Safrano. If this is true, then Victor Verdier was not a Hybrid Perpetual, but a Hybrid Tea, and the first of this modern class. It was classed as an H.P. in accordance with the then current practice because its seed parent was an H.P. and an important one, Jules Margottin, which featured next in Ellwanger's list. This bright carmine variety was raised in 1853 by its namesake whom we have already met in connexion with the Bourbons. It makes a fairly tall, upright bush with conspicuous red-brown prickles. The blooms are neither very shapely nor very fragrant, except under certain conditions, but they come freely and for this reason it was much favoured for growing as a standard.

In Fig. 2 I have given a family tree showing the supposed relationship between these patriarchs of the class. With the exception of those already mentioned, only Prince Camille de Rohan is still grown, mainly for its colour, a rich, deep maroon. The blooms are quite small and the plant lacks vigour, a noticeable failing in so many of this shade. There are among the H.P.s a few honourable exceptions in Gloire de Ducher (1865), Souvenir d'Alphonse Lavallée (1884). Both make big, willowy plants which can be treated as pillar roses if desired, although they flower more profusely if the shoots are left at full length and are then pegged down to a horizontal position.

The remainder, Charles Lefèbvre, Sénateur Vaisse, Alfred Colomb and Duke of Edinburgh (the only English-raised founder of a family), are no longer seen. They were all in shades of red and crimson and were favourite exhibition varieties. Indeed, it was the arrival of large-flowered Hybrid Perpetuals such as these from the middle of the nineteenth century onwards which gave rise to that very pleasant summer activity which is still with us—the rose show. Coupled with the revolution in transport brought about by the railways and the relative affluence when the general level of "real" wages rose on an average of twenty-five per cent above those of

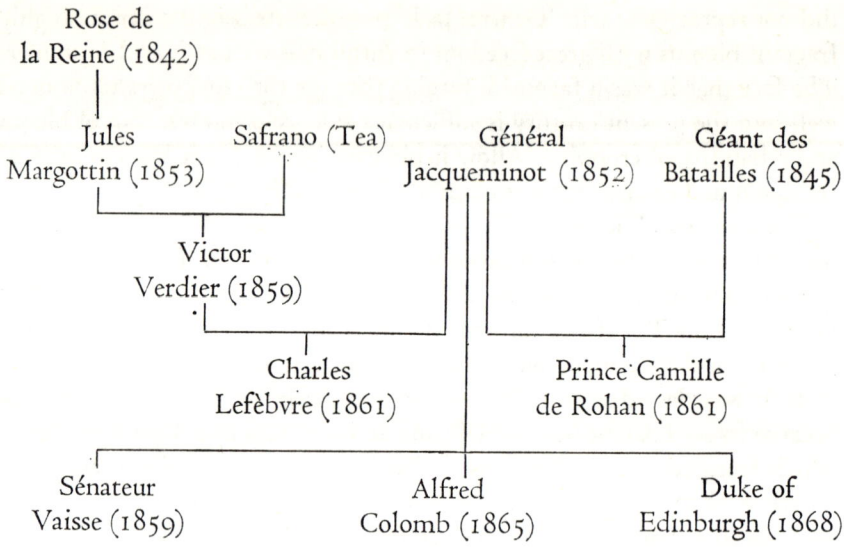

Fig. 2 Family tree showing the relationship between Ellwanger's "Founding Fathers" of the Hybrid Perpetuals.

"The Hungry Forties", the spirit of friendly (and occasionally not-so-friendly) competition developed. In his classic, *A Book about Roses*, Dean Hole gives a charming and revealing picture of the rose-growing activities of the Nottingham artisans in the late 1850s which encouraged him to think of competitive rose-showing in nation-wide terms.

Of the groups who took up rose growing as a hobby, none did so more enthusiastically than the incumbents of country rectories. The Rev. Honywood D'Ombrain founded the then National Rose Society in 1876 and became its first Honorary Secretary, an office he held for twenty-five years; Reynolds Hole, then a Canon, became President and remained so until his death in 1904, while several other clerics were elected to the first Committee. Many of these reverend rosarians wrote books of greater or lesser length, all with a style and vigour that came from composing sermons. With only a few exceptions, they were primarily concerned with assessing exhibition qualities. So obsessed with this aspect was the Reverend Foster-Melliar that in lengthy individual descriptions of over a hundred H.P.s, his remarks about colour are frequently confined to "good", "bad" or "indifferent"; presumably the actual colour of a variety was a detail too unimportant to convey to his readers.

Of recent years, it has become fashionable to dismiss the Hybrid Perpetuals on the grounds that they were not truly remontant; that they gave only a limited amount of repeat bloom. While it is true that among the 2,500 or so that were raised there were many which were known to be poor autumnal flowering, most of the writers who make this sweeping assertion today, do so without any experience of growing them. There are still quite enough varieties of this class available for putting to the test. For some ten years I kept day-to-day records of the blooming of all the roses in my garden, totalling some hundred and eighty varieties of all classes. Of the few H.P.s among them, the best were *more* remontant than *any* of the H.T.s, while the worst were less than half-way down the list. There is a limit to what a single plant can produce in the way of bloom in a single season. If the flowers are small, there will be more of them than if they are large, and many of the H.P.s—Paul Neyron for instance—were, even by today's standards, very large indeed.

The Hybrid Perpetuals, having swept all before them in their heyday, were themselves driven out in their turn by the Hybrid Teas, which first began to make their presence felt in the eighties of the last century, and had, as shown in Fig. 3, won a decisive victory by the first decade of this.

There were several reasons for this change in fortunes. The typical H.P. flower was inclined to be globular and "cabbagy" as compared with the long buds and high-centred flowers of the best H.T.s. Their colour range, too, was limited to shades of red from deep maroon to pale pink, most with a tendency to developing a distinctly bluish tint with age, and a few whites. Of yellow, orange, scarlet or salmon-pink varieties there were none. (There were, however, a number of striped roses, of which two, Vick's Caprice and Ferdinand Pichard, are still available. The latter has the more pronounced colourings, pale pink splashed with bright crimson and ranks with the gallica, Rosa Mundi, for a startling effect.) The growth habit of the H.P.s also left something to be desired, tending to the production of long, whippy canes, too long to stand without support but not long enough to train as a climber. These are usually dealt with in the way recommended earlier, known as "pegging down". By fixing the tips to pegs or short, stout canes driven firmly into the ground at the required distance from the plant so that the shoot is held in the horizontal position, a single plant can be made to cover quite a large area. Blooms are then produced at every lateral with a magnificent display, as can be seen in the beds of Hybrid Perpetuals grown in this manner at The Royal Botanic Gardens, Kew.

Class	1st Edn. 1848	2nd Edn. 1860	9th Edn. 1888	10th Edn. 1903
Portlands or Damask Perp.	84	—	—	—
Hybrid Chinas	170	41	25	9
Hybrid Bourbons	57	17	8	7
Bourbons	218	124	84	33
Hybrid Perpetuals	106	339	661	226
Chinas	97	43	41	41
Teas	115	115	227*	215*
Noisettes	74	44	41	15
Hybrid Teas	—	—	27†	133†
Total	921	723	1114	679

* Includes Dijon Teas raised mainly between 1868–1885.
† Includes Climbing sports occurring from 1881 onwards.

Fig. 3   Table to show the rise and decline of various classes of roses developed during the nineteenth century.

(Source: William Paul, *The Rose Garden*, various editions.)

Chapter Six

THE AGE OF HYBRIDS

The Late Nineteenth Century and After

THE HYBRID TEAS

As we have already seen, the first of the Hybrid Teas came into existence as long ago as 1815, which is a year before even Rose du Roi appeared, and more than twenty years before Laffay produced the first of his Hybrid Perpetuals. By 1836, Boitard was able to list four of the class in his book, *Manuel Complet de l'Amateur des Roses*, a work shamelessly pirated by the English novelist, Mrs. Catherine Gore, and issued two years later as *The Rose Fancier's Manual*. The four were Brown's Hybrid Tea (which was presumably the same as Brown's Superb Blush, the pioneer of 1815), Duc de Choiseul from Vibert of Angers in 1825, Celestial Tea Rose, raised in London by an unknown hand at an unknown date, and Thé à fleurs chagrinées, also from Vibert.

If these were all, in fact, hybrids, we may be reasonably sure that they were all once-flowering and very sterile. If they had been fertile, a second generation raised from them would have included at least a few perpetual varieties, and the Hybrid Tea class as we know it today might have started on its career fifty years before it did.

In the year 1864, Guillot *fils* of Lyons sowed, according to his custom, a large quantity of Tea Rose seed which he had gathered indiscriminately from all his different varieties in cultivation, and among the seedlings which arose from them was one which differed markedly from all the rest. He cherished it with great care, and in November, 1867, sent it out as La France. That this rose was a Hybrid Tea is unquestionable, even though its pollen parent was unknown and undiscoverable. That it was *not* the first of its class is equally unquestionable. Its only real claim to priority lies in the fact that it was the first Hybrid Tea of such superlative excellence as to draw attention to the possibilities of the class. An extraordinary tradition has grown up, and still persists, that La France was raised from a cross between the H.P. Mme. Victor Verdier—not to be confused with her husband, discussed in the previous chapter—and the Tea Rose, Mme. Bravy. Who invented this wholly mythical parentage I have been unable to discover; it is enough to say that the account I have given of the origin of La France was that given by Guillot himself in the *Journal des Roses* for March 1879. La France was, and still is, a very fine rose, with large, very double blooms of a pale bluish pink with a magnificent scent. It seems to have lost much of its former vigour, but if I were restricted to a dozen H.T. varieties, La France would be one of them. Being a triploid, as would be expected, it is very infertile, but not completely so.

The great English rose authorities of this period, Thomas Rivers and William Paul, beside a number of lesser men, have much to say on the subject of deliberate hybridisation and cross-breeding by artificial pollination. Unhappily for their reputations, they say too much and betray their own ignorance. Rivers plainly knew little more about the subject than that a transfer of pollen from one variety to another was involved in some way. Cranston laid it down that one should wait until a flower was fully expanded before applying the strange pollen—by which time self-fertilisation would almost inevitably have occurred. It is not surprising, therefore, that the first of this later generation of Hybrid Teas to appear in England was an accidental one, Cheshunt Hybrid, which came from the seed of the Tea Rose Mme. de Tartas which was believed to have been pollinated by the H.P. Prince Camille de Rohan. This was was of very tall growth, a pillar rose. A few specimens still exist, but it is no longer offered in the catalogues. Like La France, it was almost entirely sterile.

In the first three quarters of the nineteenth century, almost all the world's new roses originated in France, but the true father of the Hybrid Tea class, the first to set about breeding them deliberately, was Henry Bennett, a farmer and cattle breeder, of Stapleford, Wiltshire, and later of Shepperton, Middlesex. In 1879, when only four now acknowledged Hybrid Teas existed, and all of these of accidental origin, Bennett sent out no less than ten new varieties, all deliberately produced, which he called "Pedigree Hybrids of the Tea Rose". No doubt he was in too much of a hurry to reap the reward of his enterprise—Bennett was a shrewd businessman, a fact which earned him some disapproval from the leisured amateurs, many of whom were drawn from the Church and who set the tone of the English rose world of the period—but it must be admitted that it was bad luck that none of his ten new introductions proved a first-class rose, so that none of them survives today.

Bennett's first splash may not have been as successful as he had hoped, but he rang the bell in the following year with another new H.T., William Francis Bennett, raised from Adam (a Tea) × Xavier Olibo (an H.P.), which he sold with exclusive rights in America for $5,000—an immense sum in those days. And three years later, in 1883, he sent out Lady Mary Fitzwilliam (Devoniensis × Victor Verdier), an excellent rose which has had more than its fair share of publicity. A few years ago, an attempt was made to convince the rose world that Lady Mary was the greatest H.T. of all time, on no better grounds than that its name appears at the head of the pedigrees of such a large number of present day H.T.s which could be used for breeding at all. As a matter of fact, Lady Mary Fitzwilliam only sired ("sired" is correct; it was the pollen parent in each case) four highly influential roses, Mme. Caroline Testout, Kaiserin Augusta Viktoria, Antoine Rivoire and Mrs. W. J. Grant. The fact that these four have something in the order of 3,000 descendants at the present day means nothing. Victor Verdier, which not only sired Lady Mary but also another early parent, the excellent Mme. Abel Chatenay, must have very many more among the H.T.s alone, beside its H.P. progeny; and Jules Margottin, the H.P. parent of Victor Verdier, must have more still.

Before leaving Henry Bennett, it is perhaps worth recalling that his career as a hybridist lasted only from 1879 until his death in 1890, yet it is remarkable just how many of the roses he raised in that short time have remained in cultivation. They are eagerly sought by collectors and are still being used for breeding by present-day hybridists such as Kordes and the Meillands.

Mme. Caroline Testout was sent out in 1890 by Pernet-Ducher, who obtained it from the Tea Rose Mme. de Tartas pollinated by Lady Mary Fitzwilliam. Mme. Testout was an enterprising Parisian *modiste*, who purchased the right to name the rose and used it for publicity purposes. She can hardly have foreseen that the rose which bore her name would still be known and loved so many years after she herself was forgotten. Kaiserin Auguste Viktoria was a fine white rose from Lambert of Trier, which came out in 1891; it would be difficult to find a specimen in England today, but it still enjoys popularity in the United States. Antoine Rivoire, a rich pink, came from Pernet-Ducher in 1895, its seed-parent being the Tea Rose Dr. Grill; Mrs. W. J. Grant was sent out by Dickson of Hawlmark, N. Ireland, in the same year. The latter was remarkable in being one of the very few roses derived from seed of La France, which it somewhat resembled. Mme. Abel Chatenay was a half-sister of Antoine Rivoire and was sent out in the same year, 1895; it also was raised by Pernet-Ducher, from Dr. Grill × Victor Verdier.

In the March issue of the *Journal des Roses* in 1877, the year of its first appearance, there was printed an article by Jean Sisley which had important repercussions on the rose garden. Sisley urged his fellow rose growers to leave their old, happy-go-lucky methods of raising hybrids and to turn to the scientific method of artificial pollination, which at that time (he said) was employed only by Ducher and Antoine Levet among the innumerable *rosiéristes* of France. (I don't know why he omitted the name of Lacharme, who also employed it.) And among the advantages to be gained from this change of method he noted the possibilities inherent in the brilliant yellow *R. foetida*, if only it could be inter-bred with the contemporary garden roses. At least two men took this advice to heart, of whom the best known, and most successful, was young M. Pernet, who married the daughter of the late M. Ducher and carried on his business under the name of Pernet-Ducher. From 1883 onwards he started trying to obtain seeds from various suitable parents fertilised by the pollen of Persian Yellow, *R. foetida persiana,* the double form of the Austrian Brier. The various forms of *R. foetida* are all very infertile, but in the fourth year he obtained some seeds and raised several seedlings in 1888, which first flowered in 1891. One of these, whose seed-parent was the Hybrid Perpetual Antoine Ducher, particularly attracted his attention; its flowers were semi-double, bright pink inside, paling to the base of the petals, and clear yellow on the outside. It flowered again in 1892, but once only, of course; as an f_1 hybrid from a once-flowering species it was itself once-flowering. He continued to cherish it, and in the following year, happening to speak of it to his friend Viviand-Morel, the latter hinted that he was exaggerating its merits, so Pernet-Ducher haled him off then and there to his rose fields to see for himself. While they were examining this plant, which was then five years old, Pernet-Ducher discovered nearby another plant which he had not noticed previously. In the following year this new-found plant proved to be both double and perpetual, with flowers which were orange-yellow inside with a yellow reverse. It was exhibited at Lyons in 1898 and marketed in 1900 under the name of Soleil d'Or, the first of the so-called "Pernetiana" roses.

This is the account of the origin of Soleil d'Or which appeared in the *Journal des Roses* in June 1900—straight from the breeder's mouth. I have given it in detail, because so many other, conflicting accounts have appeared in print from time to time. Pernet-Ducher, and the rest of the rose world with him, took it for granted that Soleil d'Or was a sister seedling to the plant which first caught his eye; the snag is that it is impossible (in so far as anything is impossible in nature) for a perpetual rose to appear in the first generation of a cross such as this. But the account gives us valid grounds for adopting another assumption. The unnamed seedling first flowered in 1891, and again in 1892; Soleil d'Or was not discovered until 1893, and as Pernet-Ducher had not noticed it before it is fair to assume that it was then a seedling in its first year of growth, probably only a few months old. It is therefore very probable that it grew from a seed of the first plant, self-sown at any time between the autumn of 1891 and the spring of 1893. We may therefore assume that Soleil d'Or was actually an f_2 seedling from the cross Antoine Ducher × Persian Yellow. To the best of my knowledge, all the later Pernetianas were raised from further crosses between Soleil d'Or and its progeny and Hybrid Teas.

Antoine Ducher was a red Hybrid Perpetual, with the "blood" of at least three different species in it; by its marriage with Persian Yellow a fourth species entered the family, and with the subsequent alliances with with H.T.s, a fifth; hence the name *Rosa pernetiana* was hopelessly invalid. Nevertheless "Pernetiana" persisted as a class name for these roses for many years, and is still occasionally encountered. Virtually all modern H.T.s have a strain of *R. foetida* in them. It is worth noting that while Soleil d'Or was the first of the Pernetianas, it was not the first yellow rose in its class, since it had a good deal of red colouring in its make-up and the overall effect is reddish gold. The first pure yellow is generally acknowledged to be Rayon d'Or (Mme. Mélanie Soupert × Soleil d'Or) which Pernet-Ducher introduced in 1910.

The same year as Rayon d'Or also saw the introduction of another colour combination hitherto unknown in garden hybrids for which Soleil d'Or was responsible. This was Juliet, the first true bi-colour raised by Walter Easlea, then employed as hybridist by William Paul and Son. Juliet's seed parent was Captain Hayward, a tall growing, sweet scented red H.P. of Bennett's, pollinated by Soleil d'Or. The seedling had large, globular blooms with the now familiar chromatic effect, red on the upper surface of the petals and yellow on the reverse. An unusual characteristic is the sweet brier scent of the foliage, which needs constant protection from black spot. There are now many healthier varieties in this colour group, although I have found none so fragrant. There is a commonly held belief, indeed, it is often stated, that the Austrian Copper, *R. foetida bicolor,* was responsible for the creation of modern bi-coloured varieties. The parentage of Juliet shows that this was not so. Furthermore, I can find no record of this species being quoted in the pedigree of H.T.s until the late 1920s, by which time many other bi-colours had already appeared, all doubtless descended from Soleil d'Or.

Pernet-Ducher's only known rival, Dr. Franz Müller of Weingarten, Germany, was less fortunate. No account of his work survives, and of the half-dozen or so of the roses of his breeding that are still to be found only the rugosa hybrid Conrad Ferdinand Meyer has won any popularity. Nevertheless, in 1902 he sent out a rose, Gottfried Keller, whose parentage is given as [(Mme. Bérard × Persian Yellow) × (Pierre Notting × Mme. Bérard)] × Persian Yellow—a complex pedigree which shows that he had twice succeeded in breeding from Persian Yellow, though to little advantage, as the final product—which was apricot in colour—made no real impact. We shall, however, meet it again at a much later date.

The year 1900, which saw the début of the first of the Pernetianas, also witnessed the arrival of the first pure white Hybrid Tea. (Kaiserin Auguste Viktoria has a trace of yellow in it.) This was Frau Karl Druschki, raised by Peter Lambert of Trier from a cross between the H.P. Merveille de Lyon, a blush-coloured sport from the pink Baroness Rothschild, and Mme. Caroline Testout. It was originally meant to be named Schneekönigin (Reine des Neiges—Snow Queen), but at its first public appearance it was exhibited at a flower show in Berlin and won the prize, which carried with it the title of the best new rose of the year, and also the obligation to bear the name of the wife of the president of the society which organised the competition, thus bestowing immortality on the otherwise not very important Herr Druschki. The earlier names were revived among the Allied countries during the First World War, and are still occasionally met with in catalogues. As Merveille de Lyon was an H.P., Frau Karl Druschki was placed in the same class; and as it possessed the plentiful foliage and tall growth typical of many members of that class, it is still widely classed as a Hybrid Perpetual. It is too well known to need description; it is enough to say that for purity of colour and perfection of form no other white H.T. has ever surpassed it, and very few have approached it. But like many white roses, it is easily damaged by rain, and its sprawling growth is certainly a drawback. It makes a fine standard, however, and it will climb to six or seven feet with support. It is one of the few roses which even the most impassioned enthusiast admits to be entirely scentless.

In 1912 came another landmark in the history of the Hybrid Teas with the introduction of Ophelia. Cinderella would have been a better name, since it was an orphan—and a foundling. Even its introducer, Arthur Paul of Waltham Cross, was uncertain how he came by it, but he supposed that it must have been included by mistake in a consignment of Antoine Rivoire, a very popular bedding rose that he had bought from Pernet-Ducher in 1909. It won no medals in that year's shows; it was thought not worth exhibiting, and Paul did not even trouble to list it with the rest of his novelties for that year. But whatever the experts may have thought of it, the general public knew how to appreciate its shapely, fragrant, shell-pink flowers, even if they were not so large as those of the medal-winners. Its behaviour as a garden subject was impeccable, and it lent itself admirably to forcing for the cut-flower trade. In a sense it may even be said to have played a part in the "creation" of the Hybrid Tea class as we know it, since of recent years it has become fashionable to refer to it as the standard of excellence in flower form. What we think of as the typical H.T. shape is not just the natural result of crossing Tea Roses with other types; H.T.s can exhibit a wide range of variation. But the fact is that rose breeding is such a hit-or-miss business that the breeder throws away a thousand seedlings for every one that he places on the market; he retains only those which are likely to do him credit on the show bench, and so long as the judges continue to accept the Ophelia shape as the best mark to aim at, so long will the breeder select new roses which conform to this shape—and a very good thing, too.

However, Ophelia's virtues were not confined to her personal beauty. She was a good parent, and her progeny today are extremely numerous. But above all, she sported—she sported unceasingly. In her Masters Memorial Lecture of 1954, Wylie gave the following figures. Ophelia herself sported twenty-three times; one of these sports, Madame Butterfly, produced eight sports, including Lady Sylvia and Rapture; these eight produced four more between them, and one of these four produced yet another, making thirty-six sports in all derived from Ophelia. But this is not the whole of the story, by any means. In America Ophelia was crossed with Mrs. George Shawyer to give Columbia, which produced over sixty more distinct sports. Talisman (Ophelia × Souvenir de Claudius Pernet) yielded thirty-nine all told. Premier (Ophelia seedling × Mrs. Charles E. Russell) yielded nineteen. Joanna Hill (Madame Butterfly × Miss Amelia Gude) produced twelve. None of the other parents involved ever showed any tendency to sport, so we are justified in attributing all these to the influence of the one rose, Ophelia. Altogether, Wylie counted 206 sports due to Ophelia, which was more than half the total number of sports recorded in the H.T. class. When I was helping to compile *Modern Roses V*, I took the opportunity to check Miss Wylie's figures, and found several that she had overlooked, and several that had occurred since her lecture was given. More still have appeared since then, and it is not improbable that the total number of sports for which this wonder rose is responsible is approaching 250.

As far as the H.T.s were concerned, the next twenty-five years was a period of consolidation and gradual improvement; but there was none of the exciting and important break-throughs that had been witnessed between 1900 and 1912. Indeed, some of the leading rosarians, such as Courtney Page and H. R. Darlington, began to wonder whether the H.T.s, like the Hybrid Perpetuals before them, might have reached the end of the line. But so long as hybridists continue their patient work, a lucky break must eventually turn up in someone's seedling bench somewhere. It came among a batch of some 800 seedlings made from the same cross on the 15th of June, 1935, by Francis Meilland, a young hybridist, of Tassin-les-Lyon, who named it after his mother, Mme. Antoine Meilland.

So much has been said and written about this rose, and far too much about its parentage. I have seen four differing versions. Below is the pedigree as given in 1966 by Henri Fessel, a close friend and collaborator of Francis Meilland's. Since Fessel was quoting from the raiser's own records, his must, I feel, be the final word.

Mme. Antoine Meilland was ready for large-scale distribution in 1939, and bud-wood had already been sent by the raiser to his agents in Germany, Italy and America (he had none in England) when war intervened and cut all communications. The patriotic Germans and Italians were reluctant to distribute a rose with a French name, but even more reluctant to lose the

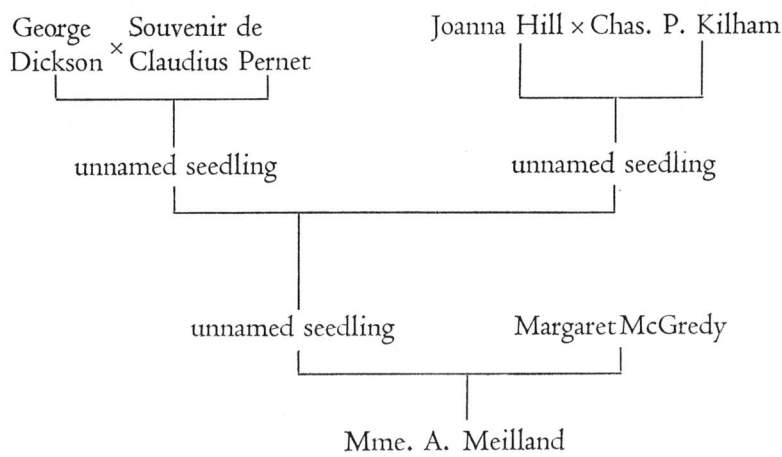

Fig. 4 Pedigree of Mme. A. Meilland (H.T.) syn. Peace.

chance of marketing an obvious winner, so they quietly changed its name, in Germany to Gloria Dei and in Italy to Gioia. In America it was held back until the end of the war, when it was rechristened Peace and launched with considerable publicity. The blooms would have attracted attention in any circumstances, from their unusual coloration, a rich but soft yellow edged with pink; but the most remarkable thing about the plant was its size. Flowers, foliage and growth all looked like a normal rose viewed through a magnifying glass. This was not an unmixed blessing. So long as it remained unique, it was a misfit among roses of normal size, while if it succeeded in establishing a line of giants like itself, they would need a good deal more space for a given number of rose bushes, with no compensating advantage. It is certainly seen at its best as a specimen shrub. If lightly pruned it grows about five feet high and as many across, and produces its huge blooms with commendable continuity throughout the season—although it is sometimes a little slow in starting. Unhappily, its scent is almost negligible.

The expected race of giants did not materialise; it has been extensively bred from and has yielded a large number of offspring, many of them very good roses. For those who want Peace with more manageable growth, Meilland kindly obliged with two of its seedlings, Grandmère Jenny, possessing longer, more shapely buds and blooms, but inheriting its parent's lack of scent, and Tahiti, of similar colour, amber edged pink, and endowed with rich fragrance and prettily serrated interior petals. The cause of the unexpected increase in size that occurred in Peace remains quite obscure; it was just a freak, although unlike most human giants, it was perfectly well proportioned and healthy (there have, however, been reports of its susceptibility to black spot in some areas of the country where the disease is particularly severe).

In 1950, it produced a climbing sport which was heralded in this country with a flourish of trumpets, but it has since been shown the back door in silence. It grows like the lianas of the tropical forest, but in this country, it very rarely flowers. In warmer climates, in the South of France and in Spain, it gives a magnificent display.

In 1943, Kordes of Germany sent out a new rose which he called Kordes' Sondermeldung ("special announcement"), but which is better known by its American name of Independence. It arose from a cross between the floribunda Baby Château and the Hybrid Tea Crimson Glory, and its proper classification has never been decided. The fact that its flowers are usually produced two or three to a stem hardly proves it a floribunda, since most H.T.s will do the same when in vigorous health. The fact that in my own garden it proved itself capable of giving flowers up to five inches in diameter without recourse to disbudding inclines me to side with those who call it a Hybrid Tea. It was the first large-flowered rose to contain in its petals the natural pigment pelargonidin instead of the normal cyanidin. Pelargonidin, as the name suggests, is the pigment responsible for the magnificent scarlet colour of the Pelargoniums or "Scarlet Geraniums". Unhappily, what is appropriate to a long-lasting flower like a geranium is less suited to such a short-lived flower as a rose; it is seen at its best for a day and thereafter fades to a dismal brick-red which becomes more and more funereal as the flower ages—and as luck will have it, the flowers of Independence are exceptionally long-lasting. In a wet autumn they hang from their excessively weak stems, upside-down, like sodden mops, for what seems like weeks on end—unless they break off from their own weight. The first appearance of Independence in this country caused something of a sensation, but its popularity waned fairly rapidly, and it has virtually disappeared from the catalogues. Seeing that twenty-five years have elapsed since it first appeared, it is strange that so few new Hybrid Teas have been produced since with the same colour. Super Star is the best so far, but its colour is weaker than a pure scarlet, as may easily be

Souvenir d'Alphonse Lavallée *(Hybrid Perpetual). Introduced by Charles Verdier, Paris, France, 1884. Raiser and parentage unknown. Medium-sized, very full, globular blooms in black-crimson, shaded maroon, usually in clusters. Very fragrant. Foliage rather small. One of the richest tinted and most vigorous of this colour, reaching a height of 5–6 ft. Profuse summer flowering, sparsely recurrent. Honours the memory of an eminent French botanist and writer. Photograph: J. L. Norton, A.R.P.S.*

Tahiti *(Hybrid Tea). Raiser: Francis Meilland, Cap d'Antibes, France. Intro-duced 1947. Parentage: Peace × Signora. Very large, well-formed solitary blooms in amber, suffused carmine at petal edges. Very fragrant. Very free flowering. Glossy, leathery foliage on vigorous, branching growth. Resembles its seed parent, Madame A. Meilland (Peace), but the growth is more restrained. An attractive but relatively little-known rose, despite its superior qualities. Photograph: J. L. Norton, A.R.P.S.*

seen by placing it side-by-side with a scarlet geranium. A cross between Independence and Peace yielded Karl Herbst, an enormous bright red rose, but it did not inherit the former's colouring, only its susceptibility to damage from rain.

Independence was a pointer to the future in another way also. It was the first of the floribunda roses (if you count it as a floribunda) to approach so close to the Hybrid Teas as to claim admission to that class. As we shall see in the next section, the floribundas have been crossed and recrossed with the Hybrid Teas until they have almost entirely lost their original character; if the process continues much longer the H.T.s will absorb them just as they have absorbed the Pernetianas. In one respect this is a good thing; the H.T.s represent the highest point of achievement in rose breeding to date, and it is well that the class should be enriched from as many sources as possible, so long as it is not degraded in the process. The name "Hybrid Tea" has ceased to have any botanical meaning whatever; there never was a time when they were exclusively composed of crosses between Tea Roses and H.P.s, as the conventional definition would have us believe, and today their ancestry is as mixed as that of any inhabitant of the Battersea Dogs' Home. Their character and standards are maintained entirely by selection in breeding, and long may it continue to be so.

THE POLYANTHAS, HYBRID POLYANTHAS AND FLORIBUNDAS

Guillot's La France, as we have seen, appeared as the result of a happy accident. It is generally accepted (though quite mistakenly) as the first of the Hybrid Teas, and it is a very remarkable coincidence that within ten years the same nursery should have been the scene of a second accidental crossing which yielded the originals—genuine this time—of another and almost equally important class of roses. I have already told the story of the origin of Pâquerette and Mignonette, the first of the polyantha roses. In 1877, Guillot raised a seedling from Mignonette which was a brighter pink than its parent, and marketed it under the name of Gloire des Polyantha. Some years later, Levavasseur of Orléans crossed this variety with the then newly introduced Crimson Rambler (itself a hybrid of *R. multiflora*) and obtained Mme. Norbert Levavasseur, which was crimson in colour and a little more vigorous than its predecessors. A seedling from this, Orléans Rose, was sent out by the same raiser in 1909.

Orléans Rose might almost be called the Ophelia of the polyanthas. In *Modern Roses* there are listed twenty-two varieties derived as sports from

G

Orléans Rose, seventeen secondary, and five tertiary sports, making a total of forty-four sports from this one variety. In 1927 the Dutch breeder, De Ruiter, sent out a crimson polyantha, Superb, whose parentage was not revealed; but that it was descended from Orléans Rose we may guess from the fact that it produced three sports, which in turn produced another seventeen (not including three climbing sports), and these three more. The pink rambler rose Tausendschön, whose parentage is anybody's guess but apparently includes Crimson Rambler and at least one polyantha, is said to have yielded two polyanthas as sports, Echo and Grete Kluis. These two varieties yielded between them another twenty-four sports all told. Here, then, are ninety-one sports, half of which were derived directly from Orléans Rose, and all of which may have been associated with that variety. In comparison, the same work of reference lists no more than forty pure-bred polyanthas known to have been raised from seed, and a hundred or so others whose origin is unknown, or at least undisclosed.

There was little development among the polyantha roses, which went on as they began; small, bushy plants, varying in height from a foot or so up to perhaps four feet in the most vigorous varieties, carrying their small, usually double flowers in large, close-packed clusters, with little or no fragrance, but very continuous flowering. In 1926, however, Superb sported to an entirely new colour, not only for the class, but for roses as a whole. To De Ruiter this seemed to be a blend of gold and salmon pink, and he accordingly christened the new variety Goldlachs—or in English, Golden Salmon. Its colour is in fact about the purest orange to be found in any rose, and it is likely—though this does not seem to have been confirmed by chemical analysis—that it is partly due to the presence of pelargonidin. Certainly this pigment was responsible for the colour of Superb's other sport, Gloria Mundi, which came out in 1929, with brilliant orange-scarlet flowers. Three years later a sport from Gloria Mundi was sent out under the name of Gloire du Midi, which did not differ importantly from the earlier variety. These two, with Paul Crampel, put out by another Dutchman, Kersbergen, in 1930, with no indication of its origin, were the pioneers of the pelargonidin-reds, which have since been multiplied *ad nauseam* among the floribundas and are now invading the Hybrid Teas.

In addition to the reddest of the reds, the polyanthas can also boast one of the bluest of the "blue" roses, in Baby Faurax, which came from Leonard Lille, a rose grower of Lyons, in 1924. This is a very dwarf plant, seldom exceeding a foot in height, with the typical pompon flowers of the class, which at their best are almost of the colour of Parma violets. Nothing was revealed of its origin, though it is in all probability related to one or other of the purple rambler roses, most of which seem to derive from Crimson Rambler. With this remarkable colour range, we can hardly hold it against the polyanthas that they have failed to produce a satisfactory yellow variety. Quite a number have been announced at one time or another, but none has stood the test of time, and as no new polyanthas have appeared since before the last world war, we are not likely to see one until or unless fashion brings them once more into popularity—which seems rather doubtful.

Among the sports so lavishly produced by the polyanthas there were quite a few climbing variants. Since the only essential feature which distinguishes the polyanthas from the ramblers also derived from *R. multiflora* is the repeat-flowering habit, one might suppose that it was the loss of this quality that caused a reversion to tall growth. Whether this is generally so I cannot say, but in the case of Princess of Orange, which is a climbing sport from Gloria Mundi, the repeat-flowering habit seems to have been retained.

It was inevitable that with the arrival of the polyanthas, a hybridist bolder than the rest would test the result of crossing them with larger flowered varieties of other classes, particularly the H.P.s and the H.T.s. Such development is usually believed not to have occurred until the twentieth century, but it is hard to accept that no-one attempted to do any breeding work in that direction for over a quarter of a century—for that is the implication. It is not surprising, therefore, that we find the first in the field to be none other than Joseph Pernet-Ducher whom we have already met as the raiser of Soleil d'Or, Rayon d'Or, and very probably Ophelia. In 1891, he sent out a seedling obtained from Mignonette × Jules Margottin named Mlle. Bertha Ludi. It produced medium sized, semi-double blooms in clusters of eight to ten; they were carmine-pink, fading to flesh-pink and were scentless. The plant was dwarf and upright, intermediate between the two parents, with many short jointed laterals giving bloom into late autumn. One might say that it was not a very prepossessing variety and it seems to have dropped out of cultivation around 1905, but from the description which has come down to us, it is easy to recognise it for what is was—the first Hybrid Polyantha in the modern sense.

In the first decade of this century, a few more Hybrid Polyantha varieties were sent out, mainly by German raisers. Two of these roses, Aennchen Müller (1906) and Gruss an Aachen (1908) are still in cultivation. Further north, a Danish nurseryman, D. T. Poulsen, was impressed with the winter hardiness of these larger flowered bedding roses compared with that of the H.T.s which needed protection during the severe winters of Northern Europe. From a cross between Mme. Norbert Levavasseur, the important and then popular polyantha pompon, pollinated by the fragrant crimson H.T., Richmond, he raised a seedling introduced in 1912 as Rödhätte—a name quite unpronounceable by any but Scandinavian lips—meaning Red Riding Hood. It made a short bush to two and a half feet with quite large, semi-double blooms in cherry-red, borne in large clusters. Once more, it attracted little attention, and with the First World War intervening, it passed almost unnoticed.

Plants had, however, been sent for distribution to France where the next development took place. In 1921, the firm of Nonin et Fils of Châtillon, near Paris, introduced a Hybrid Polyantha called Joseph Guy. There are several points of interest about this seedling which showed a good grasp of the principles of plant breeding and, perhaps unconsciously, of the new science of genetics, too. Rödhätte was a triploid and therefore sterile, or nearly so. It could not be used as a seed-parent and its pollen was probably defective. Nevertheless, a back-cross to Richmond, this time as seed parent, evidently succeeded. The result was a short, bushy plant with very large clusters of medium sized, semi-double blooms in bright carmine-crimson, produced abundantly and continuously. Unlike its predecessors, it was not overlooked except in England. In continental Europe and in the United States (where it was introduced in 1924 and renamed Lafayette), it was extensively used for bedding. From its paternal grandmother, Mme. Norbert Levavasseur, it inherited strong tendencies to mutate and over the next twelve years, a whole range of colour sports occurred from purple through varying shades of red and pink to white; there are no yellows because no rose of this colour is in its ancestry. Apart from these sports, Joseph Guy has no known seedling descendants and it is safe to assume that it is a sterile triploid.

From time to time in this account, the words "sterile triploid" have cropped up without any explanation of them being offered. This avoidance has been deliberate because it is only at the point of time we have now reached that the causes of sterility which baffled the raisers of the nineteenth and early twentieth century were beginning to be understood. Let

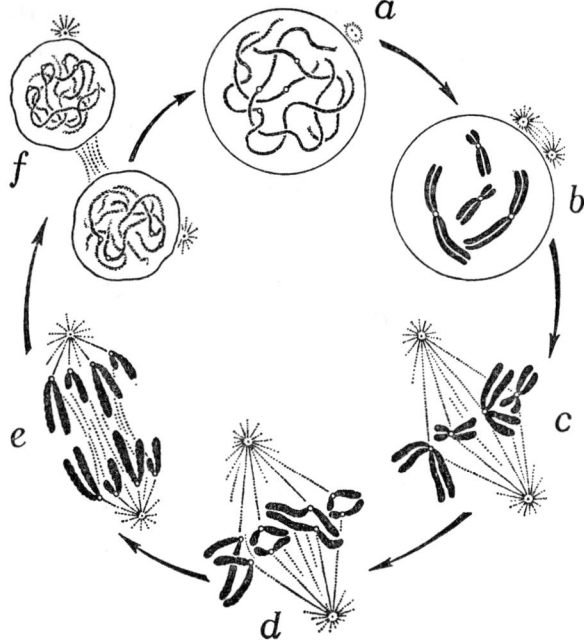

Fig. 5.   The process of growth

Diagrams to show the process of growth by division of the body-cell (technically known as mitosis). In this illustration, only two pairs of chromosomes are shown; in a rose, there would be not less than seven pairs and the great majority of modern hybrids would contain fourteen pairs.

(a) The two pairs of chromosomes appear as thread-like bodies. In animals and some fungi, but not in plants, there is a centrosome as shown here, just outside the nucleus.

(b) Centrosome divides and begins to move to opposite poles; the chromosomes contract but remain joined.

(c) The nuclear membrane has now disappeared. Centrosomes are now in position at the poles, and the chromosomes, still joined, are aligned at the equator of the spindle.

(d) The chromosomes have split longitudinally and one half of each begins to move towards its respective pole.

(e) The chromosome halves have completed movement to their poles.

(f) The nuclear membrane re-forms, enveloping each set of "daughter" chromosomes which are identical to each other and to the parent. The chromosomes elongate again as in (a) and appear as a tangled mass. The directional arrow at the lower cell indicates the repetition of the process which the cell will undergo. The upper cell will, of course, also continue the process.

us, therefore, pause at this juncture to see how and why this barrier of
sterility is set up every so often to disconcert the breeders and slow down
development.

*   *   *

All living organisms begin as a single cell. Inside the cell is a nucleus,
roughly spherical in shape which in turn envelops a group of rod-like
bodies called chromosomes, a name derived from two Greek words meaning "coloured body", given by Waldmeyer, a biologist who first discovered
them in about 1890 and found that they would readily absorb chemical
stain—a fact that has greatly helped in the study of them. Growth of a
plant (or any other living matter) is by the division of the cells. The first
phase of this process is the disappearance of the wall or membrane surrounding the nucleus. At the same time, a small, darkly-staining centrosome which exists just outside the nuclear membrane divides and moves as
two separate "daughter" centrosomes to opposite poles of the nucleus
until they are 180° apart. The chromosomes, which are at first a mass of
tangled threads, contract, becoming shorter and thicker; they move round
in a seemingly haphazard fashion but eventually all congregate in the
centre. When the last chromosome is in position, they all simultaneously
split in two lengthwise, separate and then each group moves along a
spindle in opposite directions towards the two poles. When each of the
two sets of chromosomes reach their destination, the nuclear membrane
reappears as two separate entities to enclose each of the two groups
of chromosomes which then resume their original tangled mass within
the two nuclei. At this point, the cell containing them divides into
two, rather as soap bubbles in a child's bubble-pipe, so that each new
"daughter" cell takes with it a nucleus containing identical groups of
chromosomes as the result of their longitudinal splitting. The daughter
cells are duplicates of each other and are exact replicas of the parent cell
from which they were formed. This is a simplified account of the process
of cell division, technically known as mitosis, an activity which is going
on inside a speck of matter too small to be seen with the naked eye.

When, however, the reproductive cells are formed (which in plants are
the male pollen and the female ovules), the process I have just described is
modified for a vital reason. In the creation of a new organism by sexual
reproduction, the fertilised germ cell, or zygote as it is termed, receives an
equal number of chromosomes from each parent. This number is called

the haploid number (haploid: from the Greek meaning "single form"). It varies widely throughout the animal and vegetable kingdoms.

At the formation of the sex cells, or gametes as they are termed, the chromosomes do not split, instead each seeks out the other member of its pair, lays itself alongside and becomes temporarily attached, rather like the closing of a zip-fastener, so that the total is effectively halved. A complex series of movements or phases then take place before the chromosomes split into pairs and move away from each other to opposite poles to form two nuclei for two "daughter" cells. Each of the daughter cells still contains the basic number of chromosomes, but each is still joined to its pair. This dual state is made good immediately. In exactly the same way as in the first division, the joined chromosomes in each of the two "daughter" cells divide to form single sets, polarise, and the nuclear membrane forms round each set; the two "daughter" cells divide once more to make four. Each of them then contains the haploid number of chromosomes, which is one half of the number in the body cells. Both the male and female reproductive cells are formed by exactly the same process known as meiosis, but quite independently of each other.

The reason for this halving of the number of chromosomes in the gametes or sex cells is easily grasped. If this reduction-division as it is termed, did not occur, every fertilised ovum would contain double the chromosome complement of the parents. The number would double again at each succeeding generation and chaos would soon result. As it is, the fertilised germ-cell contains exactly the same complement as its parent, although there is one very important and significant exception and it is more accurate to say that each fertilised ovum receives half of the chromosomes from the male parent and half from the female parent. This distinction will soon become clear.

Since the pairing of the chromosomes is an essential feature of the reduction-division, it will be easily understood that the wild species are generally characterised by an even number of chromosomes; fourteen, twenty-eight, forty-two or fifty-six.[1] Such roses are known as diploid, tetraploid, hexaploid and octoploid respectively, which is only the geneticist's shorthand way of saying that their body cells contain twice, four

[1] With the remarkable exception of the *Caninae* Section, which are pentaploids with thirty-five chromosomes in each body cell. The way in which these roses overcome the problem of pairing in the reproductive cells to ensure fertility is unique, but too complicated to describe in detail here.

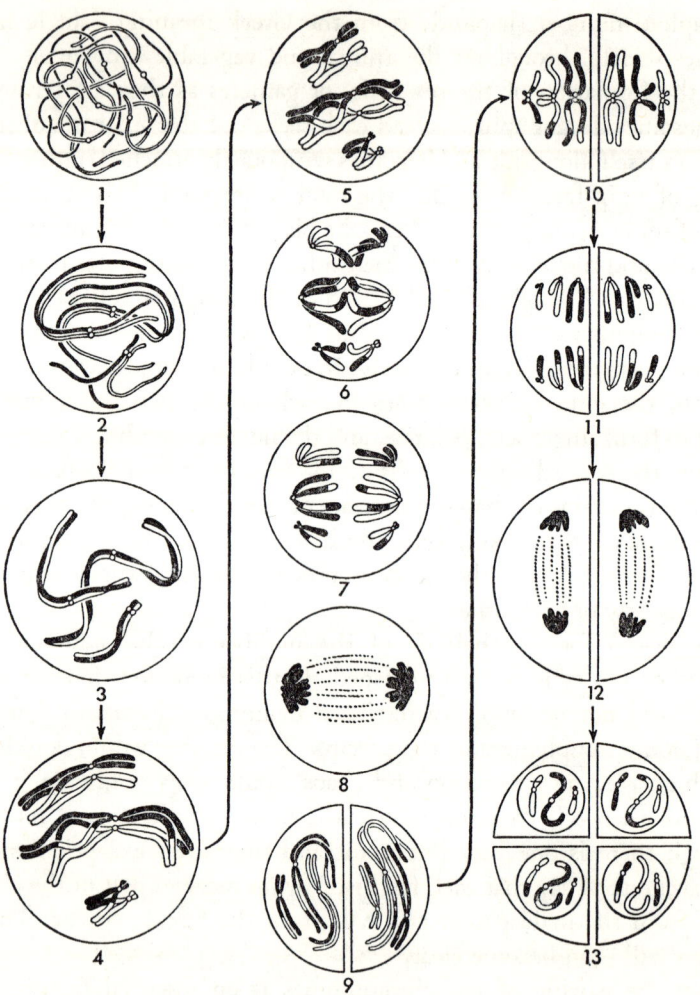

Fig. 6.   Formation of sex or reproductive cells

Diagram to show the process of formation of a sex or reproductive cell (technically known as a gamete) contained in the pollen and ova of flowering plants.

The drawing has been simplified to show only three pairs of chromosomes. In a rose, there would be not less than seven pairs, and in modern hybrids usually fourteen pairs. The three chromosomes received from the female parent are shown in white and the three from the male parent in black. Every organism receives an equal number of chromosomes from each parent.

1. Chromosomes appear as tangled threads within the cell nucleus.
2. Chromosomes, one from each parent, begin to pair off.
3. Pairing complete. Chromosomes now joined all along their length, twisted rather like two-ply wool.
4. The three chromosomes begin to separate. The sets in the diagram have made a reciprocal exchange of some of their material; all three divide longitudinally and appear four-stranded.
5. Chromosomes contract and become thicker. At this phase, the nuclear membrane around the nucleus disappears.
6. Chromosomes move towards the equator still joined.

7 and 8. Chromosomes break apart and move towards each pole. At this stage, there are six chromosomes.

9. Nuclear membrane re-forms around each set of chromosomes. Unlike the "daughter" cells of growth, they are not identical.
10. The three chromosomes in each cell begin to move towards the equator as in 6. Nuclear membrane disappears and spindle forms.
11. Chromosomes divide for a second time as in 7 and begin to move along the spindle towards the poles.
12. Chromosomes have contracted and completed polarisation.
13. Nuclear membrane reappears and envelops each of the sets of four "daughter" chromosomes to form four daughter cells. The haploid number of three has been created, but in contrast to the formation of body cells, the four cells are all genetically different as a result of the reciprocal exchange of material which occurred in 4.

The diploid (or in the case of modern roses, tetraploid) number is restored at fertilisation.

Sterility in certain rose hybrids. It will be readily seen why some rose hybrids, especially those with twenty-one (three sets of seven) chromosomes in their body cells and called triploids, are sterile. They are unable to reduce to exactly one-half the number of their chromosomes in the creation of the reproductive cells (or gametes). The female ova are consequently defective and the male pollen lacks potency. Occasionally, however, in the formation of the pollen cells, which are much more numerous than the ova, the chromosomes fail to separate properly at the second reduction division (drawing 11). A few pollen cells will then receive fourteen chromosomes and are thus potent.

times, six times and eight times the basic number of seven. The great
majority of our garden roses are tetraploids with twenty-eight chromosomes in their body cells and fourteen in their gametes or reproductive
cells. There are some diploids and these include most of the Chinas and
the Teas as well as the multiflora ramblers and their derivatives, the polyantha pompons. It is a significant feature that the majority of the roses
which had their origins in the Far East are diploids while the majority
originating in the Near East, Europe and America are tetraploids. These
include the gallicas, centifolias, and Damasks. When the Asiatic
roses, the Chinas and the Teas, were crossed with the western gallicas and
Damasks, the offspring received seven chromosomes from the Asiatic
parent and fourteen from the western, so that they were triploid with
twenty-one chromosomes in their growth cells. Since twenty-one chromosomes cannot arrange themselves in pairs, this pattern interferes with the
reduction-division in the formation of the sex cells or gametes at meiosis.
Such triploid roses, therefore, produce few, if any, viable gametes;
that is to say, triploid roses as a group are highly sterile. We can now see
why the Hybrid Chinas (Chinas × gallicas and Damasks) and the Hybrid
Bourbons (China × Bourbons) were sterile. Similarly, the early Hybrid
Teas (Teas × Hybrid Perpetuals) were very infertile.

It does, however, occasionally happen that the gametes, as a result
of a failure in the reduction-division, do manage to secure a full set of
fourteen chromosomes and become capable of normal development.
Up to thirty or forty years ago, few rose breeders knew anything
about chromosomes so they continued to try to breed new varieties by
crossing these triploid sorts with fertile tetraploids (they did not, of course,
recognise the latter as such, but as good seed-bearers). The result was that
every so often, they caught a triploid with viable gametes and succeeded in
raising a new seedling. If the gamete happened to have fourteen chromosomes, then the new plant would be a tetraploid with a reasonable chance
of being fertile and capable of giving rise to fertile tetraploid offspring.
In this way, the sterility barrier was breached and progress followed.

*   *   *

As we have seen, the Hybrid Polyanthas resulted from the crossing of
the dwarf polyanthas which were diploids with tetraploid H.T.s so that
most of the early members of the class were triploid "mules", of which

Joseph Guy is an example. In 1924, three years after the arrival of Joseph Guy, Svend Poulsen, son of D. T. Poulsen, sent out two new Hybrid Polyanthas, Else and Kirsten Poulsen. Both were derived from the same cross, Orléans Rose, the famous poly. pompon, and Red Star, a bright red, semi-double H.T. In England, these two did attract attention, the first with bright pink blooms of ten petals in large clusters on a tall plant, the second even taller, with bright red single blooms. Both flowered with great freedom and continuity and they remained firm favourites for many years despite some susceptibility to mildew.

A number of good Hybrid Polyanthas followed during the late 1920s and 1930s, many from English raisers such as Le Grice of North Walsham, whose Dainty Maid (1938) is often regarded as one of the finest of its type, and the excellent bright scarlet-crimson Donald Prior (1934) from Prior of Colchester. By one of those rare chances, Dainty Maid turned out to be tetraploid, a fact which has been seized upon by many hybridists. Else Poulsen, although a triploid, also proved to be partially fertile, and in the hands of Kordes, using a pink H.T., Sir Basil McFarland, as pollen parent, Else produced Rosenelfe (1937), the first Hybrid Polyantha with clusters of small, H.T.-type blooms with which we are so familiar today. It is a pretty rose in La France pink but is seldom seen nowadays; it is, moreover, fragrant—which is more than can be said for so many of its successors.

Yellow appeared late among the Hybrid Polyanthas. The first was Poulsen's Yellow, bred by Svend Poulsen from the polyantha pompon Mrs. W. H. Cutbush and Gottfried Keller, Dr. Müller's hybrid which failed to win the race for the first yellow H.T. Its consolation prize came in the new class. I have never seen Poulsen's Yellow which was first distributed in 1938 when men were already thinking of less civilised pursuits than rose growing, but I am told that it made a plant of medium height with glossy foliage. The semi-double blooms were bright yellow in the bud but quickly faded to a paler shade on opening. By the time the world had regained its sanity, better yellow varieties such as Goldilocks (1947) appeared, but it was not until Le Grice sent out Allgold (Goldilocks × Ellinor Le Grice) in 1956 that a true unfading deep yellow was achieved. Others have followed and there is now a fairly representative selection in this colour.

One other variety deserves mention for adding to the gaiety of nations, and that is Masquerade, raised in 1949 by the American Boerner from

Goldilocks × Holiday. This is a fine, vigorous, healthy plant, and when it opened its very first bud Boerner must have thought that he had raised a very good yellow; but the flower which is yellow when it opens is salmon-pink the next day, rose-red the next, and dies a deep crimson. It is a pity that in the last phase of its metamorphosis the colour becomes blotchy and spotty, with large areas of petal left colourless; but this is a small price to pay for such a continuous variety show, and the rose has earned consider-able popularity. In its colour changes it is a throw-back to the distant ancestor *R. chinensis mutabilis*; it has passed on this queer characteristic to one or two descendants, such as Circus, but none is quite so effective as Masquerade.

In about 1950 the American name "floribunda" for this class became current in this country, and was officially adopted by the R.N.R.S. a year or two later. It met with considerable opposition at first; the main argu-ment levelled against it was that it was botanically invalid, which was perfectly true; the name *floribunda* had already been used (incorrectly) for a rose species, and although no longer current, its adoption for any other purpose was forbidden by the international pundits. As, however, exactly the same objection could be applied to the name "polyantha", which was an obsolete synonym for *multiflora* as a specific epithet, this was not a very cogent argument. The name "hybrid polyantha" was worse still, since these were not hybrids of the wrongly named *R. polyantha*, but hybrids of the (also wrongly-named) polyantha pompon roses, which were already hybrids anyway. The new name "floribunda" had one overriding ad-vantage. Not one rosarian in ten thousand had any idea what particular species the name had once been applied to (it was in fact *R. helenae*, a close relative of *R. multiflora* and *R. wichuraiana*) and in consequence the name did not in fact convey any suggestion of affiliation with any one species; it simply designated a class of bedding roses producing smallish flowers in clusters, instead of the larger and solitary flowers typical of the H.T.s. The botanists had had their chance to produce a valid and consistent system of classification for our garden roses, and a consummate hash they made of it; we really cannot condone their dog-in-the-manger attitude, that because they have no further use for the name "floribunda", no-one else must ever be allowed to use it.

Having earned our gratitude for the name floribunda, the Americans promptly went on to earn our execration by introducing another new name, "grandiflora", which was not only invalid and unnecessary but actually misleading as well. It requires very little knowledge of Latin to see that "grandiflora" means "large flowers", whereas it was applied to a class of roses which differed from the Hybrid Teas in little beyond having flowers that were rather smaller. It may seem a little ungrateful for an Englishman to speak in this way, when the name was coined for and first applied to the variety Queen Elizabeth; but as a matter of fact, the name was little more than a trick of the trade. It was at first maintained that a grandiflora rose was one which produced H.T. flowers, both singly and in clusters, on plants six feet or more in height; but this pretence was soon dropped, and when a few of them had been grown in this country for a year or two it was seen that they were not essentially different from any others of what the R.N.R.S. clumsily, if more accurately, styles "Flori-bunda-H.T. Type". Both their ultimate height and manner of flowering depend chiefly on the sort of treatment they receive. In the climate of California most roses grow to greater heights than they do in England (or many other parts of the U.S.A.)—while in Texas, as everyone knows, they have to use a step-ladder for pruning. At least one so-called grandiflora was a pure H.T., with no floribunda blood in it at all, and not a specially tall H.T. at that.

The pelargonidin pigment, which has now become nothing less than a public nuisance in the floribunda class, did not enter it through any of the orange-scarlet polyanthas. It first appeared in Independence (if you count that as a floribunda) which inherited it—or rather, the ability to produce it—from its seed-parent Baby Château. The latter rose was a normal crimson in colour, and was descended from the so-called "Hybrid Musk", Robin Hood, which was raised in 1927 by Pemberton from an unnamed "Hybrid Musk" seedling pollinated by the polyantha Miss Edith Cavell, one of the numerous sports from Orléans Rose; so there is little doubt that it is to the polyantha line that the introduction was due. In 1954, Kordes did much better with Korona, a very different type of rose whose parentage has not been revealed; its flowers were a good deal smaller than those of Independence and less double, but much more shapely, with as fine a scarlet colour as any of its innumerable followers, and better than most. Even so, the contrast between the colours of the newly opened flowers and those that have been open for two or three days is very noticeable, and rather painful to those who are unduly sensitive to "clashes" of colour. Since then the gates have opened and a flood of these screaming-scarlet roses has poured through, with little to choose between many of them.

THE RAMBLER ROSES

This is not a strictly-defined class, although for most of us the character-istics of the ramblers are more uniform than those of most others. They are more or less vigorous climbers, producing all their flowers in one burst, usually in the form of large clusters of small flowers (though a few of the most popular have flowers as large as a medium H.T. and correspondingly smaller clusters). These are the characteristics of the section of the genus *Rosa* known as the *Synstylae*, of which our only native member, *R. arvensis*, is not typical, since its white flowers, as big as those of the Dog Rose, only come singly or in groups of two or three.

The first rambler to be cultivated was the old Musk Rose which differs from all the rest in its exceptionally late flowering season, as we have already seen. The first hybrid rambler was probably Champney's Pink Cluster, though there is no evidence that this rose ever came to Europe; but in the early part of the nineteenth century the Ayrshire Rose, a superior form of *R. arvensis*, was taken into cultivation, and a number of hybrids appeared, to form a class of Ayrshire Roses. One of these, Ayrshire Queen, deserves mention. It was semi-double, of a purplish-crimson colour, and worthy of remembrance as one of the very few hybrids raised by Rivers, who wrote so much about hybridisation, and achieved so little. It was said to have come from seed of the Blush Ayrshire pollinated by the deep crimson gallica Tuscany. Dundee Rambler, a very double pinkish rose, was said to be a cross with the Blush Noisette. Jacques, the raiser of the first Bourbon Roses, also produced two ramblers, Adélaïde d'Orléans in 1826 and Félicité et Perpétue in 1827; these were derived from *R. sempervirens* (another of the *Synstylae* native to the south of France) but whether as hybrids or sports is not known for certain. The former was semi-double and pale pink, the latter very double and creamy white; both are still available in cultivation. (The name of the latter variety has caused a good deal of misunderstanding. It has nothing to do with the perpetual-flowering habit; the rose was named for the Saints Felicity and Perpetua, who are commemorated on the 6th of March, which was, I believe, the birthday of his patron's daughter Adélaïde.)

A Chinese importation which might be mentioned here is the Banksian Rose, *R. banksiae*, which also bears small flowers in clusters, although its habit of growth is not that of the typical ramblers and it is not a member of the *Synstylae*. The wild, single white form was first introduced in 1796, but remained no more than a botanical specimen for nearly a century; in 1807 came the double white (*R. banksiae banksiae*), and in 1824 the double yellow (*R. banksiae lutea*); the single yellow (*R. banksiae lutescens*) did not arrive until fifty years later. It was named for Lady Banks, the wife of Sir Joseph Banks (1743–1820), traveller and naturalist, the companion of Captain Cook, President of the Royal Society, and founder of the Royal Horticultural Society. Lady Banks' Rose, as it is sometimes called, is tender and needs a warm wall to enable it to flourish in our climate—a situation in which the true ramblers are usually very unhappy, being martyrs to mildew unless the wind is allowed to blow freely through their branches. In 1850 a hybrid of this rose, *R × fortuneana* (probably *R. banksiae × R. laevigata*), arrived from the Far East; it has double white flowers like the Banksian, but larger, and it only too often passes under the name of the double white Banksian.

There was not a large choice of climbing roses in the nineteenth century, but a large proportion of them—the Noisettes, the more vigorous Bourbons and H.P.s, Dijon Teas, and others—were perpetual, with large flowers, so that the ramblers were not very highly esteemed. But in about 1890, Turner of Slough acquired a rose which had been received in Scotland several years earlier from Japan and had been named The Engineer's Rose, in honour of its finder, Robert Smith, first Professor of Engineering at Tokyo University. Turner sent it out in 1893 as Turner's Crimson Rambler. It was a hybrid of *R. multiflora*, of unknown origin, and the brilliance of its display took the rose world by storm. It was not a first-class rose by modern standards; its double crimson flowers "blued" badly as they faded, and it was even more prone to mildew than most ramblers. But it caught the public fancy, and for the next twenty years or so the Martian astronomers must have puzzled their heads over the unexplained red coloration which covered a large area of Europe for a few weeks every year. It was crossed with a number of polyanthas. With Gloire des Polyanthas, as we have seen, it yielded the important variety Mme. Norbert Levavasseur, the parent of Orléans Rose; with Blanche Rebatal it gave rise to the deep crimson rambler Non Plus Ultra, sent out by Weigand of Germany in 1904, which sported in the nursery of Nonin of Châtillon to a violet-coloured variety which was sent out under the name of Améthyste in 1911. In 1909, Schmidt of Erfurt had sent out a Crimson Rambler seedling, Veilchenblau, which was even bluer, though its effect was somewhat spoilt by the white centres to the flowers; it is, however, a very good rose, practically thornless, and of immense vigour. Its self-seedling, Rose Marie Viaud (1924), is a better colour, more double, and less vigorous. The variety Violette marketed by Turbat of Orléans in 1921 is perhaps the best purple of all roses, fully double, and though less blue than Veilchenblau a magnificently deep and rich violet at its best. (When not in health the flowers "ball" and often come pale pink or even white.) The origin of Violette was not disclosed, but there can be little doubt that it derives from Crimson Rambler.

Almost simultaneously with the arrival of Crimson Rambler a species was introduced into this country from the Far East, under the name of *R. wichuraiana*, in honour of its discoverer, the German botanist, Wichura. It crossed the Atlantic without delay, and there its potentialities as a parent of hybrid ramblers were first demonstrated when Horvath crossed it with the crimson China Rose, Cramoisi Supérieur, to yield Pink Roamer, which was placed on the market in 1897. Universal Favorite, with Pâquerette as its pollen parent, followed in the next year. These roses were introduced by W. A. Manda, a New Jersey nurseryman; in 1899 he put out three more of Horvath's hybrids, Evergreen Gem (from Maréchal Niel), South Orange Perfection (a sister seedling to Pink Roamer) and Manda's Triumph (a sister seedling to Universal Favorite), together with two of his own raising, Gardenia and Jersey Beauty, both from the yellow Tea Rose, Perle des Jardins. Meanwhile, Barbier of Orléans also took a hand, and in 1900 he sent out the still deservedly popular Albéric Barbier, from the yellow Tea Rose, Shirley Hibberd. (Yellow roses, Teas and Noisettes, seem to have been specially favoured as pollen parents, perhaps because white, pink and red ramblers were already fairly plentiful by now; but they never succeeded in fathering a good yellow rambler; those that were yellow in the bud faded rapidly to off-white as soon as they opened.) In 1902, came the introduction by Jackson and Perkins of the immortal Dorothy Perkins, whose pollen parent was the pink H.P., Mme. Gabriel Luizet. Dr. Walter van Fleet of Maryland gave us American Pillar in 1902, from (*R. wichuraiana* × *R. setigera*) × a red H.P. Of other well-known ramblers, Walsh's Lady Gay (from Bardou Job, a climbing H.P.) appeared in 1905, and Excelsa (parentage undisclosed) in 1909; van Fleet's Dr. W. van Fleet—(*R. wichuraiana* × Safrano) × Souvenir du Président Carnot (H.T.) —in 1910; Barbier's François Juranville (from the pink China, Mme. Laurette Messimy) in 1906, and the popular Albertine (from Mrs. Arthur Robert Waddell, one of the early Pernetianas) in 1921.

A fine floribunda, **Dainty Maid.** *Raiser: E. B. LeGrice, North Walsham, England. Introduced 1937. Parentage: D. T. Poulsen seedling. Medium-sized (3 in.) single blooms in silvery-pink, deeper on the reverse, in large, long-stemmed, well-dispersed clusters. Not fragrant. Semi-glossy, rich green foliage. Very healthy. Vigorous, tall and branching growth. Profuse flowering and especially good in autumn. One of the best of its type. Portland (U.S.A.) Gold Medal 1941.*

Don Juan *(Climber). Raiser: Michele Malandrone, Sessant d'Asti, Italy. Introduced 1958. Parentage: New Dawn seedling × New Yorker. Large (4–5 in.), long-stemmed blooms, solitary and in clusters of 2–3. Very well-formed in dark, velvety red with a distinct and penetrating fragrance. Dark green, leathery foliage. Free, recurrent flowering. Vigorous growth to an eventual height of 10 ft. Rarely seen in the United Kingdom, but a leading exhibition rose in the United States. Photograph: J. L. Norton, A.R.P.S.*

It has been stated from time to time that Barbier did not use *R. wichuraiana* for breeding his ramblers, but its close relative *R. luciae*. These two species are very similar in appearance, so much so that they were frequently confused; *R. wichuraiana* was first described in the *Botanical Magazine* under the wrong name of *R. luciae*. All things considered, it seems much more likely that Barbier's species was, in fact, *R. wichuraiana*, even though he himself may have known it by the name of *R. luciae*.

English breeders have not contributed greatly to the rambler class. Sanders' White deserves a mention, as one of the best of the white ramblers, whose small, fully double flowers have a strong fragrance suggestive of lilies-of-the-valley rather than roses. It came from Sanders and Sons of St. Albans in 1912, but no other contributions to the rose garden can be traced to this firm. Paul's Scarlet Climber achieved immediate popularity when it was first introduced by William Paul and Son of Waltham Cross in 1915, and is still widely grown, but it is not an easy rose to train satisfactorily; it does well against a wall, being less mildew-ridden than most of its kind, but is apt to produce a long bare stem with all its flowers at the top. Its globular, bright red flowers are practically scentless, like most ramblers. England can also claim to have produced what are sometimes described as the two best yellow ramblers, Emily Gray (Jersey Beauty × Comtesse du Cayla (China), raised by Dr. A. H. Williams of Horsham, in 1916, and Easlea's Golden Rambler (parentage undisclosed, from Walter Easlea of Leigh on Sea, 1932). These are certainly yellow roses, but in flower and growth they both resemble climbing H.T.s rather than typical ramblers.

It is interesting to note that both Dr. W. van Fleet and Emily Gray were derived from crosses which could have yielded perpetual roses, though in fact they did not. But in 1930 Dr. W. van Fleet made up for it by producing a perpetual form as a sport, which was given the name of New Dawn, and had the honour of receiving the first plant patent issued in the U.S.A. As was to be expected, the perpetual-flowering habit altered its pattern of growth considerably; its canes were shorter and more branched, and it sometimes takes two or three years before it really starts to climb, though once it is established it shows much vigour, putting out new canes eight or ten feet in length. But the charming, blush-pink flowers were unchanged, and in a mature specimen, they are produced from June to November without a break. New Dawn, in fact, is not a rambler, but a climbing Hybrid Tea (its "maternal grandfather" was a Tea Rose, and its "father" was a Hybrid Tea) and a very good one, too.

One or two other roses sometimes listed as ramblers may be mentioned here. The first is Elmshorn, whose pink flowers are somewhat reminiscent of Dorothy Perkins, whence for a short time it was known as Perpetual Dorothy. It came from a cross between the so-called Hybrid Musk, Hamburg (which actually had no claim even to that wholly inaccurate class name), crossed with a polyantha Verdun. It is a vigorous, remontant shrub, which can be persuaded to climb, with patience, but has no real resemblance to the typical rambler roses. Next there is Phyllis Bide—whose reputed parentage, Perle d'Or x Gloire de Dijon must be regarded with great suspicion, since it is a diploid—which has small pink and yellow flowers in clusters; but it is remontant and not a tall grower.

THE RUGOSA HYBRIDS

One form of *R. rugosa*, known botanically as *R. rugosa kamtchatica*, is said to have been introduced into this country as long ago as 1770; but the form with which most of us are familiar as the "Japanese Rose", with its wide, silky, magenta-pink flowers, *R. rugosa rubra* or *R. rugosa typica*, did not arrive here until the middle of the last century, presumably from Japan, though it is said to be native to the mainland also. It is very hardy, and genuinely remontant (in my own garden a specimen went from the 29th of April to the 31st of October in 1961 without ever being without at least one flower), which is remarkable in a wilding. As I have pointed out elsewhere, the perpetual habit is a serious disadvantage in the wild; *R. rugosa* gets over this by producing enormous, tomato-like hips, each containing as many as fifty or sixty seeds, which ripen exceptionally quickly.

The first man to try his hand at hybridising the Japanese Rose was apparently that Dr. Müller of Weingarten whom we have already seen as a rival of Pernet-Ducher's in the race to produce a hybrid from the Persian Yellow. In 1886 he sent out a variety Thusnelda, obtained from seed of the white form, *R. rugosa alba*, pollinated by Gloire de Dijon. It had semi-double pink flowers, and according to the records it flowered only once a year, which was surprising—though I have known the same result from a cross with a China Rose. In 1899 he followed this up with Conrad Ferdinand Meyer, from the same pollen parent; the seed parent was probably Thusnelda. This was a very vigorous rose, capable of climbing to about ten feet, and producing its fully-double pink flowers at midsummer and intermittently thereafter. It is still popular with those who can find room for it; in 1907 it sported to a white variety, which was given the name of Nova Zembla.

Meanwhile others had been busy. In France, Bruant of Poitiers had produced Mme. Georges Bruant in 1887 from a cross with the Tea Rose Sombreuil, and Cochet-Cochet of Coubert raised Blanc Double de Coubert, allegedly from the same parents. In the U.S.A., Dawson of Arnold Arboretum, Massachusetts, used Général Jacqueminot as pollen parent to give Arnold in 1893, and a few years later he crossed *R. rugosa* and *R. wichuraiana* to give a trailing rose which he named Lady Duncan. This latter rose had a curious history. It came out in 1900, but did not catch the public fancy and soon disappeared from the catalogues. In 1919, a Mr. Bowditch of Connecticut found a trailing rose growing in a neglected garden which seemed to be a cross between *R. rugosa* and *R. wichuraiana*, and which was almost certainly a specimen of Lady Duncan; but knowing nothing of this obsolete variety, he gave it the name of Max Graf and re-introduced it into commerce. Its great hardiness attracted the attention of Herr Kordes, who has always specialised in breeding hardy roses, but its almost total sterility prevented him from breeding from it. In 1940, however, his plant set a few seeds by self-fertilisation and he was able to raise two seedlings in the following year, only to lose one of them in the following winter. The other survived and grew into a plant with semi-double deep pink flowers which proved completely fertile; subsequent examination revealed that the chromosomes had spontaneously doubled in number, thus fixing the characteristics of the plant and eliminating its sterility. It was recognised as a new species, under the name of *R. kordesii*. It has been used by Kordes to produce his Kordesii Hybrids; in most cases the other parent has not been disclosed. On their first introduction, they were often referred to as "perpetual ramblers", but the expression has now been changed to Kordesii Climbers. I have only grown one of them, the pale yellow Leverkusen (1954), and after trying to induce it to climb for three years, I finally gave up and shifted it to a shrubbery where it made a large, rounded bush reminiscent of its rugosa ancestor, which was pleasant enough, but anything less like a rambler, or even a climber, would be difficult to imagine.

A number of rugosa hybrids have been produced in the present century, but no important development has taken place in the group. The trouble is that the first generation of such hybrids always inherits much of the character of its rugosa parent, but owing to the unfortunate choice of pollen parents they nearly always proved sterile, thus failing to yield the huge hips that are one of the attractive features of the species, and also, of course, preventing further breeding. Considered as a shrub, *R. rugosa* in its various forms is a splendid plant. The best hybrids are those which most closely resemble the rugosa parent, such as Frau Dagmar Hastrup in light pink and Scabrosa (purple).

THE HYBRID SWEET BRIERS

The Sweet Brier, *R. eglanteria* (synonym, *R. rubiginosa*), is a native of this country and the continent of Europe, and has been valued from time immemorial for its scented foliage. In the sixteenth and seventeenth centuries a double form was widely grown, but this seems to have disappeared. In the early part of the last century, Lee of Hammersmith offered another double form under the name of Lee's Duchess, but this, which is better known today by its French name of La Belle Distinguée, is apparently a hybrid, of lower growth than the species and with bright crimson flowers; its leaves have little fragrance. At about the same time—before 1832, at any rate—appeared Manning's Blush, which had small, very double flowers, almost white in colour. The origin of both these roses is obscure.

In 1892, George Paul of Cheshunt sent out Janet's Pride, with semi-double white flowers edged with deep pink. This rose was said to have been found growing wild in a Cheshire hedgerow. In the U.S.A. it masquerades under the name of Clementine.

In the meantime, Lord Penzance had put in hand a serious breeding programme with the Sweet Brier, and by 1895 he had raised some fifteen or sixteen hybrids, which were named after the female characters in Scott's romances and are known collectively as the Penzance Briers. If he hoped in this way to introduce the scented foliage into our garden roses, he was disappointed. Owing to the abnormal mode of reproduction which *R. eglanteria* shares with the rest of the *Caninae* section, it does not obey the normal rule that it makes no difference which way round a cross is made. When it is employed as seed parent, its own character is preserved almost entirely in the offspring; and since, owing to the ideas on heredity current at the time, Lord Penzance invariably did use it as seed parent, his hybrids are all Sweet Briers in everything but their flowers. With an understanding rare in his day, Lord Penzance tried raising second generations from such of his hybrids as were fertile, but his enterprise went unrewarded; he reported that in general the f_2 resembled the species even more closely than their parents. This is only what we should expect, though it is not impossible that improved forms should arise in later generations; but the odds are much against it, and I would not recommend this as a line of research for the amateur unless he has unlimited patience (and garden space) to bestow on it.

The actual pollen parents used by Lord Penzance have not all been recorded, but in two important cases they are known; these are the varieties for which he departed from his ordinary naming scheme and dubbed them Lady Penzance and Lord Penzance respectively. The former was due to the Austrian Copper, *R. foetida bicolor*, and the latter to the plain yellow Austrian Brier. Lady Penzance has small single flowers of a bright cerise pink with a yellow centre, giving an effect of bright scarlet at a distance; Lord Penzance has lemon-yellow flowers washed with pink, which gives them a fawn tint. The lady is the better rose, in my experience, not merely because it is rather taller and more vigorous, but because it comes into flower earlier—usually the last week in May, in north Norfolk—flowers more freely, and goes on for a longer time, often as much as six or seven weeks. But regarded as "improved Sweet Briers", which is just what they are, all the Penzance briers are good plants; for an impenetrable hedge they are unequalled. They all possess the characteristic "baked apple" scent in their leaves, but are somewhat liable to black spot.

In 1909, Paul of Waltham Cross sent out a new hybrid, Refulgence, with large, semi-double, bright red flowers and exceptionally fragrant foliage; its origin was not revealed. This seems to have been the last of the class to appear. But in 1916, Hesse of Germany produced a rose which he called *R. rubiginosa magnifica*, which by the rules of nomenclature ought to represent a variety of *R. rubiginosa (eglanteria)*. It was not, however; it was a seedling from one of the Penzance briers, Lucy Ashton. Magnifica, as the rules compel us to call it, had semi-double flowers of purplish-red, and was used, by Kordes and other German breeders, rather on account of its hardiness than any other qualities. The best-known of its offspring in this country is probably Kordes' Florence Mary Morse, which is a perfectly normal floribunda, and a very good one, too. Other shrubs were derived from Magnifica but none of them has the characteristic leaf scent.

THE "HYBRID MUSKS"

I have put that name in inverted commas because, as is now generally admitted, it is totally false and misleading. The true Musk Rose, *R.*

moschata, played no significant part in the formation of these roses. In 1896, when ramblers were fashionable, Schmitt of Lyons raised one by crossing *R. multiflora* with the Noisette Rève d'Or, and called it Aglaia. A few years later Lambert of Trier crossed this rose with the Hybrid Perpetual Mrs. Sharman Crawford—but the evidence of the chromosomes shows that the cross did not "take", and the resulting seedling, Trier, was evidently a self-seedling from Aglaia. Just as the once-flowering rambler Champney's Pink Cluster when selfed produced the perpetual semi-climbing Noisette Rose, so Aglaia yielded a perpetual semi-climber. Trier was semi-double, with pale yellow flowers flushed with pink, and grew to a maximum height of about six feet.

Between the years 1912 and 1928, this rose Trier when crossed with a number of different roses, mostly H.T.s, gave rise to the new class of "Hybrid Musks". The Rev. J. H. Pemberton, of Havering-atte-Bower, must be given the credit for creating the class; to him also must be given the blame for giving it such a misleading name. As may be seen from the family tree in Fig. 7, even the earliest of these was eight generations removed from the Musk Rose. The records are not complete, and the parentage of all his roses is not now discoverable, but it can safely be said that a "Hybrid Musk" was a cross between Trier and a Hybrid Tea. The very close affinity between the new class and the floribundas is plain. Each class arose from a cross between a H.T. on the one hand and an f_2 from a cross between *R. multiflora* and a perpetual rose on the other. The only important difference lies in the fact that the second parent was a semi-climber in one case and a dwarf in the other; hence the Hybrid Musks are really no more than taller versions of the floribundas.

As with the earliest floribundas, development of the "Hybrid Musks" was hampered by sterility. Only two of the typical hybrids are recorded as playing a part in further breeding, Daphne (1912) whose parentage has not been published, and Danaë, said to be a cross between Trier and the H.P. Gloire de Chédane-Guinoisseau—though, as Wylie has pointed out, this parentage is improbable, and Danaë was more likely a self-seedling from Trier. In 1927, Pemberton tried a change, by crossing one of his unnamed seedlings with the polyantha pompon Miss Edith Cavell, to yield Robin Hood. The seedling's own parentage is not recorded; all we know of it is that it bore the code number 172/11; but it is a fair guess that it, too, was derived from Trier, and that Pemberton used it because it had the rare property of being fertile, even though he didn't think it good enough to

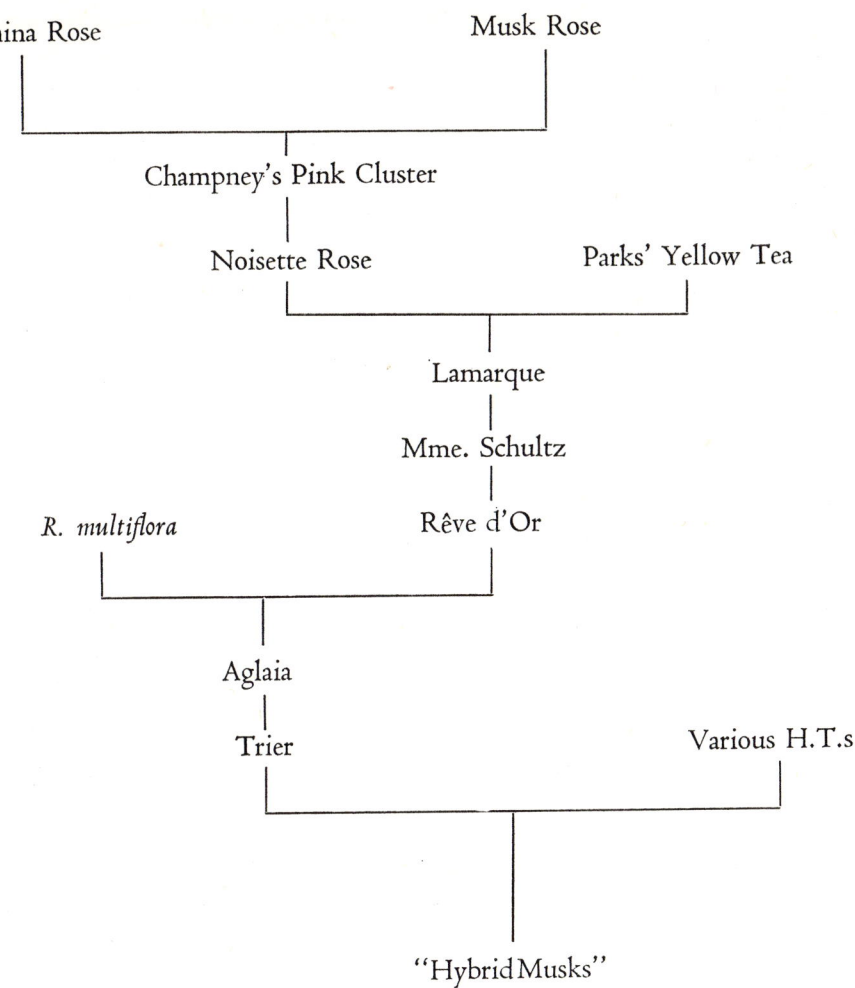

Fig. 7 The origin of Pemberton's so-called "Hybrid Musks".

put on the market. As was only to be expected, Robin Hood was indistinguishable from a tall floribunda.

In Germany, this class of roses is sometimes referred to as "Lambertiana" (which is, of course, just as invalid a name as Pernetiana) after Peter Lambert, the raiser of Trier, who also raised some hybrids from it. But Lambert did not restrict himself to a single line of breeding; he cast his net wider than Pemberton and his shrub roses show a greater variation in consequence and do not fall into any definable class. Not that any class-names mean much, anyway; our rose classification is past praying for. In fact, the "Hybrid Musks" give an excellent example of how little these class-names really mean. Fig. 8 shows three lines of descent from the variety Eva, a complete mongrel raised in 1933 by Kordes, and always classed as a "Hybrid Musk". Two of these lines, fathered exclusively by H.T.s, have yielded roses classed as floribundas, but the longer one has finally given a so-called Hybrid Tea; the third, fathered by floribundas, has yielded only "Hybrid Musks". What's in a name?

THE CLIMBERS

Strictly speaking, a rambler is no less a climber than any other rose; but the characteristics of the ramblers are so well-known and well-defined that it is convenient to have a separate name for the rest. The basic difference between them is that the ramblers are characterised by supple canes and relatively small blooms in clusters and flower once only on new wood formed the previous season, whereas the climbers have stiffer growth, usually longer blooms, borne on laterals formed in the current season. Bearing in mind that to get the best performance out of our ramblers we prune away the whole of one year's growth as soon as it has flowered, whereas the climbers need little in the way of pruning except the periodical removal of diseased, exhausted or unwanted growth, we might describe the former as "annuals" and the latter as "perennials".

The first of the climbers to appear were the Hybrid Noisettes Lamarque and Jaune Desprez. Thereafter, during the long reign of the Hybrid Perpetuals, few good new climbers appeared. I know of only one of that class which was a climber from birth and that is Bardou Job—which is often classed as a Bourbon, with little reason, since Nabonnand obtained it (in 1883) from a cross between the unclassifiable Gloire des Rosomanes and the famous H.P. Général Jacqueminot. But a number of the more vigorous H.P.s and Bourbons were trained up walls and trellises and

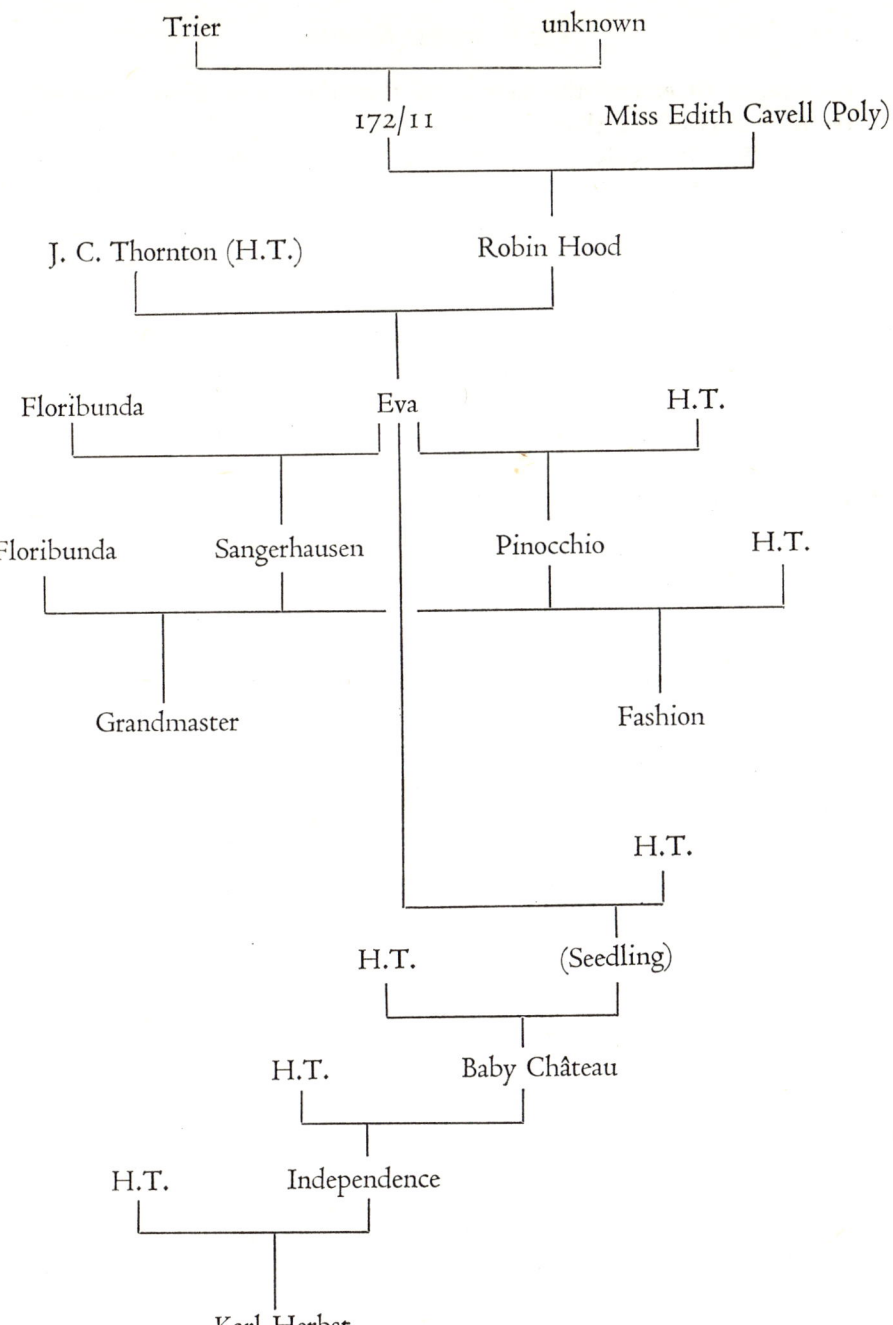

Fig. 8 Divergent lines of descent from the rose Eva. Sangerhausen and Grandmaster are classed as "Hybrid Musks"; Pinocchio and Fashion as floribundas; and Karl Herbst as a Hybrid Tea.

encouraged to extend themselves, so that they were quite reasonably regarded as climbers, though not very tall ones.

The China Roses also produced a few climbers, of which the best known is probably the climbing sport of Cramoisi Supérieur, a form of the old Crimson China. Fellemberg, another old crimson variety, is usually grown as a bush, but it can be persuaded to climb some distance with a little encouragement. On the other hand, the climbing sport of the hybrid Cécile Brunner is a vigorous grower, which will cover a sizeable wall; the solidity of its main stems is astonishing to anyone who knows it only as a dainty bush.

The Hybrid Teas have proved the main source of our new climbers over the past sixty years. Some have been climbers from birth, such as Lady Waterlow, Mme. Grégoire Staechelin and Paul's Lemon Pillar, of which the last two are among the Climbing H.T.s which persistently refuse to repeat. But not the least of the virtues of the incomparable H.T.s is the fact that so many of them have produced climbing sports, so that one may take it for granted that a climbing form of any good new introduction will appear in due course. These climbing sports are identical with their dwarf counterparts in everything but growth; they are all potentially perpetual flowering, but very few of them repeat quite as well as the corresponding dwarf, or bush forms. In consequence, they are now being largely superseded by the newer, deliberately bred Long-flowering Climbers (in the United States they are referred to as "Ever-blooming Climbers") of more restrained growth but giving greater continuity of flower. Of the climbing roses I have grown, I can vouch for the remontancy of the following:

Aloha	*Geheimrat Duisberg	*Mrs. P. S. Du Pont
Allen's Fragrant Pillar	Gruss an Teplitz	New Dawn
Conrad F. Meyer	Gloire de Dijon	Pink Cloud
*Crimson Glory	High Noon	Réveil Dijonnais
Danse du Feu	Honour Bright	Royal Gold
*Devoniensis	*Lady Hillingdon	*Shot Silk
Don Juan	Lady Waterlow	*Snow White
*Ena Harkness	*Mme. Edouard Herriot	*The Doctor
*Etoile de Hollande	Mme. Alfred Carrière	Zéphirine Drouhin

Of these, Aloha, Gruss an Teplitz, High Noon and New Dawn have occasionally gone through the whole season up to the end of October without once being entirely without flowers, while Danse du Feu, Etoile de Hollande, Lady Hillingdon, Snow White and The Doctor have on all occasions exceeded 150 flowering days in a season—which is much better than many of my best performers in the dwarf H.T.s. The varieties marked with an asterisk are climbing sports. Devoniensis, Gloire de Dijon, Lady Hillingdon, Mme. Alfred Carrière, New Dawn and Zéphirine Drouhin, all "classics" of the rose garden, have already been mentioned in their own sections. Danse du Feu and Gruss an Teplitz are mongrels which cannot be placed in any botanical class; they both produce smallish red flowers in clusters of two or three; the latter's are crimson and the former's almost scarlet.

There is a curious superstition attached to the climbing sports to the effect that if they are pruned hard in the first year after planting, the shock to their systems is liable to cause them to revert to a dwarf form. There is not a word of truth in this. I have discussed the point in detail in Chapter Nine, so I won't elaborate here. The Long-flowering Climbers, represented in my list by Aloha, Don Juan, High Noon, Pink Cloud and Royal Gold, should not, however, be hard pruned in their first season. They climb relatively slowly; in fact they build up rather than climb, and need to be treated differently from the others. If the main shoots of a maiden plant as received from the nursery are reduced to the two strongest and are then pegged down in the manner recommended for the Hybrid Perpetuals, new basal growth produced the following season will attain quite quickly a height of seven to eight feet, which is about the maximum that can be expected from the majority—one or two, such as High Noon, will add another couple of feet to their stature. At the end of the first season, the old nursery growth can be cut out completely and the new shoots trained in gentle coils round the pole or whatever structure has been provided. I have also found that the Long-flowering Climbers budded on laxa understock put on height much more satisfactorily than on any other understock. The probable reason is that roses worked on laxa tend to put out one or two very long shoots from the budded scion instead of several shorter shoots as appear, for example, on multiflora. The Long-flowering Climbers, then, are not really climbers but Pillar Roses. One occasionally meets the term "semi-climber", which is a handy way of describing a rose which doesn't climb as much as we should like it to; but taken by and large, it has very little meaning, and one would be reluctant to recognise a class of semi-climbers.

Class	1899	1908	1912	1920	1930	1935
Teas and Chinas	187	150	134	71	32	21
Hybrid Perpetuals	504	201	115	73	46	25
Hybrid Teas	117	401	579	668	1003	1464
Pernetianas*	—	6	12	33	64	107
Polyantha pompons	36	60	64	79	102	106
Hybrid Polyanthas†	1	1	2	2	25	39
Climbing H.T. sports	8	10	16	21	42	64
Multiflora Ramblers	9	30	36	54	36	30
Wichuraiana Ramblers	—	36	52	67	80	94
Hybrid Musks	—	—	—	7	15	22
Total	862	895	1010	1075	1445	1972

* Class merged with the Hybrid Teas about 1938.

† Name changed to floribunda in the U.K. about 1950; the older name persists on the continent of Europe.

Fig. 9   Table to show the rise and decline of various classes of garden roses during the first third of the twentieth century.

(Sources: T. W. Sanders, *Cultivated Roses* and *Roses and their Cultivation*, various editions 1899–1930; A. J. Macself, *The Rose Grower's Treasury*, 1935. Neither author claimed his list to be exhaustive, but included all varieties known to be in commercial cultivation in the year prior to publication.)

Note the rapid decline of the Teas, Chinas and Hybrid Perpetuals coupled with the spectacular increase in the Hybrid Teas after 1899. The multiflora ramblers reached their peak of popularity around 1920 and the

Polyantha pompons about 1930. Note, also, the very slow development of the Hybrid Polyanthas due to triploid sterility.

THE MINIATURE ROSES

These all originated in various forms of the species *R. chinensis minima*, which is generally similar to the pink and crimson Chinas but reduced in size so much that a mature plant may stand no more than four or five inches high. According to the R.H.S. *Dictionary of Gardening, R. c. minima* was known in this country as early as 1762, but most other authorities prefer a later date; the commonest story relates that the first specimen was imported into England in about 1810 from Madagascar, of all unexpected places. It is not a native of that island, but came originally from the Far East, where it probably originated in cultivation. Different varieties have cropped up in different places at different times—and under different names. In England it was known for some time as the Fairy Rose, Miss Lawrence's Rose, or *R. lawrenceana*. In France, in the 1840s, it was a popular pot-plant under the name of Pompon de Paris. A very similar variety brought from Switzerland by one Major Roulet passed, and still passes, under the name of *R. rouletii*. There is even a climbing sport of Pompon de Paris, which retains all the delicacy of its prototype while reaching a height of five or six feet.

In the 1930s or thereabouts, one or two breeders, notably Pedro Dot of Spain and Jan de Vink of Holland, made a few crosses between these miniatures and other roses, polyanthas and even H.T.s, which retained the characteristics of *R. c. minima* to a surprising extent. These roses caught the public fancy and created a demand for more of them, which the breeders did their best to satisfy. The public may not actually have cried out for "bigger and better miniatures", but that was what they got. Several of the modern hybrids are not more than very dwarf polyanthas; others have flowers that are disproportionately large for the size of the plant. Estrellita de Oro (Baby Gold Star), for instance, makes a neat and compact little bush about eight inches high, and then thrusts its two-inch flowers several inches higher—looking like dandelions growing through a bed of parsley.

The chief difficulty with these delightful little plants—as the best of them still are—is to know where to grow them. They are perfectly hardy, and can—indeed, must—be grown out of doors; they will not flourish as house plants. But if they are grown in ordinary beds, one has to go down on one's knees to enjoy them. If one is not the fortunate possessor of a terraced garden which will allow them to be grown at something like eye-level, perhaps a raised trough is the best solution; but in that case it will have to be at least fifteen inches deep, with good drainage.

MISCELLANEOUS HYBRIDS

Two interesting hybrids of *R. spinosissima* arose, by accident, in the early part of the last century. The first was Harison's Yellow, evidently a cross between *R. spinosissima* and Persian Yellow, the double form of *R. foetida*, which was sent out by Harison of New York in 1830. It has small, semi-double flowers of a good bright yellow colour, and its great hardiness made it very popular in the United States, where it is still widely grown. It is, of course, once-flowering only. The second was Stanwell Perpetual, sent out by Lee of Hammersmith in 1838. This generally resembles *R. spinosissima*, but has medium-sized, double pale pink flowers which are produced at midsummer then intermittently throughout the season. Its origin is quite unknown, but it is supposed to have derived its remontance from an Autumn Damask. At about this time, or rather earlier, there was quite a boom in varieties of the Scotch or Burnet Roses, and it is said that over 300 varieties were once to be found in the catalogues; some of these must certainly have been hybrids, but so few have survived to the present day that we can find out little about them. In recent years, Kordes has bred some fine new shrub roses by crossing the central Asian form of this species, *R. spinosissima altaica* with various garden roses, to give tall, arching plants, six or seven feet high, bearing flat, single or semi-double flowers in various shades of pink and yellow. They can be recognised in the catalogues from the fact that they all bear German compound names beginning with the word Frühling (Spring).

One or two of these roses of Kordes' show a trace of remontance; but none of them can compete in garden value with the mysterious hybrid Nevada, which covers itself with large, flat, white semi-double flowers, sometimes flushed with pink, at its first flowering and then goes on to repeat as reliably as any rose in the garden. (In 1960, my own specimen was continuously in flower from the 21st of May to the 1st of November.) I call it mysterious on account of its parentage. The raiser, Pedro Dot, sent it out in 1927 and said in all good faith that he had obtained it from a seed of the Hybrid Tea La Giralda pollinated by *R. moyesii*. But by all the rules, such a cross ought to produce a once-flowering rose and a pentaploid;

whereas Nevada is determinedly perpetual and a tetraploid. (I do apologise for introducing these horrible technical terms, but one can't entirely avoid them. Their meaning is quite simple, and has been explained earlier in this chapter and in the glossary; I am afraid there is nothing to be done about their ugliness.) It has been suggested that instead of the normal *R. moyesii*, Dot may have used its tetraploid variety, *R. moyesii fargesii*; but while this would account for its tetraploid character, it still cannot account for its remontance. Of recent years a pink sport of Nevada has appeared called Marguerite Hilling. It is not, I think, an improvement on the original.

The variety Marie Léonida appeared in about 1832, a climber with double cream-coloured flowers, which is said to have been a hybrid between *R. bracteata* and *R. laevigata*. It was once-flowering and rather tender, and not of any great importance. It can still be obtained, however. In 1918, Paul of Waltham Cross did better with the climber Mermaid, from *R. bracteata* pollinated by an unrecorded yellow Tea Rose. This has pale yellow, single flowers as much as six inches across, which leave an attractive bunch of golden stamens when they have fallen. It is a vigorous, though somewhat temperamental, climber with attractive glossy leaves, and reliably perpetual, but it must be admitted that the flowers are not produced as freely as one might wish. Like its predecessor, it is wholly sterile, thus closing the road to further development.

One or two hybrids have been raised from *R. gigantea* pollinated by various garden roses; Belle Portugaise, La Follette and Sénateur Amic are all obtainable in this country, but they are really too tender for our climate, and hardly worth persevering with when so many better roses are available. They only flower once.

Apart from these, innumerable odd hybrids have cropped up from time to time in the course of rose history. All of them were of interest, even if of little value aesthetically or commercially, but the great majority of them have found their way to the rubbish-heap, leaving the rose world much as they found it. I am not one of those who believe that there is still a wealth of untapped resources in the many wild species which have not yet been bred into our garden hybrids. When one looks at a perfect bloom of, say, Paul's Lemon Pillar, Frau Karl Druschki, Mrs. Sam McGredy or Shot Silk, it is not easy to suggest in what way they could be improved. No doubt there will be changes in fashion—though the present-day cult of ugliness and silliness in art has not yet, thank God, entered the rose garden. But while there are a number of desirable secondary characters which might with advantage be injected into our H.T.s, if we should ever reach the point where every garden rose is as hardy as an oak-tree, as uniform in growth as a field of wheat, and as free from disease as a surgeon's hands, they will be no more beautiful than they are today. And they will be much less fun to grow.

Part Two

DESCRIPTIVE

Chapter Seven

SCENT

The morning rose, that untouch'd stands,
Armed with her briars, how sweet she smells!
Sir Robert Ayton (1570-1638)

It is a very commonly heard remark, that "roses haven't got the scent that they used to have". This is a very old criticism, which has passed current, to my own knowledge, for over forty years. Whether it was true in the past I cannot say; the rather surprising fact is that today it is true.

I don't ask the reader to take my word for this; he can verify the fact for himself very simply. Take any representative list of Hybrid Teas that are still grown today—a catalogue issued by one of the larger growers will do admirably, or one of the lists published from time to time by the R.N.R.S.—and jot down the numbers of different varieties which fall into each of the following classes: (i) pre-1945 roses described as "scented" or "strongly scented"; (ii) pre-1945 roses described as "slightly scented" or "scentless"; (iii) post-1945 roses described as "scented" or "strongly scented"; (iv) post-1945 roses described as "slightly scented" or "scentless". Count up the numbers in each class, and you will find that the well-scented roses form a higher percentage of the pre-1945 class as a whole than they do of the roses produced in more recent years. I am sticking my neck out in claiming this, without knowing what list you propose to work on; my confidence is based on the fact that I have tried it with every list I could lay hands on, and the facts were so in every case, even though there were innumerable disagreements over the rating of individual roses. In Fig. 10 I give a table of the results obtained from eleven such lists. I have restricted the analysis to the H.T.s since it is against them that the criticism is usually levelled; the number of well-scented floribundas is still quite small. The inference seems inescapable, that for some years past, the H.T.s have been losing their scent.

| | Pre-1945 | | Post-1945 | |
	A	B	A	B
List I	89%	11%	78%	22%
List II	74%	26%	40%	60%
List III	84%	16%	65%	35%
List IV	85%	15%	72%	28%
List V	81%	19%	76%	24%
List VI	87%	13%	47%	53%
List VII	90%	10%	80%	20%
List VIII	40%	60%	30%	70%
List IX	65%	35%	44%	56%
List X	80%	20%	72%	28%
List XI	70%	30%	64%	36%

A. Percentage of roses described as "scented", "strongly-scented", or equivalent.
B. Percentage of roses described as "unscented", "slightly scented" or equivalent.

It will be seen that in every list, A is higher for the pre-1945 roses than for the later introductions.

Fig. 10   Table showing falling-off of scent in Hybrid Teas.

The blame for this is not to be laid upon the breeders; it rests squarely on the public. If the ordinary amateur rose grower refused to buy scentless roses, they would not be put on the market. The breeder has no control over the scent of his roses; the factors which govern its appearance in new hybrids are quite unkown. So long as he knows that his best roses are still eligible for the highest show awards even though they may have no scent at all, we can hardly expect him to discard some of his finest seedlings and perhaps rob himself of a gold medal, however much he himself may regret their lack of scent. After all, he has a living to make; he is not a professional philanthropist. There is, as a matter of fact, one special prize, the Henry Edland Memorial Medal, which is available for annual award by the Royal National Rose Society to the best new scented rose. But it is one thing to recognise the present trend, and quite another to arrest and reverse it.

However, there are plenty of good scented roses in the world still, and good new ones appear from time to time, even if not as frequently as we could wish. One cannot dogmatise about scent. It varies from one strain to another of the same variety; a striking instance of this is Ena Harkness, of which the original plants were so fragrant that they did receive the Clay Cup (which was formerly awarded for fragrance), but many plants of this variety are now completely scentless. It varies between different plants of the same strain. It varies from year to year; I once gave away half a dozen plants of a variety of my own breeding, apologising at the same time for their lack of scent, but the recipient took me severely to task the next year, assuring me that they were deliciously fragrant. And it very noticeably varies from hour to hour of the day in the same individual flower.

If the reader wants to be certain that the roses in his garden are scented, there is only one thing for him to do and that is to visit the grower's fields and find them for himself. But he must remember that the scent is due to volatile oils secreted by the flower, and that a rose growing in the middle of a field, exposed to the unbroken rays of the sun and all the winds of heaven, may be robbed of its sweetness more quickly than it can replace it. If one goes for the half-opened flowers and sticks one's nose well down into the hearts of them one can usually find what one wants, if it is there to find; but a rose without scent is not necessarily a scentless rose; it may be a well-scented rose which is temporarily exhausted. For this reason it is always best to make a visit, if one can, on a cool, cloudy and windless day.

*   *   *

The scent of flowers in general seems to have come into being, under the influence of natural selection, in consequence of the activities of insects. Indeed, the flowers owe their very existence to this. In the high and far-off times before the first insects appeared on the face of the earth there were no flowers. Green vegetation there was in plenty; but its reproductive organs were not conspicuous, and were either self-fertilised or dependent upon the wind for the transport of their pollen. But when the insects first appeared and some of them developed a taste for pollen as food, their movements from plant to plant resulted in increased cross-fertilisation, with consequent increased vigour and a better chance of survival. If one plant sported a freak growth which made the pollen sources more conspicuous, it reaped an advantage which in course of time allowed it to multiply at the expense of its less conspicuous neighbours; and through countless ages, these freak growths developed until they culminated in the gorgeous advertising banners that we see in the flower garden today. The additional attractions of nectar and scent must have arisen in the same way; though we cannot be sure that the first secretion of flower scent was, so to speak, a brilliantly original idea of the flower; it may have been only copying the insects. Many of those insects—chiefly moths—which are effective pollinators of scented flowers do themselves possess scent glands which yield an odour closely resembling that of the flowers that they frequent. These glands are always restricted to one sex or the other, which suggests that they were primarily a mating guide, and that their function as a foraging guide was a later development.

If this is true, it was probably the insects which first developed scent, and the flowers which followed suit; but in such questions it is not always easy to distinguish between cause and effect. Those plants which are normally fertilised by the night-flying moths often yield no scent at all in the daytime; sometimes their flowers do not even open until the light begins to fail. But whether they exhale their perfume at night because that is when the moths are about, or whether the moths fly at night because that is when the flowers are most scented, is a question not easily decided. The association between flowers and insects has always been very close.

It may seem to border on the miraculous that a plant which previously lacked these adjuncts should suddenly begin to secrete nectar and scented oils, but as a matter of fact this does not call for any radical change in its internal economy. Every growing plant contains large quantities of sugar, which it uses for its own purposes, and it can easily afford to let a drop or two of syrup ooze on to the surface for the delectation of insect visitors; while the chemical substances which are the source of flower (and insect) perfumes are closely related to other substances which are present in all living things, and have much more vital functions to perform in the plant's internal chemistry. In fact, unpleasant as it may seem, the secretion of fragrant oils by plants and the excretion of waste products by animals are closely allied processes. The substance indole, which has one of the vilest stenches known to man, is present in and partly responsible for the smell of the faeces of flesh-eating animals; yet the same substance, greatly diluted, is largely responsible for the scent of jasmine, jonquils and wallflowers. The transition from scent to smell, and from smell to stink, is often only a matter of degree; though happily most of the scented substances found in flowers, while often quite unpleasant at full strength, are not nauseating like indole.

I have set down these things, because they seem to me to form an interesting, if at times disconcerting, background to the subject. But I must admit that they have little direct reference to the rose, which produces no nectar to speak of, and does not depend upon insects for its pollination. That it yields a fragrance second to none in the garden must be due either to the survival of a habit which has outgrown its usefulness, or else to the mere fact that its waste products happen to be exceptionally sweet to the human nose. Insects are not especially attracted to it.

*   *   *

The rose looks fair, but fairer we it deem,
For that sweet odour which doth in it live.

Shakespeare

The scent of roses is lovely but fleeting, and from the earliest times means have been sought of preserving it. More than four thousand years ago some unknown genius noted the fact that fats and oils have the power of absorbing and retaining the vapours given off by strong-smelling substances—a discovery which many a young housewife makes afresh for herself when she stows the butter too close to the kippers—and so led the way to the preparation of that oil of roses which for centuries was the stock toilet adjunct of the civilised world, serving the combined functions of soaps, toilet creams and perfumes—and medicinal salves. It was made by steeping and heating rose petals in a vegetable oil, usually almond, sesame or olive; and Pliny, in his *Natural History*, describes the special precautions taken in the preparation of the oil to reduce its own smell to a minimum and guard against its turning rancid.

It was not until nearly a thousand years after Pliny that roses were first distilled to extract their scent, either in India or in Persia; both countries claim to have originated the process, but the records do not allow one to decide with certainty. The rose petals were placed in a closed vessel filled with water, which was brought to the boil; the steam was led off through a pipe, cooled to cause it to condense, and the resulting water was found to be impregnated with a delicious perfume. It was in fact "Rose-water", whose mode of preparation is substantially unchanged today.

Rose-water does not smell very much like roses. This is not surprising when one considers that not less than a dozen different constituents have been identified in the essential oil of roses and that only one of these is appreciably soluble in water, and hence gives its scent to the rose-water. The attar is composed of the remaining eleven constituents, some of which are affected by the heat of distillation, together with wax from the surface of the petals and, of course, other minor impurities. Attar of roses has been rather over-romanticised in literature, partly on account of its "Arabian Nights" background, and partly because of its supposed fabulous price. It is indeed expensive, since it takes the produce of about an acre of roses to yield a pound of attar—its current trade price is about twenty-five pounds an ounce—but when all is said and done, it is only one of many highly-prized and highly-priced ingredients used by the professional perfumer. It is much too powerful—and too sickly—to be used by itself.

Attar of roses was, and still is, produced in many eastern countries. In the sixteenth century, when the Turks over-ran Bulgaria, they introduced the practice of rose distilling into that country, where it took root and flourished; so much so that by the present century the Bulgarian attar was acknowledged to be the best in the world. Down to the outbreak of the last war it was a peasant industry, the roses being grown in small plots and distilled in rather crude apparatus in the fields; so crude, in fact, that the rose-water yielded as a by-product was quite worthless and was thrown away. Improved methods were introduced from time to time by foreign experts; since the absorption of Bulgaria into the orbit of Soviet Russia, the industry has, of course, been nationalised, and its output has fallen off —though it is only fair to add that the diminished output has been accompanied by an improvement in quality which has to conform to a predetermined standard of purity.

The centre of the Bulgarian industry is at Kazanlik, which is not so very far removed from the "place known as the Gardens of Midas" where the sweetest roses in the world grew wild in the days of Herodotus. It is tempting to imagine some relation between these antique roses and the present day Bulgarian material, though they cannot be one and the same; Herodotus's roses had sixty petals, while the Bulgarian rose of today is *Rosa damascena trigintipetala*—"the Damask rose with thirty petals", sometimes known by the varietal name of Kazanlik. Where this rose originated we do not know.

In the south of France, in and around the town of Grasse, which is the centre of the French perfume industry, a small quantity of roses is distilled, but only for the sake of the rose-water; the attar produced in the process is made use of by the local perfumery houses. The great bulk of the roses grown in this part of the world are not distilled, but have the essential oils extracted from them by means of solvents—usually petroleum spirit. The rose petals are steeped in this and gently agitated until all their oils are dissolved, when the solvent is drawn off and evaporated, at low temperature and under reduced pressure, leaving behind a waxy residue not unlike the attar produced by distillation; but this *concrete*, as it is called, contains all the essential oils of the rose, both those which go into the attar and that which is dissolved in the rose-water. Moreover, the product obtained in this way runs no risk of being altered by the heat of distillation, and—a point of considerable importance—something like ten times as much *concrete* is extracted from a given quantity of roses as could be obtained by distillation. It is true that about fifty per cent of the *concrete* consists of nothing more than the wax which forms a thin layer over all the external surfaces of the flower; but by extracting the *concrete* with pure alcohol, which dissolves the oils and leaves the wax, they obtain what is called the *absolute*, a sticky, brownish oil, which represents the final stage in the purification of the rose scent. The wax is not a waste product; it is sufficiently impregnated with scent to fetch a high price from the manufacturers of cosmetics.

The scent of the rose *concrete* and *absolute* is much closer to that of the flower itself than that of the distilled attar; it comes as something of a surprise to find that this "true" scent is not of great importance to the perfumer. The explanation is that all commercial perfumes are blends of many constituents, and it is of less importance to the perfumer that any one of these should closely resemble the scent of the flower it is obtained from than that it should be constant, so that he can repeat his blends in the certainty of producing the same result every time. There are some flowers, such as jasmine and violets, whose *concretes* do reproduce the natural scent with great fidelity, though even then a measure of blending is necessary in order to produce an acceptable jasmine or violet perfume for the market. Other flowers, such as carnations, yield a *concrete* whose scent bears little or no resemblance to their own, though it still finds a place in the armoury of the expert blender. Yet others—lilac, for instance—give an evil-smelling product which is of no use to man or beast and the required fragrance is obtained synthetically. Today, when simple flower scents are out of fashion and most perfumes have to be marketed under fanciful names which are either meaningless or sexually suggestive, there is hardly one which does not contain a proportion of either the attar or the *concrete* (or *absolute*, as may be more convenient) of roses; the inferior "rose" scents, on the other hand, are mostly obtained from geraniums, tropical grasses or synthetic products.

The best attar is always produced from *R. damascena trigintipetala* and no other. *R. alba* is also used to a limited extent. It is usually planted as a hedge around the rose fields, and being taller and hardier than the Damask Roses, it helps to protect them from the icy blasts which descend from the neighbouring mountains in winter. The quality of the attar from *R. alba* is invariably reduced, and its price on the world's markets is accordingly less.

Neither the Damask nor the white rose has any part to play in the French perfume industry. The staple variety there is the old pink cabbage rose, *R. centifolia*, locally known as the Rose de Mai. This yields a smaller quantity of attar when distilled in the oriental manner, but when extracted with spirit solvents the yields from this and the Damask are much the same, both in quantity and quality, so that the French have no incentive to give up the use of their old Rose de Provence. Other varieties have been tested from time to time; a variety known as Professeur Émile Perrot, a Damask similar to but not identical with the Bulgarian variety, was introduced from Persia by its namesake, but had no material advantage to offer. There is even a record of a *concrete* having been extracted from our old friend Frau Karl Druschki, though all I could learn of it was that the yield was only about one-tenth of that from the Rose de Mai; no particulars were given of its scent—presumably there wasn't any. It is interesting to note, however, that it yielded much less wax than the Rose de Mai, which presumably accounts for the Frau's liability to rain damage, her petals being less waterproof than the average. There is, however, another variety which sometimes finds its way into the vats of Grasse and that is the fine old Hybrid Perpetual Ulrich Brunner Fils. It yields less *concrete* than the Rose de Mai, and of an inferior quality; but it is extensively grown locally for the florists' trade, and it is only added to the pot when a glut compels the florists to unload their surplus stocks cheaply.

Roses are grown widely in the less arid parts of Morocco, and the city of Marrakesh has for many years been the centre of a trade in rosebuds, picked before they open and dried in the sun, from which a local variety of rose-water is distilled. Both Damask and Cabbage Roses are employed, in what was until recently no more than a cottage industry; but of recent years at least one enterprising Frenchman has taken advantage of a climate even better than that of the south of France, combined with substantially lower labour costs, to initiate an industry on French lines. The Moroccan rose fields have already demonstrated their ability to equal the quality of the French *concretes*, and it may be that they will supersede them altogether in course of time.

*   *   *

In the table (Fig. 11) I have given a list of all the different constituents which have been identified in the essential oil of a Cabbage Rose, together with the proportions in which they are to be found in a good sample of French rose *absolute*. These proportions are approximate only; they vary from sample to sample, and those items marked with a query may be anything from one or two per cent down to a mere trace. But the effect of each constituent is not to be measured entirely by the proportion present; some smell more powerfully than others, and a small difference in quantity may make a big difference to the overall effect. Moreover, although it is known that there are no important differences between the composition of the oils of Cabbage and Damask Roses, there is no knowing whether other substances may not be present in the secretions of other species and varieties.

The constituents as listed are sufficient to explain the many variations to be found in the scents in our rose gardens. There can be little doubt that a slight preponderance of eugenol or methyleugeonol would account for the "spicy" scent attributed to many roses, including those alleged to smell of musk. (The clove-scented carnations were formerly called "musk-gillyflowers".) The "fruity" scent resembling that of muscatels (a word, incidentally, also derived from musk) which is to be found in, for example, Etoile de Hollande, can probably be accounted for by supposing that these varieties secrete a slight excess of citral. Farnesol or linaloöl could account for the scents of such varieties as Sanders' White Rambler and Premier Bal. Even variations in the proportions of the first five constituents would give rise to different scents, since although I have characterised them all as being "rose"-scented, this is only for lack of a more precise description. The smell of phenylethyl alcohol is familiar to anyone who has ever smelled rose-water, since this is the one constituent which enters into its composition; the others are all vaguely rose-like, but distinguishable among themselves none the less. The "tea-scent" which is supposed to be characteristic of the Tea Roses I personally believe to be an illusion, but if I am mistaken, there is the fact that geraniol is present both in roses and in green tea to explain it. On the other hand there is no doubt at all that the muscatel scent, which is ascribed with general agreement to the "fruity" roses and not the Teas, was very clearly apparent in the best Darjeeling tea. But one must be on one's guard against carrying this game of spotting resemblances too far; one is liable to range farther and farther afield, via such harmless fantasies as the "caramel toffee", until one arrives at such ridiculous images as "burnt string beans", which I encountered in an American publication not long ago. Even if it could be proved to be literally and exactly true, it would be of little use or interest to those of us who are not in the habit of burning string beans. That way madness lies—or at any rate, fatuousness.

Substance	Scent	Proportion	Also found in—
Phenylethyl alcohol (soluble in water)	Rose	50%	Hyacinth Orange blossom
Citronellol (Rhodinol)	Rose	30%	Geranium Eucalyptus
Geraniol	Rose	10%	Geranium Jasmine Orange blossom Wallflower Green tea
Nerol	Rose	3%	Cyclamen Orange blossom Tuberose Wallflower
Nonyl aldehyde	Rose	?	Ginger Cinnamon Orris root
Eugenol and Methyleugenol	Clove	1%	Cloves Bay leaves Hyacinth Parma violet Tuberose
Citral	Lemon	?	Lemon peel Lemon verbena
Farnesol	Lily of the Valley	?	Cyclamen Jasmine Lily of the Valley Mignonette
Linaloöl	Lily of the Valley	?	Jonquil Lavender Orange blossom Wallflower
Carvone	Caraway seeds	?	Caraway Mint
Menthone (?)	Mint	?	Mint Pennyroyal

Fig. 11   The constituents of rose scent.

Chapter Eight

COLOUR

Roses, damask, white and red . . .
Michael Drayton

The newcomer to rose growing, when he pays his first visit to a rose nursery and sees the flowers that he has read of in books and catalogues spread out for his admiration, is often struck by a sense of disappointment. The colours that he sees hardly come up to his expectations; with few exceptions they are all either yellow, pink, white or red. Where are those wonderful confections of scarlet, cochineal-carmine, cinnabar, copper, silver and what-have-you that he has read about? The answer is, that most of them exist only in the writers' minds. This is not, I hasten to add, because professional rose growers are more given to exaggeration in their descriptions than members of other trades; on the contrary, most of them (that I have had any dealings with) are remarkably modest and honourable persons, and some of their catalogues are startlingly frank and honest in their admission of the shortcomings of some of their goods. The exaggeration and misrepresentation of colours in the rose world is simply a convention which has grown up over many years, and experienced growers take it in their stride without giving a thought to the way in which it must strike an outsider. The underlying causes are twofold.

In the first place, the rose is a very fleeting flower. Most of our garden flowers move fairly rapidly from the bud stage to the fully open flower, and then remain in that state for days or even weeks before they begin to fade and fall. But the unfolding of a rose is an almost continuous process from birth to death; her petals expand more widely with every passing hour, and in the heat of summer the whole process may take no more than two or three days. Now this is a great embarrassment to those who exhibit roses at shows. If the rose were cut at the climax of its expanding beauty, it would be already past its best when it came to be judged, and if the show lasted two days, it might be fallen and dead before the exhibition closed. Roses for exhibition are, therefore, cut when they first begin to unfurl their petals; and since the judging is completed before the public is admitted, they are necessarily judged when in this half-opened state. It is true that a half-opened rosebud has an exquisite beauty of its own— though to insist, as some hardened pot-hunters have done, that this is its "most beautiful" state is merely silly. Beauty is where you find it. But it is an unfortunate fact that at this stage the colours of a rose are almost always more intense than when it has unfolded sufficiently for us to see it whole. And since books are written and catalogues compiled almost exclusively by exhibitors, it has become an established habit to describe a rose in print as it appears when it is only half open. That is why you will find, for instance, Mrs. Sam McGredy described as "scarlet", "copper" and "orange", when it is actually salmon pink. Some roses change more than others as they open; one can lay down no universal rule; one must just be on one's guard against this innocent deception.

The second cause of much innaccuracy is to be found in the element of wishful thinking which enters into the descriptions of so many specialist flowers. Whatever colours a flower may exhibit in nature, the first wish of the breeder is to produce something different. Hence the never-ending search for blue and black tulips, blue roses, pink delphiniums, pink flag irises, etc. Human nature being what it is, every tiny step towards the desired aim is hailed as a full achievement. Down to about forty years ago, a true scarlet was a colour almost unknown in roses; but being a bright and popular colour, the word was used to describe many roses whose colour was bright and free from blueness, though few of them approached as near to scarlet as blood-red. But when the pigment pelargonidin appeared by a natural accident in the rose, it gave rise to a spate of scarlet roses—and the experts, having misused the word for so long, did not know how to describe them. For the most part they fell back at first on the words "vermilion" and "cinnabar", which didn't really help things in the least. Neither of these words is the name of a colour; vermilion is a pigment prepared for painters by refining a natural ore of mercury; cinnabar is the ore from which vermilion is prepared; but the colour of both of them is scarlet. Today these roses are usually described as "orange-scarlet", or even "orange"—which suggests that none of the persons concerned can ever have passed by a fruiterer's shop.

True orange-coloured roses are still scarce. The polyantha Golden Salmon, or its sport, Golden Salmon Supérieur, are probably the best. What their raiser, De Ruiter of Holland, had in mind when he christened them I cannot say, but it is a pity that in so many English catalogues they are described as "golden salmon" in colour. History repeats itself; the word orange being now monopolised by the scarlet roses, a new description has to be invented for the real orange colour. The best orange-coloured H.T. is probably Mev. G. A. van Rossem, though on close examination its colour is seen to be due to red veining on a yellow ground.

The "blue" roses are in rather different case. There never has been, and quite possibly never will be, a rose which can honestly be described as blue. The word was fairly widely used—though for very shame it was usually printed in inverted commas—in the early 1950s to describe such varieties as Prélude and Lilac Time which had a faint suggestion of mauve in their coloration, but today they are more usually said to be "lavender", which is an improvement inasmuch as it is a tacit admission that the colour is not blue; but even this is misleading. So far as the Hybrid Teas are concerned, "lavender" must normally be taken to mean a dusky or dusty (I had almost written "dirty") pink inclining towards what is more commonly called "lilac". Among the old-fashioned roses there are a number of varieties whose colour approaches to a true violet or mauve. To see them at their "bluest" one is urged to examine the older, faded flowers at dusk— which seems to invite the comment that all cats are grey in the dark. The best violet colours are found in the polyantha Baby Faurax and in a few of the ramblers, of which Veilchenblau and Violette are about the best.

I cannot discuss all the misleading words used to describe the colours of roses; this would take a book in itself. Most of those likely to cause difficulty will be found in the glossary at the end of this book. All I want to do here is to warn the reader that there are certain descriptive words applied to roses which bear a different meaning from that which we ascribe to them in everyday speech. It is only in the most exceptional cases that they are used with a conscious intention to deceive; for the most part they have become simply conventional, and in some cases quite meaningless. But the principle *caveat emptor* still applies; if you want to know the colour of a certain variety, go and see it growing.

I have already pointed out that the colour of the bud is usually more

High Noon (Climber). Raiser: Dr. W. E. Lammerts, Livermore, California, U.S.A. Introduced 1946. Parentage: Soeur Thérèse × Capt. Thomas. Chrome-yellow buds on long stems, solitary and in small clusters, opening loosely. Moderate, sharp scent. Profuse flowering from early summer until late autumn. Vigorous, upright growth from 8–10 ft. Foliage mid-green, some-what sparse. All-America Rose Selection 1948. Photograph: J. L. Norton, A.R.P.S.

A rose of many uses, **Ulrich Brunner** *fils (Hybrid Perpetual). Raiser: Antoine Levet, Lyons, France. Introduced 1881. Parentage: Anna de Diesbach seedling. Large (4–5 in.), globular blooms in cherry, flecked with carmine, lighter on the reverse. Strong fragrance. Matt, mid-green foliage which is plentiful and highly disease-resistant, on tall, upright, almost thornless canes to 5 ft. Abundant bloom, summer and autumn. A favourite exhibition rose in Victorian times, still grown as a cut flower and for perfumery in France on account of its high oil yield. Named for a Swiss nurseryman. Photograph: J. L. Norton, A.R.P.S.*

intense than that of the open flower; not infrequently the colour actually changes in hue, as well as fading, as the flower ages. No matter what the catalogues may say, all red roses fade, though some fade more than others, and in the process of doing so their hue shifts in some degree towards a bluer colour; in fact this is often spoken of as "blueing". One or two of the China Roses, however, display what we think of as a national habit of doing things the wrong way round; the pink Miss Lowe's Variety becomes deeper in colour as it ages, while *R. chinensis mutabilis* opens as a yellow rose, but begins to develop a red colour shortly afterwards, which deepens progressively until it finally swamps the yellow entirely. The same remarkable behaviour is now familiar to us in the floribunda variety Masquerade, which has thrown back to a remote Chinese ancestor in this respect. Yellow roses generally grow lighter with age, especially those which derive their colour from a Tea Rose ancestor rather than from *R. foetida*, such as the rambler Albéric Barbier, which is almost white by the time the flowers are fully open; but even the earlier yellow floribundas such as Goldilocks, which was only two generations removed from *R. foetida*, faded very badly indeed. Many of the red and yellow and red and white bicoloured roses have an annoying habit; the sharply contrasted colours of the upper and under sides of the petals seem to percolate through and merge, so that they fade through light orange to salmon-pink. Trade Wind and Gay Crusader are outstanding for their avoidance of this fault; they maintain the distinction to the end.

As if this were not enough to complicate matters, the colours of roses often change with changing seasons. The first flowers put out by Geheimrat Duisberg are often little deeper in tint than Paul's Lemon Pillar, but its autumn blooms are quite a rich gold. Mev. G. A. van Rossem, on the other hand, is a fiery orange from June to October, but flowers which open later (and sometimes those that come unusually early in a mild spring) are pale yellow, with no trace of the red veining responsible for the normal appearance. Many others show less striking differences than these. Differences in soil and aspect may also cause differences in colour. Some varieties give their brightest colours under a blazing sun; some seem to be bleached by sunlight and show their richest tones in cool, damp weather.

It is worthwhile to note the difference between the colour effect produced by a rose as a whole and the details of its coloration when viewed closely. I have already given an instance in Mev. G. A. van Rossem, which

K

appears pure orange when viewed from any distance, but which on close inspection is seen to consist of red veining on a yellow ground. Very few roses show an absolutely uniform coloration throughout; there is usually some gradation of tint from the tip to the base and often a complete change of hue, as in that still unsurpassed beauty Shot Silk, whose petals shade from pink to gold at the base. (It does not exhibit any true "shot-silk" effect, however, whatever the catalogues may say.) That lovely rose Polly, whose yellow buds open to a pale cream flower, shows in its earlier stages a glow of deeper colour, sometimes pinkish, sometimes orange or gold, deep down in its heart; its distant ancestor Devoniensis shows the same effect. Unhappily, the colour disappears as the flower ages.

Many of the older roses were characterised by a deeper colour in the centre than in the outer petals. Mme. Abel Chatenay is still a popular example of this effect, even at seventy years of age; Burnaby is a similar example in yellow. The effect is persistent, and must not be confused with the normal fading of the opening petals.

Quite a number of roses, mostly among the deeper reds, exhibit a shading on the petals which looks like the bloom on a grape. It is usually purple in colour—I have seen a half-opened flower of Crimson Glory whose inner petals were a pure, rich violet from this cause—but sometimes, as in such varieties as Charles Mallerin, Josephine Bruce and the climber, Don Juan, it is almost black. This is not a dust which can be rubbed off the petal, but a sprinkling of minute points where the natural pigmentation is greatly concentrated and deepened in colour. It tends to fade as the flower fully expands. The purplish bloom is not especially advantageous, as its effect is chiefly to shift the colour of the rose as a whole towards the blue, which is generally reckoned a disadvantage; but in its black form it can be very decorative, deepening the colour of the flower without spoiling its hue and enhancing the brilliance of those parts from which it is absent. It is probably an extension of this to the whole petal which is responsible for the colour of the deepest "reds" of all, such as Bonne Nuit and Papa Meilland, which are not so much red as a deep maroon. At their best they are entrancingly lovely, but I have not been fortunate enough to obtain many flowers at their best; I do not know one variety in this colour which is a really solid, vigorous plant. Most of them have thin, wiry stems and are notorious sprawlers in their growth. The best H.T. in this colour is probably the climber Guinée. Among the H.P.'s, Prince Camille de Rohan and Souvenir d'Alphonse Lavallée are well spoken of, though I have not grown them—I cannot recommend Empéreur du Maroc from my own experience; the semi-double gallica Tuscany si probably the finest of all.

Amongst the H.P.s and H.T.s it is almost true to say that there is only one pure white rose, and that is Frau Karl Druschki; and even she commonly shows a few splashes of red on the outer guard petals in the bud. But the open flower is so white that it almost seems to sparkle, like new-fallen snow. The popular Virgo often has a flush of pink in the bud, and sometimes retains the colour when open. The newer Message is better, but cannot approach the glistening purity of Frau Karl Druschki. For many years white roses have had a bad reputation for "balling"—that is to say, failing to open and rotting on the stem—in wet weather. This seems to be due to a deficiency in the wax which normally covers the petals of a rose; it is undoubtedly the case with Frau Karl Druschki, but it is not peculiar to that rose, or to the white roses as a class. There are only too many in all colours which dislike rain; it was particularly the case with the older pale yellow exhibition roses such as Mrs. Charles Lamplough, Sam McGredy and Mrs. C. H. Rigg. In the wet summer of 1957 my plants of the last-named failed to open a single flower throughout the whole season.

The description "bicolour" is usually restricted to those roses which have petals which are red above and yellow or white beneath. It could, of course, be applied to any rose which displays two colours, however arranged, but I prefer to use it only of those which show a contrast between the two sides of the petals. In the red and yellows the red is always uppermost. Good examples are My Choice and Gail Borden; the latter has rather globular flowers, which are not generally popular today, but its luscious "strawberry and vanilla" colouring is irresistible. Orange above and yellow beneath is best seen in L'Arlésienne, another lovely but difficult rose; McGredy's Sunset and Marjorie Le Grice both show much gradation in the upper colour, from yellow to scarlet. Quite a number of pink roses have a much deeper tint on the lower sides of their petals, of which the best known are probably the old favourites Betty Uprichard and Lal, and the floribunda Dainty Maid. The first is sometimes accused of having too few petals, but the open flower displays its two-tone finish to perfection, where a fuller one would tend to hide it. A similar effect among the yellows is rarely discernible.

Striped roses are found mostly among the old-fashioned varieties, especially among the gallicas. Rosa Mundi, *R. gallica versicolor*, is the best of all, its wide, flat, semi-double flowers providing a perfect ground for the display of its light pink and carmine stripes. Most of the rest are smaller and more double, which detracts from the effect. Ferdinand Pichard is a very vigorous H.P. with similar-coloured stripes, and is very popular among those who like it. There are several striped H.T.s, Modern Times, with pink stripes on red, and Ambossfunken (Anvil Sparks), which is said to be orange breaking into red stripes, but they do not seem to have caught the public fancy to any extent. The Damask Rose, York and Lancaster is not striped but parti-coloured; its flowers are either all white, all pink, or one blotched with the other.

There are no blue roses, and no prospects of any. Prélude was once advertised (in the pages of *The Times*, no less!), as a blue rose; I used to point it out to visitors to my garden with the remark, "That is what is called the blue rose", which invariably brought the puzzled query, "Why?" The best H.T. of this colour at present is probably Blue Moon, raised by Tantau, and known on the continent as Mainzer Fastnacht and Sissi.

There is, however, a green rose, *R. chinensis viridiflora*. It is commonly said that in this rose "the petals have been transformed into leaves", but that is not quite accurate; they are still recognisable as petals, since they lack the typical veins of the leaves and are not always shaped like them, but they are a good deal narrower than normal, and are often pointed at the tips and partly, but not entirely, serrated at the edges. The flower, which is fully double but seldom exceeds one and a half inches across, is of course a pure freak—a monstrous growth—but it can sometimes be quite attractive, especially when it comes much paler than the ordinary leaves, which it often does; but its appearance is usually spoilt by a red pigment which suffuses the petals and makes them look brown and withered. It has one virtue denied to more conventional roses; it lasts anything from two to three months on the plant. The plant is perfectly healthy—a typical China, rather taller and more vigorous than the Old Blush; but it is only worth growing as a curiosity.

*   *   *

The colours of our roses are due to two chemical substances, one of which is yellow and the other red. The yellow one, which goes by the name of xanthophyll, is insoluble, and is present in the form of minute solid particles in the cells of the petals—and also of the leaves, though its colour there is normally hidden by the green of the all-important chloro-phyll, and is only seen in those few roses whose leaves lose their chlorophyll just before they die, and so turn yellow in autumn. *R. rugosa* is the most familiar example. What may be the importance of xanthophyll to the plant is obscure; perhaps it has no function, but is only the end-product of more important chemical changes. Its importance to us lies in the fact that in various degrees of depth and permanence it provides us with a host of lovely yellow roses, besides modifying the colour of the red pigment when both are present together.

The red colouring matter, cyanidin, is a much more versatile substance. It is one of a group of three related chemicals, pelargonidin, cyanidin and delphinidin; the first is found in the pelargoniums, and is responsible for the typical hue of the "scarlet geraniums", which are properly pelar-goniums; the last takes its name from, and gives the blue colour to, the delphiniums; while cyanidin (whose name, just to make things more difficult, is derived from a Greek word meaning "blue") is found in roses, and many other plants beside. In fact these three substances are between them responsible for practically all flower colours except yellow. They achieve this versatility by their remarkable property of changing their own colours through a wide range, depending upon the acidity of the solution they are dissolved in, and also the nature of other substances, chiefly sugars and tannins, with which they habitually combine. As regards acidity, they behave much like the familiar litmus of the chemical laboratory, being red when acid and blue when alkaline, but their ranges of hue are not identical. Pelargonidin passes from scarlet to violet-blue, cyanidin from crimson to mid-blue, and delphinidin from magenta to a greenish blue. The effect of combination often over-rides the effect of acidity or alkalinity. In roses, whose sap is slightly acid, the cyanidin has a typical crimson colour, but in cornflowers, whose sap is more acid than that of the rose, the same substance is a beautiful blue. And since corn-flowers may be red, or at least pink, as well as blue, there seems to be no reason why roses should not be blue as well as red—if we only knew how to bring it about. Only we don't.

When, some thirty-odd years ago, a new pigment appeared in roses, for the first time, so far as we know, for thirty million years, it was unfortunate for the blue-rose enthusiasts that it turned out to be, not delphinidin, but pelargonidin. Yet we should all be very grateful that this was so. In xantho-phyll and cyanidin we already have the necessary ingredients for the production of a complete range of colours from canary-yellow to cornflower-blue—if we only knew how to produce it. The new pigment has brought about a flood of screeching-scarlet roses, it is true; but the flood will abate when the fashion takes a new turn. While if it had been delphinidin, the flood would have been composed of magenta roses, which is a dreadful thought.

The few roses we have whose colour lies among the purples and violets owe this to cyanidin in combination with tannins; but the condition is not inherited directly. I have myself raised a number of self-seedlings from both Baby Faurax and Veilchenblau, but none of them departed noticeably from the normal rose red or pink. Nevertheless it is interesting to note that both departures from the normal, the cyanidin violets and the pelargonidin scarlets, are seen at their best in roses having a strain of *R. multiflora* in them, and quite possibly, of the particular multiflora rambler Crimson Rambler. If the records of its various matings are correct, the latter must have been a hybrid, in which case the significant connexion—if there is one—might be with *R. multiflora* itself, or with the unkown other parent of Crimson Rambler. This is only the vaguest speculation, but it may give a pointer to the direction in which we ought to look for new colours. At all events, I recommend a study of Crimson Rambler to any amateur hybridist who, like myself, prefers to poke around in unfamiliar corners to see what happens, rather than slavishly following the latest fashions in the hope of making a fortune.

Chapter Nine

GROWTH AND PRUNING

Addish-, Subtrac-, Multiplica-tion.
Lewis Carroll

The rose plant adds to its stature by the natural process of growth; we subtract from it by the process of pruning, which seems unnatural enough, though in fact it only takes the place of Nature's method of removing unwanted, worn-out parts of the plant by death and disease. We adopt it because Nature's methods are too slow—and too liable to involve plants that we want, even if Nature doesn't. A rose plant as a whole is not mortal, as an animal is mortal; it is tolerably certain to die eventually, but this will not be from the essential process of ageing, but from some concatenation of circumstances which could be avoided if it could be foreseen.

One quite often sees or hears it said that since roses are multiplied by "vegetative propagation"—that is, by taking a small part of the original plant and growing it into a new one, either by putting it into the ground and letting it put out new roots and shoots, or by grafting a portion, usually a single bud, on to some other stock, so as to supply it with a ready-made root system—it follows that all plants of a particular variety are actually parts of the original specimen; and that therefore they are bound to take part in that plant's ultimate deterioration and death. The fallacy in this reasoning is easily exposed. Of the bud which is inserted in the stock, the part which actually grows on is a cluster of minute cells, weighing less than one thousandth of an ounce. In one season's growth, this can easily give rise to ten ounces of new plant, which can therefore only contain one ten-thousandth part of the substance of the original plant. After ten repetitions of the budding process, the growing part of the bud from the last plant would contain a quantity of original substance amounting to a fraction of an ounce represented by a figure one over a number composed of a one followed by forty-three noughts. This is very much less than the weight of the smallest particle of matter that can possibly exist; in other words, by the time you reach the tenth "bud generation" the new plants contain none at all of the original substance. As a matter of fact, this is equally true of the second generation: the original bud merely acts as a "template" and decides the nature of the rose which will grow out of it, whose own structure is wholly made up of new material built up from the foods taken in by the roots and leaves. The prototype plant may eventually deteriorate and die off, though not simply from old age; but whatever happens to it, it cannot possibly affect the other plants which have been budded from it.

An interesting instance of this is given by the once-popular variety, Dame Edith Helen, introduced by Dickson in 1926. In the past twenty years or so, this rose has often been quoted as an example of a variety which has deteriorated through age—in this country. Yet long after the deterioration had been observed here, this same variety was barred from competition with other varieties in shows in Queensland, Australia, because it flourished so luxuriantly that anyone could produce a prize bloom with no trouble. There is no doubt that the present stock of Dame Edith Helen has deteriorated in England, but whatever the cause may be, it cannot be connected in any way with the age of the original specimen, otherwise all plants would be affected equally, in all parts of the globe.

I said just now that a rose plant should not be regarded as an individual; nevertheless, if we restrict our attention to a single one of the basal canes of the plant one finds that it does work out a life-history which is characteristic of all of them. For simplicity's sake let us choose a rose in its natural state in the wild, or one of the once-blooming ramblers, which have retained the growth habits of their wild ancestors unchanged. The cane starts its life as a bud low down on the plant, just above the "crown" which marks the position of the original junction between the scion and the stock. The bud swells, bursts, and gives rise to a vigorous shoot which grows straight upwards, unbranching, and bearing leaves at regular intervals. The growth all takes place at the tip of the shoot; if you make a mark on it near the ground, you will find that this mark remains in the same place and does not rise up as growth progresses. As the cane grows longer, the water with its dissolved nutrients taken in by the roots has farther and farther to travel before it reaches the growing tip, with the natural result that the rate of growth gradually falls off; the cane tapers down, and the distances between successive leaves is gradually reduced. The size of the leaves also falls off, but not in the same proportion; there is a normal size for the leaves of any one species or variety, and they do not vary much from this whether they spring from a thick or a thin part of the cane. This growth continues so long as conditions are favourable to it; in a normal year it is finally stopped by the first frosts, which kill the delicate growing tip and wither up the leaves, causing them to drop, but in an exceptionally mild winter it is not unknown for a cane to go on growing without a break until the following March, when the new year's growth absorbs all the available energy and leaves none for further growth at the tip. Under normal conditions, the cane passes the winter as a bare stem; but at each point where a leaf originally grew—these points are known as the "nodes" of the stem, and in some plants, carnations, for example, they are marked by a distinct swelling—there is a bud, ready to burst into growth when spring brings in the new season's activity.

When the spring brings new life to the garden, these buds expand and give rise, not to leaves, but new shoots, which for obvious reasons are called "lateral shoots", or laterals for short. As there may be a score or more of these laterals competing for the nutriment which all went into the growth of the main cane in the previous year, their growth is naturally less vigorous; they are thinner than the stem from which they spring, and their nodes are a bit closer together; but their most important difference lies in the fact that after they have passed a few nodes—as a rule, the farther from the base, the fewer the nodes—each of which is marked as before by a leaf, the tip develops into a flower bud, or a bunch of flower buds. This of course puts an end to further growth. In due course the buds expand and open, the flowers fall, and the available energies of the cane are concentrated on forming the hips, with their enclosed seeds. As with the leaves, so with the flowers; there is a normal size which does not greatly vary; the more vigorous laterals produce more of them, that is all. The next winter sees the fall of the leaf, leaving the canes bare once more, but now the "eyes", as the undeveloped buds at the nodes are called, are to be found on the laterals and not on the main canes, unless, as not uncommonly happens, some of the original eyes have failed to develop into a shoot.

The third year sees a resumption of growth from the eyes, as before, but now the system begins to break down. Many of the eyes are located on stems so thin that they simply cannot support the growth of a flowering "sub-lateral", as the side branches from the laterals are called. This is primarily due to the fact that the size of the leaves and flowers is not reduced in proportion to the size of the stem which bears them. What usually happens is that one eye at the base of each lateral gives rise to a sub-lateral approaching in size and vigour to the lateral from which it springs, while the rest either fail to shoot at all, or at best give rise to small, twiggy growth bearing a leaf or two, but no flowers. In its third year, therefore, the cane is more bushy, but bears rather fewer flowers. Meanwhile, the lower portion of the cane is beginning to develop signs of age. The outer skin which in the first year was smooth and green—being in fact composed of similar substance to the leaves, and capable of the same functions—grows brown and wrinkled and dry, and will eventually become bark. If, as not uncommonly happens, a new basal cane should spring from a point low down on the old one, this will compete with its forerunner for the available supply of nutrients; the old cane will languish, and sooner or later it will fall a victim to one or other of the parasitic fungi that lie in wait to devour it, and it will die and rot. The part below the new cane is protected by its bark from attack by fungi; it continues to thrive and to support the new cane, and any successors it may have, growing thicker and more rugged with the passage of time.

This, then, is the life-history of the cane. In its first year it bears leaves only; in the second, laterals and a plentiful crop of flowers; in the third, sub-laterals—mostly twiggy growth—and fewer flowers; and thereafter, increasing deterioration until death supervenes, though not from old age, be it noted, but from disease on top of semi-starvation. The deterioration is more marked in our garden ramblers than in the wild species, since their flowers are in general larger and more disproportionate to the small growth of the third and successive years. None the less, this account is correct in principle for all roses, though it is profoundly modified in the case of those roses which flower perpetually, as we shall see shortly.

These observations are not new; they have been known to observant rose growers from the earliest times. In ancient Greece, as Theophrastus records, it was the practice to leave a rose to its own devices for five years before "pruning" it in the drastic manner he describes. Sir Thomas Hanmer, in 1659, was more specific; he recommended pruning every other year at least, "for the young second yeare branches beare most flowers". It is all the more difficult to understand why so many modern writers recommend that the shrub roses and species should not be pruned at all, when the need for it has been so clearly and correctly recognised for over two thousand years. As a matter of fact, they usually qualify their advice by recommending that the plants should not be pruned "except for the removal of diseased and unwanted growth"; and as the removal of diseased and unwanted growth constitutes the whole art of pruning where any rose is concerned, the reader is little the better for the advice.

Be that as it may, the reader should now be in a position to understand both why and how we should set about pruning any rose which conforms strictly to the rambling or climbing mode of growth that I have outlined. We want to see the most luxuriant crop of flowers that the plant can yield, and to that end, we must cut out every basal cane as soon as its first crop (in its second year of life) is over, thus allowing the plant to concentrate all its energies on the new canes which are growing up in the same year, preparatory to flowering in the year following. The canes should be cut right out, either down to the base of the plant, or to the point where a new cane has sprung from the old one, if such is the case. In the ordinary way, the new crop of canes will be well in evidence by the time the old ones are due for removal. If, as may happen with some varieties of rambler, not enough new canes are coming on to furnish the plant adequately, one or more of the old ones may be left in place, but all its laterals must be cut back to the main stem, thus in effect putting it into the same condition as the new crop. In the following year, one may hope to see a single sub-lateral spring from the base of each former lateral, and being freed from unwanted competition, it should grow with little less vigour than its predecessor, and bear almost as many flowers. It will be, in fact, not so much a sub-lateral as a new lateral taking the place of the old one which has been cut off.

In species of a more moderate growth, the basal canes seldom exceed about four feet in height, though in compensation there are usually more of them, so that the plant as whole forms a fairly compact bush. The laterals, especially those which spring from low down, tend to grow more vertically and more strongly, so as to bring their tips level with the tips of the basal canes. The distinction between canes and laterals is not so clearly marked, but the fundamental rule still holds good, that the first growth bears nothing but leaves, the flowering shoots springing from the eyes which mark the positions of the leaves on the earlier growth. The greater size of the flowers on roses of this kind is largely offset by their smaller number, but it is also compensated by the stouter growth of the laterals, which are often thick enough to produce sub-laterals equally capable of bearing flowers. But the same basic rule for pruning still applies; a cane should be allowed to bear its quota of flowers, and then it should be cut out, down to the base; though in this case it may be three years or even more instead of two before the cane has given all the best of which it is capable.

The perpetual-flowering habit in roses is best regarded as a form of hereditary disease. However welcome the habit may be to us, to the rose itself it brings no good at all. Its chief symptom is that every shoot, including the first-year growth, bears, or tends to bear, a flower bud. Since the presence of a terminal bud effectively puts a stop to any further extension of the shoot, the consequence is that the basal canes of a perpetual rose do not continue to grow throughout the first season, but complete their initial growth comparatively early; thereafter they produce flowers. When the flowering is done, they are left at a loose end, so to speak, while the plant as a whole is still in an active state of growth. The result is that their eyes begin to shoot and they produce laterals in the same year, which also flower in due course. To a rose struggling for existence in the wild, this alteration in its habit is a threefold disaster. In the first place, the restricted length of the main canes means that they may fail to penetrate their encroaching neighbours in their search for the life-giving light and air. Secondly, the shorter canes will bear fewer flowers, and so produce a smaller crop of seed, with a smaller chance of perpetuating its kind. And thirdly, the late blooming of the secondary crop of flowers means that the seed that they set will have small chance of ripening, thus still further reducing the hope of progeny. A rose so affected will have small chance of competing with its normal kindred, so that a wild rose which sported to the perpetual form would almost inevitably succumb to competition and die out. It is significant that *R. rugosa*, which is almost the only true species which displays the perpetual habit, is not a climber but a bush rose, and its hips ripen with exceptional speed, so that all but the latest flowers are capable of yielding ripe seed. We do know that the true wild form of *R. chinensis*, the China Rose which introduced the perpetual habit into our gardens, is once-flowering.

It seems that this "disease" which afflicts our roses and adorns our gardens can occur in both severe and mild forms. This is most clearly apparent with the climbing roses of predominantly Hybrid Tea ancestry which have largely ousted the ramblers from the modern rose garden. With a few exceptions, all of these are potentially perpetual-flowering, but some of them—Climbing Etoile de Hollande is an example—show little sign of it when young. Its basal canes are vigorous and tall, and while they may terminate in a flower bud, these are often the only flowers they produce in their first season—if any. But once the plant is fully established, the flowers come thick and fast from laterals and sub-laterals, so that in the year 1961, the last specimen that I grew was in flower for no less than 161 days between the middle of May and the end of October. This is a longer flowering period than I have been able to record for any dwarf rose. At the other extreme is the splendid New Dawn, which has taken the "disease" very severely. It usually flowers well from the start, but is very reluctant to climb, so that it may take two or three years before it reaches as much as five feet in height; but given time it will cover a space ten feet by ten without difficulty. I have more than once known it to go through a whole season without once being without a flower. New Dawn is of special interest, since it is the only recorded example of a rose which has sported from once-flowering to the perpetual habit in cultivation. Its story has been told in Chapter Six.

The pruning of perpetual roses is not such a simple, clear-cut business as it is in the case of the once-blooming ramblers. Their growth is not so systematic, and the distinction between canes and laterals not nearly so clearly marked; nor, for that matter, is it so important. But the basic principles are still valid. Every stem tapers in its growth, and every stem is thinner than the one that it springs from; hence, as growth continues, the new shoots become thinner and thinner until finally they are too flimsy to support a good flower. When this stage is reached, then is the time to cut out the cane entirely, to be replaced by younger canes which have sprung from the base of the plant more recently. Keep your plants young. The ideal to aim at with a dwarf rose is to maintain from four to six healthy canes, cutting out an older one for each new one that makes its appearance. The actual number must depend upon the health and vigour of your plants; and as with the ramblers, if insufficient new growth appears, one can mend matters by cutting back the laterals or sub-laterals which have borne flowers and so restore the older canes to something approaching their pristine state. Since the leaves require sunlight in order to perform their function of furnishing fuel and raw materials to the plant, growth tends to be concentrated at the upper ends of the canes, and it may often be found that while the upper half of a cane has developed to the point where nothing more may be expected but blind, twiggy shoots, the lower half has still a number of eyes that have not yet produced laterals. If the production of flowers is all that you expect of a rose bush, you may if you choose, confine your pruning to cutting back the cane to a point immediately above the highest of these unshot eyes, which will normally produce a new shoot which becomes in effect the upper half of a new cane; but it will be a most unsightly, dog-legged affair, which quite destroys any symmetry that the plant may possess.

Pay no attention to anything you may read or hear about the way in which pruning "stimulates" this, that or the other sort of growth in roses. Pruning does not stimulate a rose at all; on the contrary, by robbing it of certain quantities of stored fuel, and by upsetting the balance between top-growth and root-growth, it weakens it, though the effect is negligible unless the pruning is carried to unreasonable extremes. It is most commonly said that hard pruning stimulates the production of new growth from low down on the plant; but if you cut off all the upper part of the plant, where else can the new shoots come from but the lower part? It certainly is not true that a hard-pruned rose puts up more true basal canes than one which is lightly pruned; in the trials conducted by the Royal National Rose Society some fifteen years ago, it was plainly observed that the plants which received the least pruning produced the most new growth from the base. That the plants which had received the least pruning, and therefore naturally grew biggest, should have yielded the most flowers is only what one would expect; but it was also observed that the best flowers that they produced were in no way inferior to those produced by the hard-pruned plants, which effectively disposes of the theory which is still held among some exhibitors that hard pruning is necessary to stimulate the production of flowers worthy of the show bench.

So far I have only spoken of that pruning which is directed to keeping the plants young and vigorous, and so ensuring the best crops of the best flowers. But pruning is also needed to preserve the health of the plant. Roses are subject to a number of fungal infections, most of which are quite incurable, in the sense that the spread of the disease cannot be checked once it has taken hold, so that, as in a number of human diseases, recourse to surgery becomes necessary. When the disease is confined to the leaves, Nature acts as her own surgeon, and the infected leaves will eventually drop off; but a cankered stem, while it, too, will eventually disappear by natural processes, will take far too long over the business, allowing ample time for airborne spores to infect neighbouring stems of the same and adjoining plants. So it must be cut out ruthlessly, as soon as the infection is observed, at a node sufficiently far below the site of infection to ensure that none but healthy wood is left in place.

There are other forms of "surgical" pruning which should be practised. If two stems have grown across one another so that they are in contact, either permanently or intermittently as the wind blows, the outer skin at the points of contact is bound to suffer damage, either from friction or from thorns, and such injuries provide especially favourable conditions for the entry of the invading fungi. One or other of the stems must be excised. Roses are also subject to frostbite, which may manifest itself in the immediate death of the affected cane, or may not become apparent until later in the year, when the apparently healthy first shoots cease to thrive and the cane dies off. In extreme cases, the cane may be actually split by the frost, when the damage is at once apparent. If you only have cause to suspect damage, snip a little bit off the tip of the cane and examine the cut surface. If the pith in the centre is a clean, greenish-white colour, all is well; but if it is brown, the cane is frosted, and you will have to go on cutting farther and farther back until you reach a point where a normal healthy colour shows that the stem is undamaged.

There is yet a third reason why we prune roses, and that is the fairly obvious one of cutting them into the actual shape that one desires. I do not suggest that one should practise topiary work with them—it is hard to imagine a more unrewarding task than trying to clip a rose bush into the form of a peacock, for instance—but some growers like to form hedges out of the bushier forms of roses, and these require a degree of shaping. In such cases, provided one has had the foresight to choose a good, tough variety, as vigorous, hardy and floriferous as possible, and little susceptible to disease —Rosa Mundi is an example which springs to mind—one can forget all about the finer points of pruning and simply have at them with the shears at the beginning of each season. So-called "hedges" which are formed by training ramblers horizontally along a supporting fence are in rather different case. Their new canes are so long and so strong that they must be left alone until the end of the season—which rather detracts from the neatness of the "hedge". If a fully-grown cane is bent down and tied into position along the top of a support, all the laterals that it produces in the following season will also turn upwards, which looks very well at first; but there will come a time when the weight of the bunches of flowers will cause the cane to twist to one side or the other, and the laterals will then all hang downwards, which is not so attractive. It matters less if the support is well above eye-level, but on the top rail of a low fence the result is rather unsightly and therefore they cannot really be recommended for the latter position.

The perpetual climbers always require a measure of shaping, even when they are grown normally—the normal practice being to train them into a quite unnatural form, flattened against a wall or trellis, or twisted round a vertical pillar. Their basal canes are not so readily expendable as those of the ramblers, and an old-established plant is often found to have developed a woody backbone like the trunk of a forest tree. Their laterals are often longer and stouter than the basal canes of a dwarf rose, and just as unwilling to submit to the distortion required to make them fit into an unnatural position. If one of them persists in growing in the wrong place or the wrong direction, there is nothing for it but to sacrifice it and cut it off. One usually wants a climber to cover the maximum possible area, but with the minimum thickness; there is no advantage in allowing it to form a tangled thicket against the side of the house. It is bad practice, too, to allow a climber to depend upon a single stem at the base; such a rose tends to concentrate all its flowering growth at the top, until one eventually finds nothing but a bare, gnarled trunk for the first ten feet or so. Most of us prefer to see a uniform display of flowers from ground-level upwards, and the best way to make sure of this is to see that the plant develops with not less than three main stems between the top-growth and the roots. One of these can be cut out from time to time, to be replaced by a new basal cane. A rose so treated will not grow as extensively as if it were allowed to follow its own devices for decade after decade, but it will produce more and better flowers.

The dwarf polyanthas are very close kin to the rambler roses, and to some extent share their propensity for putting up a regular supply of new canes from the base. They will therefore stand being cut hard back without complaint, and as their uninhibited growth is apt to be straggly and uneven many people prefer to treat them like this, especially if uniformity is desired in a number of plants. The same applies to the earlier floribundas,

Blue Moon, *syn.* **Mainzer Fastnacht, Sissi** *(Hybrid Tea). Raiser: Mathias Tantau, Uetersen, Holstein, Germany. Introduced 1964. Parentage: Unnamed seedling of Sterling Silver × unnamed seedling. Large (4 in.), high-centred blooms of 40 petals in dove-grey, overlaid lilac. Very fragrant. Free flowering. Dark green, matt foliage on vigorous, upright growth. The most satisfactory large-flowered rose of its colour. Rome Gold Medal 1964. R.N.R.S. Certificate of Merit 1964. Photograph: J. L. Norton, A.R.P.S.*

One of the best of modern bi-colours, **Piccadilly** (Hybrid Tea). Raiser: Sam McGredy IV, Portadown, Northern Ireland. Introduced 1960. Parentage: McGredy's Yellow × Karl Herbst. Large (4–5 in.) blooms in scarlet, base and reverse mid-yellow. Little fragrance. Very free flowering. Dark green, glossy foliage on vigorous, branching growth. A very good bedding rose and for cultivation as a standard. Gold Medals: Rome, Madrid, R.N.R.S., 1960. Photograph by courtesy of S. McGredy and Son Ltd.

which were derived from the polyanthas; but the later members of this group have so much Hybrid Tea in their make-up and resemble this side of the family so closely that they are better treated just like the Hybrid Teas, each cane being allowed to fulfil itself before being cut out.

The taller and more upright shrub roses, like the unsurpassable Nevada and Kordes' spinosissima hybrids, offer one a choice in their shaping. They start life with a few graceful canes, which cover themselves in due course with large, flat, almost single flowers on short stalks, holding them close to the main stem. If left to themselves they will become more bushy and eventually form quite thick shrubs, usually rather irregular in shape, though this slight drawback is more than offset by the breath-taking beauty of their first flush of flowers. If one wants a plant of the maximum size, with the maximum number of flowers, give them the minimum of pruning and allow them to develop in this way; alternatively, if one prefers the more delicate beauty of the young plant one may treat them like the H.T.s, cutting out an old cane for each new one that appears.

R. sericea pteracantha has thorns as much as an inch wide at the base and on the young growth are bright red in colour and translucent, like stained glass. If one values this property above others, one should prune it hard back every year. The older growth is not very attractive—the thorns lose their translucency in a month or two, and the plant is distinctly ungainly in growth—nevertheless its unique, four-petalled white flowers, borne on such short stalks that they seem to come direct from the main stem, are very beautiful, and doubly welcome in that they are usually the first of all to arrive, often opening at the end of April in a forward season.

But I must not go on discussing special pruning methods devoted to the special needs of special plants, or I shall never have done. What I have tried to do is to give the reader an idea of why we prune roses, and what the effect of pruning is. The only pruning which is actually necessary is that which is devoted to maintaining the health of the plant, which I have called "surgical pruning". It is a pity that the reports on the pruning trials carried out a few years ago by the Royal National Rose Society were so worded as to convey the impression that the early death of the unpruned plants was due to absence of pruning. It was not. They did not die from absence of pruning but from the presence of disease, due to (deliberate) neglect—not only the absence of surgical pruning, but the absence of any measures at all to keep disease at bay. They seem to have been most severely affected by black spot, which is not normally controlled by any

L

special pruning methods but by spraying with fungicides to kill the fungus spores before they have a chance to invade the leaves. Neither spraying nor pruning has any effect on disease once it is established. The former acts by preventing infection, and the latter by removing the diseased parts altogether. An unpruned or lightly-pruned rose will grow bigger and throw out more leaves than one which is hard-pruned and therefore offers more scope for the entry of disease spores; hence, if disease is common in a locality, the less you prune the more important it is that you should spray; but you will never avoid disease by pruning alone.

Apart from surgical pruning, you are perfectly free to follow your own sweet will. Prune your roses to suit yourself; and the better you understand the practice, the quicker and more certainly you will achieve the aim you have in mind, whatever it may be. The only right method of pruning is the one which brings the results you want.

Two points remain which I should deal with in this chapter. The first is the oft-repeated statement that climbing sports of dwarf varieties must not be pruned after planting in their first year, or the shock caused by pruning may cause them to revert to dwarfs. That this belief must be nonesense is shown at once by the undoubted fact that plants do not possess either brains, nerves or hearts, and therefore cannot suffer from surgical shock. Moreover, any such reversion as this entails a fresh mutation—sporting, as we call it—in the plant, in the opposite direction to that which caused the climbing growth in the first place. But all sports have their origin in a single cell, and can only manifest themselves in the cells which grow out of this one. Sports can be caused by physical damage (though none, I think, has ever been recorded among the roses) though they are only found in growth which originates at the point of damage; but neither pruning nor any other form of treatment could conceivably cause a simultaneous and identical mutation in every one of the billions of mature cells composing a year-old rose plant.

This superstition has arisen as a result of bad reasoning on top of bad observation. It is an undoubted fact that many climbers do exhibit a reluctance to climb in their early years, and even later in life if they have been seriously damaged by accident. This reluctance may sometimes persist for a very long time. I had a plant of Pink Cloud which never got above three feet in the five years that I kept it in my garden, and another of Réveil Dijonnais which behaved in much the same manner. But if anyone had suspected that they had "reverted" to a (non-existent) dwarf form, this could easily have been disproved; buds or grafts or cuttings from these plants would have shown that they still retained the climbing habit, even though it was temporarily in abeyance. The fact was that, like the millions of undersized and mis-shapen children who disgraced our so-called civilisation a hundred years ago, they were suffering from the results of starvation.

A climbing rose, whether it is a climbing sport or a climber by birth, starts its life as a bud inserted under the bark of an understock in a nursery. This understock is a fairly young plant with (at this stage) a not very extensive root system. As the top-growth expands, so also does the root-system; each has an essential part to play in the growth of the plant as a whole, the leaves supplying all the necessary energy (derived from sun-light) and a large proportion of the raw materials, in the form of carbon derived from the carbon dioxide in the air, while the roots supply all the water required (itself an essential raw material) together with the various mineral salts necessary to life. Hence a maiden plant of a climbing variety does not normally make very strong growth in its first year. At the outset it is entirely dependent upon the reserve supplies of food laid down in the roots in the previous year, but these were laid down by a comparatively small plant and are not very large; while it has to manufacture all its own leaves before it can derive any benefit from the light-energy and carbon that they can supply. It is therefore in a state of what the economists call "marginal subsistence" most of the time, and by the end of the growing season the roots will not have grown beyond what is needed to support the moderate growth above. At this stage, it is dug out of the ground, often entailing some loss to the root system; then packed and dispatched to the purchaser, which may entail a measure of drying-out and further damage. Finally, it is re-planted in your garden, with yet more root loss and damage. The consequence of this is that when the next growing season starts—the first one in your garden—the poor rose is in a worse state than it was a year before. The impoverished root-system cannot supply enough to support an adequate top-growth, and the inadequate top-growth cannot supply enough to repair and replenish the damaged roots. If, on top of this you have pruned it hard after planting, you have robbed it of the reserve supplies stored in the stems cut away, while giving it even more leeway to make up. It is not surprising that such a plant may make no more growth in its second year than it did in its first. While if, to cap it all, the plant wastes its own substance in producing flowers while it is still struggling to grow, this may well prove the last straw. It probably will not die; roses are very tenacious of life; but it can and very likely will continue for four or five years, putting out nothing more than a handful of leaves and a few flowers every year.

Fortunately, ours is a variable climate. Sooner or later an unusually favourable season will come along; the plant, being kept in a state of activity for a few extra weeks, is enabled to add that little extra to the normal reserve supplies laid down each year for the initiation of the next year's work which makes all the difference; a new cane makes its appearance at the beginning of the next season, and at once sets in train a chain-reaction. The slight increase in top-growth provides scope for the roots to grow longer; the extended roots provide for further increases in top-growth, which in turn supports further extension of the root-system, and so on, until in a couple of years the plant is shooting skyward like a rocket.

But you don't have to wait for Nature to correct your mistakes for you. It is a good rule never to prune any newly-planted rose, climber or dwarf, more than is necessary to remove any parts that may have been damaged in transit. Hard pruning at this stage may not do any harm, but it cannot possibly do any good. While if your climbers are reluctant to climb, don't accept any nonsense about "reversion", but do the best you can to cure the starvation from which they are suffering. See that they are not suffering from unfair competition by neighbouring plants—or weeds; see that they are not being over-shadowed and robbed of the life-giving sunlight; ensure that they are fed, and if necessary watered, generously (which doesn't mean excessively); and finally, remove all flower buds as soon as they make their appearance. Better no flowers in the first year and a hundred in the next than five a year from a stunted plant for an indefinite period.

Curiously enough, true dwarf plants do sometimes arise from buds taken from certain varieties of climbing sports—though not from all, and never from climbers which have not come into existence as the result of sporting. But this change does not occur in your garden, and certainly not as a result of pruning or any other treatment. It is due to the fact that many—probably most—of our roses which originated as sports are what are called *chimaeras*. A chimaera is a plant composed of the tissues of two different varieties or species, or even genera. But when a rose sports, it sometimes happens that the new variety so produced is itself a chimaera, inasmuch as the sported tissues do not permeate the whole of the plant;

parts of it are still composed of unsported cells. If a bud is taken from a part of the plant which has not sported, it will grow out into a new plant of the original variety, not the sport; and this is what sometimes happens with certain of the climbing sports. But it is not strictly a reversion, because it is made up of cells which have never sported at all.

The second point I mentioned has to do with the removal of flower-heads after the petals have fallen. One is often urged to do this on the score that to allow the rose to concentrate its energies on setting seed operates to reduce the later crop of flowers. In theory there is a measure of truth in this; but in practice the great majority of our modern garden roses set little or no seed so it is really a needless precaution. Nevertheless, the dead flower-heads are unsightly, especially in those naughty varieties which do not drop their petals cleanly but leave them clinging in a mop-head of rotting vegetation to the top of the stem, and their removal does improve the appearance of a rose bed. They would—or should—fall naturally in due course, since the flower-stalk is provided with an "abscission layer" at its foot, just as the leaves are, which grows across the stalk and cuts off communication with the living plant below. The flower-head begins to rot soon after it dies, but this is the one instance where surgical pruning is not vital, as the infection rarely if ever crosses the abscission layer. The layer is situated at the topmost node of the stem, which is marked, not by the usual leaf, but by a smaller leaf-like growth called a "bract"; and even before decay has set in, it gives a brittleness to the stalk, which is easily snapped off at this point. It is much better to break off the flower-heads at this point, rather than to cut lower down with the secateurs; it looks better, and also avoids an unnecessary wound, which is always a possible entry site for infection.

*   *   *

A word or two about the ways and means of pruning. You may sometimes be assured by an old hand that you can prune better and more quickly with a knife than with secateurs; but he is mistaken. What he means is that he can do better with the knife; but if you try it, without previous experience, you will tear your hands and clothes to shreds and probably do a lot of damage to your roses. It is quite a mistake to suppose that a knife is less liable to crush the stems than secateurs. The young stems of a rose are very like bamboos, a thin tube of brittle wood with nothing in the centre but pith, and when you press them against your thumb with the blade of the knife it is only too easy to crush and split them. If you want to enhance your prestige with the Joneses, do it by buying the most expensive secateurs you can find, not by doing without them altogether.

There are two basic types of secateurs on the market, the "anvil" type, in which a straight blade is forced down on to a flat brass anvil, which holds the stem while the blade is cutting through it, and the "scissors" type, in which the cutting blade is curved like a parrot's beak and slides past the other blade; but as the other blade, in the best makes at least, is also quite flat, the difference between the two is more apparent than real. Both types are quite capable of crushing and splitting a stem on occasion, though probably not more often than a knife would. Both types, if given the care and attention they deserve, will give years of satisfactory service. They must be kept sharp, but don't attempt to sharpen them yourself unless you are quite certain that you can make a good job of it; send them back to the makers if they are blunt. And they must be kept scrupulously clean at all times; if you have just cut through a diseased cane and go straight to a healthy one, you are taking the best means of injecting disease into it. Always clean the blades immediately after dealing with any infected material, and always wipe them carefully with an oily rag before putting them away after use, oiling the joints at the same time. Treated like this, they will last you a lifetime.

In addition to a pair of secateurs, you will also need a small pruning saw—the smaller the better if you are only going to use it for roses. The woody base of an old cane an inch thick is beyond the capacity of most secateurs, and you will only damage them if you try to make them do more than they are meant to; moreover, it often happens that the canes are so close together that it is difficult or impossible to introduce the secateurs to get a good bite on even a small cane, where a saw can be inserted without difficulty. See that you restrict your sawing to the cane that you mean to cut, and don't excoriate its neighbours at the same time.

At any point between the base and the tip of a shoot, the cut should always be made directly above an eye. That is where any future growth will spring from, and any length of stem left above it will remain leafless and bare until it soon becomes very literally a dead end, inviting infection. If the cut is made slanting at an angle of about forty-five degrees, running from behind the eye and at the same level to a point on the same side as the eye but as far above it as the stem is thick, the wound will heal with the minimum scar and with no projecting snag to die and rot. (See Fig. 12.)

The shape of your bush will be greatly influenced by your choice of eye at which you make your cut. As a general rule, the strongest new growth will spring from the eye immediately below the cut. The common rule of "prune to an outward eye" is perfectly sound in most cases, but it makes even more sense if you render it, "prune to an eye facing in the direction in which you want the new shoot to grow". Some of our roses, such as Josephine Bruce, are inveterate sprawlers, whose stems may take up almost any position between the vertical and the horizontal. There is little you can do to make a shapely bush of such a variety, but you can at least avoid pruning to an "outward" eye which is pointing almost vertically downwards. Generally speaking, you can judge how a new shoot is going to behave by seeing how its predecessors have grown on the same plant. You may prevent the entry of disease spores at the cut surfaces by giving them a dab of shellac, white lead paint, or one of the special protective preparations marketed for the purpose, but this precaution is seldom necessary in this country.

As regards the time of year when pruning should be done, there is only one rule: prune whenever is most convenient for you. It makes no difference to your roses. I have already said that the ramblers should be pruned as soon as their burst of flowers is over; with these tall plants the lower parts of the stems are not much hidden by the foliage, and even if they were, the inconvenience of this would be nothing compared with the inconvenience of disentangling the old growth from the new which has grown up and mingled with it, if one defers pruning until winter. But the ramblers apart, it is the merest common sense to put off pruning until all or most of the leaves have fallen, so that one can see what one is doing. There is a school of thought which advocates pruning in late autumn or early winter, which at least has the advantage of reducing the amount of top-growth which is left exposed to winter gales, especially if one practises hard pruning; on the other hand, a spell of hard frost in January or February will mean that one has to go over the roses again to discover and cut out any damaged wood. I have heard it argued that when pruning, one should cut out any young, sappy growth, such as is most liable to frost damage, so that early pruning prevents—or at least avoids—major damage from frost; but it seems almost perverse to cut out a healthy young shoot on no better grounds than that it may be frosted later. Why not leave it and see? On the whole I prefer to leave my roses unpruned until the new growth has started in the spring; then one can see which eyes are yielding

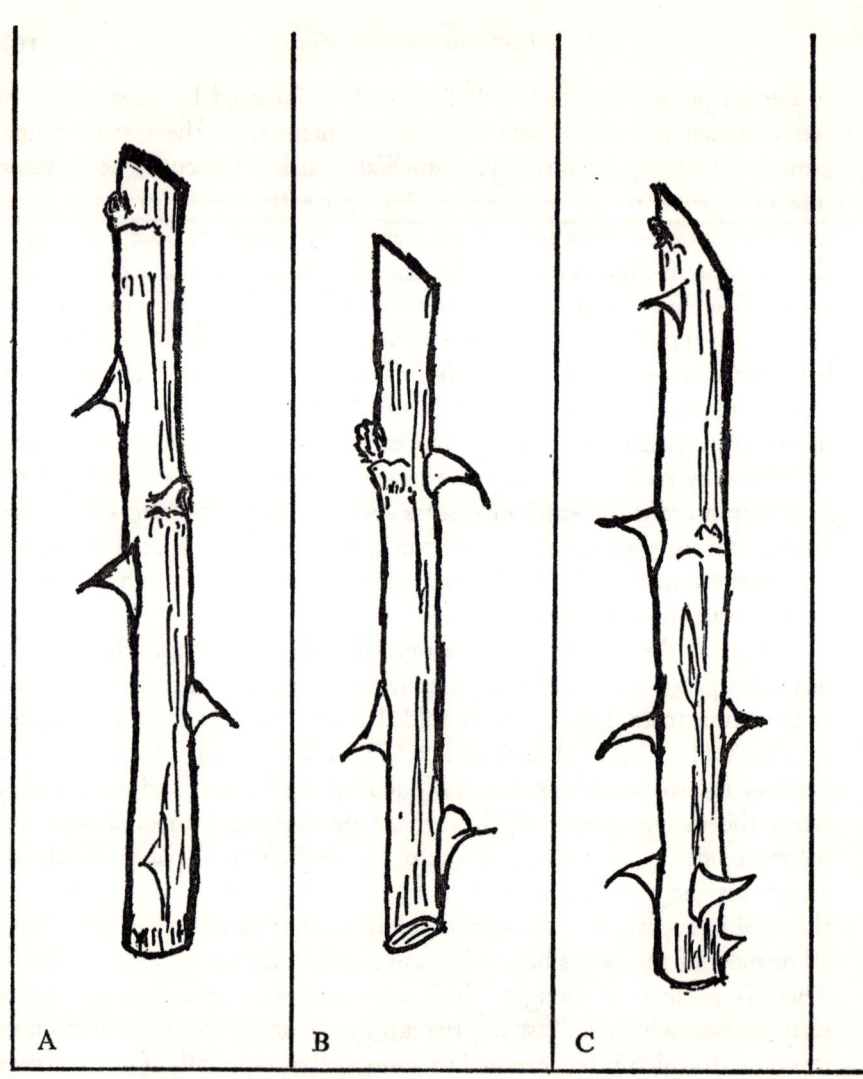

A. CORRECT CUT $\frac{1}{4}$ inch above bud and parallel to its direction of growth.

B. INCORRECT Cut made too far above bud. Whole area above will die back, including bud itself.

C. INCORRECT Angle too steep and projects behind bud, which will die back.

Fig. 12 The incorrect and correct methods of pruning.

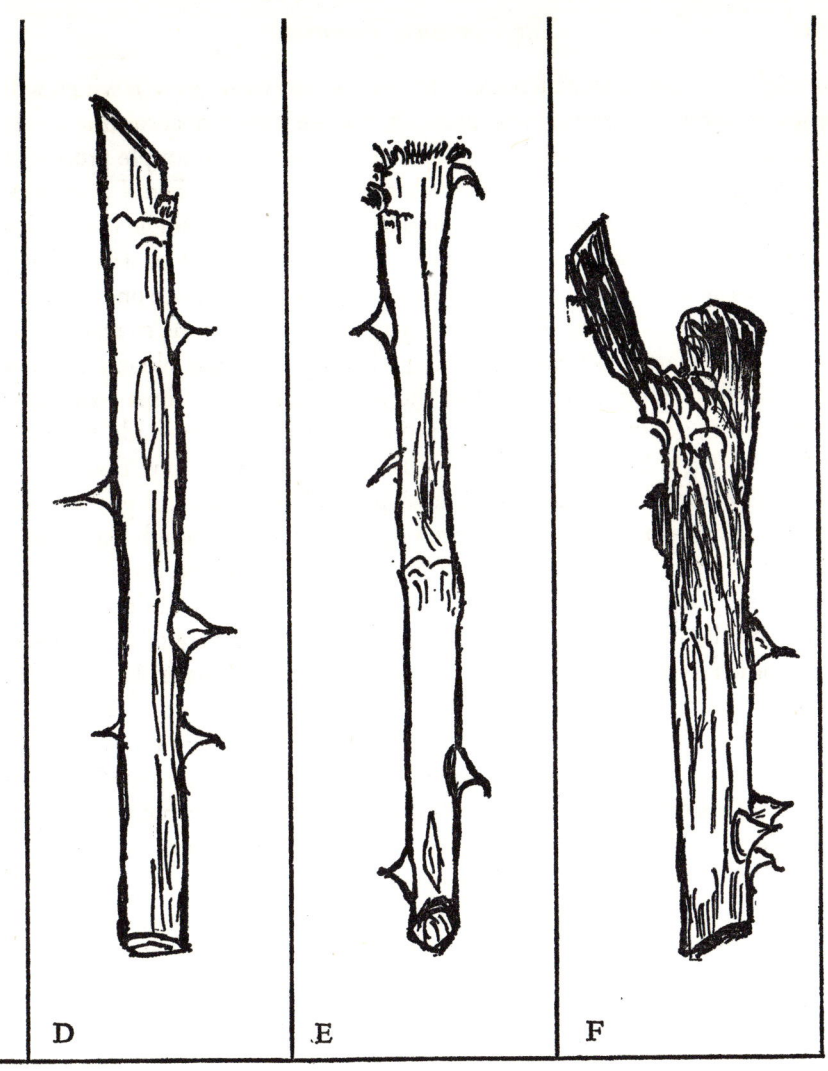

D

.E

F

D. INCORRECT Angle of cut made
in wrong direction.

E. BAD PRUNING Cut made with
blunt blade, and not made at
an angle. It would have helped
if the prickle behind the bud had
first been rubbed off.

F. THE RESULTS OF BAD PRUNING
Main stem has died back and the
bud shoot with it.

strong new shoots and which are only putting out weak growth which will probably prove "blind", and pruning can be adapted accordingly. At this stage, too, a great deal of shaping can be done by the simple process of "rubbing out" unwanted shoots with the fingers. This should always be resorted to when two shoots are seen to be coming from a single eye, which often happens when the earliest growth has been checked by a late frost; such twin shoots seldom flourish, and it is better to eliminate one of them.

If you aim to shine as an exhibitor, you will quickly come to realise that one of your major problems is timing—having your best blooms in their best condition on the day of the show. In years past, some exhibitors succeeded in deceiving themselves into the belief that they could time the arrival of their blooms by timing the spring pruning, but there is no doubt that they were mistaken. A hard-pruned rose bush will give its first flowers later than one which has been lightly pruned—though these latter flowers, coming from the eyes on the thinner parts of the canes near the top of the plant, are less likely to be of exhibition quality—but there is no exact correlation between the date of pruning and the date of first flowering. Some recently published figures[1] supplied by a consistently successful exhibitor purported to show that there was a fairly constant interval of thirteen weeks between pruning and flowering, but timing to about a week is no sort of use; you need to time your roses to the exact day—and as a matter of fact, these figures showed a difference of eighteen days between the intervals from pruning to flowering in roses pruned on the same day in two successive years. The weather conditions dictate the date of opening of your roses, and you cannot forecast them three months in advance, so it is better to avoid disappointment by refusing to entertain any false hopes of timing by pruning.

There is a form of "pruning" which is universally practised by exhibitors, and that is the disbudding of shoots bearing more than one flower bud. This is absolutely necessary because the rules insist upon it; the judges will unhesitatingly reject any bloom which has a subsidiary bud on the same stem. They will also penalise you for leaving even traces of such a bud, so make sure that the unwanted ones are rubbed out as soon as they appear, so that the scars will have vanished before the bloom opens. But whether such disbudding does, in fact, add to the size of the remaining flower is a much more open question. It is natural to suppose that if only one flower is left where two or three grew before, the energies of the plant

[1] *Roses for Enjoyment*, by Gordon Edwards, p. 155.

will be concentrated on the sole survivor, which will naturally grow bigger in consequence. But this is not the whole story. A rose does not expand on its stem like a soap-bubble expanding on a child's clay pipe, in response to forces applied from without. The power which causes the flower to expand is developed in the flower itself, and does not pass through the stem, which is no more than a "pipe-line" conveying the necessary fuel to the "power-station". If the stem is capable of supplying all the needs of two or three flowers, then those flowers will grow to their maximum size—which will be determined by other factors—independently of each other, and disbudding will have no effect on the survivors. If, on the other hand, there is a measure of competition between them for the available supply of nutrients, then disbudding may be expected to cause the survivor to grow bigger than it otherwise would. When a rose throws up, as it sometimes will, a great candelabrum-spike, carrying as many as twenty or even thirty flower-buds, competition is certainly present, and the flowers are seen to be small and often defective. But when, as more often happens, there is only one or a pair of side-buds below the centre flower, all three usually develop quite normally, and we have no grounds for assuming as a matter of course that the central one will grow larger if the side ones are removed; while it is quite certain that your garden will be the poorer for two good flowers if you do disbud. As with most aspects of pruning, it depends on what you want. If you want roses for cutting or for exhibition, then disbud by all means, but if you want them for the glorification of your garden, leave the buds alone. Candelabrum growth can be a nuisance, and if you see it developing you can sometimes nip it in the bud, literally, by pinching out the growing point of the shoot before it has formed too many flower-buds.

Chapter Ten

FOOD AND DRINK

I sometimes think that never blows so red
The Rose, as where some buried Caesar bled.

Omar Khayyám

The old division of the world into three kingdoms, animal, vegetable and mineral, still serves well enough for B.B.C. parlour games and the like; but in other departments of learning there is a tendency nowadays to increase the number of kingdoms to four, allowing a separate one for the microbes instead of dividing them arbitrarily between the animals and the vegetables—with neither of which they show any great affinity to anyone but the specialist. The change has no doubt been brought about by, and for the benefit of, the scientists, but it has its advantages for us, too, since it helps to clarify Nature's great scheme of Eat and Be Eaten, which rules the living world. Thus:

1. The mineral kingdom, comprising nothing but inert matter, requires no food.

2. The vegetable kingdom obtains all its food from the mineral kingdom.

3. The animal kingdom obtains all its food from the vegetable kingdom; animals either eat plants, or the flesh of other animals which do so.

4. Microbes feed indiscriminately upon both plants and animals, converting their substance back into the mineral form in which it originated.

We can see from this how foolish is the old argument about the relative efficacy of "organic" and "inorganic" plant foods. Strictly speaking, there is no such thing as an organic plant food; plants cannot feed on either animal or vegetable matter. When you add "organics" to the soil, it is not the plants you are feeding but the soil bacteria, and it is not until these have broken down the organic substances into inert mineral salts that the plant can absorb them. It doesn't make a ha'porth of difference to the plant whether these come from a rotting dunghill or from a chemical fertiliser factory; they are identically the same substances whatever their source.

However, before we go further into the question it will be as well to get clear in our minds exactly what we mean by "food" in relation to plant life.

In the vegetable kingdom, water is a prime necessity for all plants, which need it for the same reasons that animals do, but beside this, water constitutes one of the most important of plant foods. Part of the water absorbed by a plant is broken down in its "chemical factories" and converted into substances which are used both as raw materials and as fuel. The other most important plant food is neither a solid nor a liquid, but a gas—carbon dioxide, which is present in the air, of which it makes up about 0·03 per cent. A plant obtains its energy, not from foods, but from the light of the sun. Sunlight, acting through the agency of the green colouring matter chlorophyll, allows the plant to break down the water and carbon dioxide absorbed and recombine their elements in the form of sugars, which dissolve in the sap and permeate the whole plant. Wherever energy is required—wherever chemical activity is going forward—part of the sugar is reconverted into water and carbon dioxide, and in the process it yields up the energy which originally went into its formation. To provide a reserve, another portion of the sugar undergoes a form of chemical concentration and emerges in the form of starch, which, not being soluble, is deposited in the form of solid granules in various parts of the plant. An immediate reserve is laid down in the leaves every day, and is reconverted into sugar at night, when the energy of sunlight is no longer available. Long-term reserves are chiefly laid down in the stems and roots where they are available to be drawn on in the spring, when a plant starts to make vigorous growth before the quantity and strength of sunlight have grown to their maximum. Yet another portion of the sugar is still further concentrated and converted into cellulose, a tough, inert material which forms a large part of the woody structure of the plant. All these substances are formed out of the elements carbon, hydrogen and oxygen—in effect, of carbon and water—hence they are known collectively as carbohydrates. Starch and sugar provide the greater part of the nourishment that animals derive from eating plants; no animals but the goat are capable of digesting cellulose. Goats apparently achieve this through the agency of the bacteria in their digestive tracts— what the biologists picturesquely call the "intestinal flora", which conjures up a very misleading picture of the interior of a goat's entrails.

Important as the carbohydrates are to plant life, there is another class of chemicals which are equally important to every form of life. These are the proteins, substances of immense complexity, which can take a large number of different forms and are present in all plant cells. Considered as chemists, the plants are greatly superior to the animals. They take in the simplest substances, air, water, and a few mineral salts from the soil, take them to pieces, and from their elements they build up the proteins, and other equally complex chemical substances, with an ease and certainty which would put to shame any merely human chemist. To suggest, as many still do, that organics are the "natural" foods of plants is not merely a confession of ignorance; it is a horrid slander on the plant world.

One happy result of this chemical skill of the plants is that it greatly simplifies discussion of their diet. We only need to find out which chemical elements are present in the plant's substance, and to supply these elements in the most conveniently available form; the plant will take care of the rest. Analysis shows that the following elements are present in appreciable quantities in plants:

Hydrogen (H)	Nitrogen (N)
Oxygen (O)	Phosphorus (P)
Carbon (C)	Potassium (K)
Calcium (Ca)	Magnesium (Mg)
Sulphur (S)	

In addition to these, there are also small traces of the following:

Iron (Fe)	Chlorine (Cl)
Manganese (Mn)	Zinc (Zn)
Copper (Cu)	Boron (B)
Molybdenum (Mo)	Aluminium (Al)

Of these latter, iron and/or manganese are the only ones that the amateur rose grower will have occasion to consider for himself. The rest of these "trace elements", as they are commonly called, are never present in more than the most minute quantities; it is not at all certain what effect, if any, their lack has on roses, but it is quite certain that many of them will kill your plants if they are present in excess. So never play around with them except on the advice of an experienced soil chemist.

Let us return to the first list. Quantitatively speaking, the first three are much the most important. About seventy-five per cent of your rose plants consist of water: that is, hydrogen and oxygen; of the solid residue, about another seventy-five per cent is made up of carbohydrates (H, O and C) and another twenty per cent of the same three elements put together in different ways; so that little more than one per cent of the total weight of the plant is made up of compounds containing the other elements. Not "of the other elements", please note, but of compounds which contain them—often in very small proportions. But in spite of the overwhelming preponderance of the first three elements, they are never mentioned in discussions on feeding roses, presumably because air and water are such commonplace things that one does not think of them, as foods at any rate. Lately there has been some discussion of the results of enriching the air with a greater proportion of carbon dioxide, but this of course can only be done under glass, and so far as I know, it has not been tried with roses. Extra water we certainly can and do supply when the natural supply fails, though we usually think of this as a remedy for thirst, not hunger—naturally enough, when all is said and done. But it is as well to bear in mind that over ninety-nine per cent of the growth of your roses is built up out of air and water, if only as a corrective to the tendency to pour on excessive quantities of "plant foods".

Calcium and sulphur are in rather a curious position. They, like all the remaining elements, are derived by the plant from the soil, and in suitable circumstances one is not infrequently advised to apply one or the other to one's rose beds; yet, like the first three elements, they are rarely discussed as foods. Probably this is because any normal soil contains more of them than any rose is capable of exhausting. Two-fifths by weight of the South Downs consist of calcium, and the same applies to all the chalk and limestone areas of this country, so there is no risk of shortage in these parts of the country at least; while as for sulphur, tens of thousands of tons are deposited on the soil every year from factory and domestic chimneys, quite apart from the fact that most chemical fertilisers contain a high proportion of it—though the fact is not mentioned in their literature, since this is not one of the elements whose presence and proportion are required by law to be declared on the label. So far as the plant's food requirements are concerned, therefore, the rose grower need not worry his head over these two elements; their importance to him lies in the fact that a high proportion of calcium tends to make a soil alkaline in its reaction, while a high proportion of sulphur tends to make it acid. These points are discussed elsewhere, in the chapter dealing with the soil.

Now—at last—we come to the three elements, nitrogen, phosphorus and potassium, which are regarded, quite rightly, as the essential ingredients of any general fertiliser. The reason for this is that they are taken up by the plant in comparatively large quantities, but are not available in unlimited quantities in the soil; hence, after a year or two's vigorous growth, there is a risk that the plant may have exhausted the available supplies, which will have to be replenished by the grower. Even so, it is as well to remember that growing roses is not like growing crops. Even if you prune your roses back to the ground every year, and avoid disease by collecting and burning every fallen leaf, still the net loss to your soil is a good deal less than it is, for example, in a row of cabbages or potatoes. It is a wise rule never to apply a fertiliser in greater quantity than the manufacturer recommends; the more of his product you use, the better he will be pleased, so you can be sure that he will not err on the side of niggardliness in his instructions.

The law in this country lays down that all fertilisers shall bear on their labels a statement of the actual percentage of these elements which is present in the product. It is a convention, which is, I believe, world-wide, that the three elements shall always be mentioned in the order that I have given; so that a fertiliser which is described as "10–8–10" would contain ten per cent of nitrogen, eight per cent of phosphorus and ten per cent of potassium. It is also a convention in this country, but not in all others, that while the percentage of nitrogen means exactly what it says, in the case of the other two elements it does not. The figure given for phosphorus is not the percentage of the actual element, but of the equivalent quantity of phosphoric acid (P_2O_5)—although P_2O_5 is not the chemical formula for phosphoric acid, but for a compound of phosphorus and oxygen which is correctly called phosphorus pentoxide and which yields phosphoric acid when combined with water. Potassium is in like case; it is declared as the equivalent quantity of potash (K_2O), although K_2O represents neither the element potassium nor the substance potash,

Guinée *(Climber). Raiser: Charles Mallerin, Varces, Isère, France. Introduced 1938. Parentage: Souvenir de Claudius Denoyel × Ami Quinard. Medium-sized, full globular blooms in deep crimson, clouded maroon, solitary and in small clusters on long, fairly pliable canes to 10 ft. Very free summer flowering with a repeat factor which is variable. Quite healthy. Photograph: J. L. Norton, A.R.P.S.*

Rosa chinensis mutabilis. Commercially introduced 1932 *but possibly synonymous with Tipo Ideale, early nineteenth century. Medium-sized, single blooms in clusters, opening chamois-yellow from orange-red buds, changing to pink and finally coppery red. Slender, vigorous growth to 4 ft. in average situations, taller in a warm, sheltered southerly position. Reddish young wood, foliage and thorns. Exceptionally free and continuous flowering well into late autumn.*

which as a chemical is potassium carbonate. I have explained them here for the benefit of anyone who may be tempted to compound his own fertilisers; but the ordinary gardener has no concern with precise quantities, and can quite safely disregard them.

Until fairly recently, magnesium was reckoned among the trace elements, but it is now recognised that plants need it in considerably greater quantities than the rest of these, though appreciably smaller quantities than the three elements we have just mentioned. A lack of magnesium in the soil is not very common, but not specially rare. The law does not require its presence to be declared, and the simpler "general fertilisers" usually contain little or none, but those which claim to contain "all the necessary trace elements" will always contain an adequate proportion of it.

To sum up, then, Nature normally supplies all the hydrogen, oxygen and carbon that our plants need, while our additions of sulphur and calcium, if any, will be governed by other factors than the plants' food requirements. To maintain our rose beds in good heart we shall have to add regular supplies of nitrogen, phosphorus and potassium, and in some soils, one or more of magnesium, iron and manganese. The rest are best left alone. The next question which crops up is, in what form should they be supplied? There are limits to the virtuosity of our vegetable chemists, which cannot accept any of these elements in their simple, uncombined form. They must be added to the soil in the form of mineral salts. Which salts are suitable for fertilisers? Let us consider the elements in turn.

NITROGEN

There are two broad classes of chemicals containing nitrogen in a form which can be used by plants: ammonium salts, in which the nitrogen is present, so to speak, in the head of the molecule, and nitrates, in which it is present in the tail. Ammonium sulphate is the commonest and cheapest of the first group, and contains twenty per cent by weight of nitrogen; it has the effect of causing part of the calcium in the soil to become soluble and so to leach out, increasing the acidity of the soil, hence it is specially suitable for alkaline soils. On the other hand, it need not be avoided on soils which are already very acid, since these will need liming anyway, and the extra lime needed to counteract the effect of the ammonium sulphate only amounts to about the weight of the sulphate added, which is normally a very small proportion. Ammonium phosphate

M

is sometimes used in very concentrated fertilisers, since it contains twenty-eight per cent of nitrogen and forty-five per cent of phosphorus, but it is very expensive. Ammonium nitrate, having nitrogen in both its head and its tail, is a rich source of the element, containing thirty-five per cent, but it absorbs water from the air and rapidly becomes an unmanageable mess, so that it must be kept in sealed containers. It is also a powerful high explosive, but a safe one, which has never, to my knowledge, been known to hoist a gardener with his own petard. But to overcome both these objections it is mixed with powdered chalk and sold under the name of "Nitro-chalk", in which form it contains only about fifteen per cent of nitrogen. It is perfectly safe, but still requires to be kept from the air, if it is to be stored for any length of time. Its large content of chalk makes its use undesirable on alkaline soils. Sodium nitrate or Chile saltpetre used to be imported in large quantities as a fertiliser, but it was very impure and contained a good deal less than its theoretical proportion of twenty-seven per cent of nitrogen; its sodium content is also undesirable on clay soils, which it renders even stickier than they are normally. Potassium nitrate or true saltpetre, containing fourteen per cent of nitrogen and nearly fifty per cent of potassium, is a very good fertiliser, but expensive; the same quantities of the elements can be obtained more cheaply from other sources. In the more *recherché* mixtures sold for foliar feeding one sometimes finds urea, which is a very rich source of nitrogen, containing over forty-five per cent; but its cost precludes its use on a large scale. As an organic substance (it is present in the urine of all animals) it would seem to contradict what I have said about the inability of plants to use organics as food; but the precise mode of its entry into the plant is not known with any certainty, while in the soil it is rapidly converted into nitrates by the microbes present. Organic substances, as one would expect, normally contain all three of the major elements in varying quantities, but there are two which have such a preponderance of nitrogen that they may be regarded as sources of this element only. These are dried blood and "hoof and horn meal", both of which may contain up to about fifteen per cent of nitrogen; but their composition is inclined to be variable, and one should consult the label on any packet before buying.

PHOSPHORUS

Phosphorus suffers from the drawback that so many of its compounds are insoluble in water, and therefore unsuitable for use as fertilisers.

The two chemicals containing soluble phosphorus compounds that are available in bulk to the gardener are superphosphate and basic slag. The former contains eighteen per cent of phosphorus (here and throughout this book I use the legal convention, so that these figures may be compared with those appearing on labels); the latter is a by-product from iron smelting and its composition varies, but as sold for garden purposes it usually contains twelve to fourteen per cent. The purchaser should consult the label. Both these materials also contain calcium, but in superphosphate it is in the form of calcium sulphate or gypsum, which does not increase the alkalinity of the soil; basic slag contains it in the form of lime, which does, so its use is not recommended on soils that are already too alkaline. On the other hand, basic slag also contains a small but not negligible proportion of magnesium, which is of value if a shortage of this element is suspected in your soil.

The stock organic source of phosphorus is animal bone, which is largely composed of a form of calcium phosphate (hydroxyapatite to the minerologist). This is prepared for the gardener in two forms, steamed bone flour and bone meal, of which the latter, containing about twenty-one per cent of phosphorus, is undoubtedly the more popular, although the former, with about thirty per cent, is the richer source and often cheaper. But bone meal seems to act like a habit-forming drug on some gardeners. There are a number of addicts in the rose world who can hardly describe the simplest operation in the rose garden without adding the instruction to "sprinkle a handful of bone meal" on the soil. It certainly does no harm, but it can do precious little good, since bone substance is one of the most insoluble of materials.

I have on my desk a bone from the finger of an ancient Briton which lay in the soil of Salisbury Plain for some two thousand years before it was dug up in my presence, and to my unskilled eye it appears completely unchanged by its lengthy sojourn below ground, apart from its darker colour. Yet chemical changes do take place in buried bones. Fresh bones contain about four per cent of nitrogen, and in the course of time this is lost to the soil at the rate of about 0·7 per cent per thousand years; and this process is regular enough for archaeologists to estimate the age of a bone by analysing its nitrogen content. But it is phosphorus that we are interested in, and phosphorus is not lost at a rate which enables the archaeologist to date his finds.

On the other hand, the anti-organicist cannot have it all his own way.

No matter how soluble the phosphorus compounds in his selected chemical fertiliser may be, the fact remains that no sooner does the solution enter the soil than the phosphorus at once begins to react with the calcium which is always present, and before long it is all converted into an insoluble form again. The important difference is that in this case the insoluble compound is now distributed in a microscopically finely-divided form on the surface of the soil particles, where the fine rootlets cannot fail to come into contact with it. Compared with this fine state of division, the particles of bone meal, and even of bone flour, are large lumps, and are easily missed. It is certain that plants can and do absorb phosphorus from the soil, though how they do it is still something of a mystery. Whatever is the case, it is clear that the more finely divided the phosphorus compound is, the more readily the plant can satisfy its needs; and in this respect the soluble forms have an overwhelming advantage over their rivals. One thing at least is certain, that no important quantity of phosphorus can be lost to the soil by being leached out.

POTASSIUM

Potassium forms a large number of soluble compounds, but most of them are ruled out on the score of price. I have already mentioned potassium nitrate; there is also offered a substance known as Chilean potash nitrate, which contains about fifteen per cent of potassium and ten per cent of nitrogen; it may be a very good fertiliser, but its analysis shows clearly that it certainly does not consist of pure potassium nitrate. The name suggests that it may also contain sodium nitrate in large quantities, which is not very desirable. Muriate of potash—potassium chloride—is also available, and contains rather over sixty per cent of potassium; but like ammonium nitrate it absorbs water from the air and becomes very messy, while the chlorine it contains is an undesirable addition to the soil. Commercial potassium sulphate or sulphate of potash contains about forty-eight per cent of potassium, is cheap, and in every way suitable for garden use. Unhappily for the organic enthusiast, there is no organic material which can serve as a source of potassium alone; the best he can do is to fall back on bonfire ashes, which may contain an appreciable quantity of true potash, potassium carbonate; though unless the fire has been fed almost exclusively on green wood the quantity will be very small, and being very soluble it will be washed out of the ashes into the ground by the first shower of rain, so they must be collected when fresh.

MAGNESIUM

Magnesium is required in smaller quantities than the former three elements, and in many gardens it may safely be forgotten altogether. Moreover, if one's soil is acid enough to require periodic dressings of lime—which in practice means either powdered chalk or powdered limestone—the use of magnesium limestone or dolomite will take care of the magnesium requirement, though it is not worth while to order it from the other side of the country, when the cost of carriage will be much greater than the shilling or two which will purchase all the magnesium needed. (The same applies to the use of basic slag as a source of phosphorus.) If magnesium must be bought separately, it comes in the form of magnesium sulphate, which is known to your chemist as Epsom Salt. An ounce or two will usually suffice for a small rose garden. The "commercial grade" of magnesium sulphate is cheaper still, but is normally sold by the pound rather than by the ounce. There is no available organic source of magnesium.

I do not intend to go into the various signs and symptoms of shortage or excess of nitrogen, phosphorus or potassium. You must make additions of these to your rose beds at reasonable intervals, and so long as you do so intelligently neither shortages nor excesses will occur. I should, however, warn you that chlorosis, or lack of green colour in the leaves, which is caused by lack of nitrogen, is also caused by many other things such as spring frosts, etc. It is often seen on the smaller leaves put out early in the year, on little blind shoots, which calls for no treatment at all. Don't start pouring on the nitrogen directly you spot a yellow leaf. That is how excesses are brought about, and they are much harder to deal with than shortages; anyone can add chemicals to the soil, but taking them out again is a different problem.

As regards magnesium, the wisest course is undoubtedly to add this regularly with the other three elements, either by mixing magnesium sulphate with your normal fertiliser or by using one of the proprietary mixtures in which it is included. It may be unnecessary, but it will do no harm. If, on the other hand, you choose to ignore it, the odds are that you will never suffer for your neglect, though you may be one of the unlucky ones whose soil is poorly supplied with this element.

The only other shortage which you are likely to encounter is that of iron or manganese, which can be discussed together. It is common in roses grown in an alkaline soil, and reveals itself in a characteristic form of chlorosis, which starts at the edge of the leaf-blade and grows inwards in wedge-shaped areas between the veins, until in the final stages the whole leaf is yellow with the veins standing out in green. If the signs first show themselves in the younger growth near the tips of the canes, then the trouble is due to a shortage of iron. If, on the other hand, it is first seen in the older foliage while the new growth is still healthy, it is due to manganese deficiency.

The trouble with this is that the symptoms are due to the alkalinity of the soil, rather than to any actual shortage of the elements; in an alkaline soil these two elements tend to become "locked up", so that they are no longer available to the plant. Hence there is little to be gained by adding them to the soil, since the new additions only become locked up in their turn. As a temporary palliative one can spray the foliage with a solution of one ounce of iron sulphate (ferrous sulphate) or manganese sulphate in five gallons of water—do not make it any stronger or it will be likely to burn the leaves—repeating it weekly until the signs disappear. But the trouble will certainly reappear the next season; it may even turn up again a few weeks after you have stopped spraying. A fairly permanent cure can be brought about by adding iron and/or manganese chelates or sequestrenes, which are compounds in which the iron and manganese are isolated from outside influences and can be absorbed by the roots unhindered by the alkalinity of the soil. These are proprietary products, and you should follow the instructions on the package. But the only really permanent cure lies in acidifying your soil; though even then you may have difficulty in maintaining the acidity if your garden overlies a chalk subsoil. The condition is rarely, if ever, fatal, and can be ignored if it is only present to a slight degree; but it is disfiguring, and a source of weakness to your plants, and you should do all you can to clear it up.

Let me sum up very briefly. Of all the elements which go to make up a rose, there are three which must be supplied in regular doses to keep them flourishing, nitrogen, phosphorus and potassium. A fourth, magnesium, may not be essential in all soils, but it is a wise precaution to add it regularly with the others. On alkaline soils the plants are likely to go short of iron, or manganese, or both, but it is little use adding them in any but the special "chelated" form, while the shortage is best cured by acidifying the soil. Next we must discuss the question of the best forms in which to supply these elements, and how much of them to supply.

✳   ✳   ✳

First let us touch on the old question of organics and chemicals. I have already said, and I repeat it for emphasis, that your roses are absolutely indifferent to the source of their food elements; it makes no difference to them whatever whether they come from a chemical works or a cow-house. But it is not a matter of indifference to the gardener. The major difference is that the chemicals are applied in a form which the plant can most easily make use of, and are therefore instantly available, whereas the organics have to be broken down by the soil bacteria before the plant can absorb their nutritive elements; hence, generally speaking, chemicals are quicker off the mark. This may be important if one is treating an individual plant which has been starved, but doesn't matter in the least in a well-kept rose garden, where the plants, one hopes, are never allowed to approach starvation point. The chemical fertilisers, being soluble, are more liable to be leached out of the soil by heavy rains; but for reasons explained in the chapter dealing with the soil, both clay and humus—and any reasonable soil contains a fair proportion of both—have the power to hold these chemicals and prevent their loss by leaching. This is not true of the nitrates, which are not retained by the soil colloids to any extent, so that continuous heavy rain is liable to cause a shortage of nitrogen, particularly on soils with rapid drainage. This, however, is not an argument in favour of the use of organics, since it is in the form of nitrates that their nitrogen content is finally made available to the plants by the time the soil bacteria have finished with them. Urea and ammonium salts are also converted, partly at least, into nitrates in the soil, so the loss is pretty general; but with organics or ammonium salts, the shortage will be only temporary.

The one great advantage of organics, more especially in their cruder forms such as farmyard manure, rotted garden compost, seaweeds, etc., lies in the fact they are, weight for weight, much poorer sources of the nutrient elements than chemical fertilisers. Only a small proportion of their bulk ever appears as available nitrogen, phosphorus and potassium; the rest rots down into the final form of humus and so greatly improves the soil. This is less true of "hop manure", in which the spent hops are normally enriched by the addition of chemicals; the hops alone are an excellent source of humus, but contain only negligible supplies of plant foods. If you have a difficult soil, either a heavy clay or a very light, dry sand, farmyard manure is undoubtedly your best bet—if you can get it. While if you choose hop manure, look closely at the label before you buy it; the degree of enrichment varies much more widely than the price.

There is nothing to be gained by making separate applications of the different elements; in fact this is a practice to be avoided, as it so easily leads to the habit of dosing roses at frequent intervals, on imagined signs of a shortage of first one thing, then another. Excess of one element not infrequently causes a deficiency of another, so the practice often ends in causing what it sets out to cure. A mixed or "general" fertiliser is better in the long run, and a good deal less trouble. The question is, what ingredients to choose, and in what proportions to mix them; also, of course, whether to mix them yourself or buy them ready mixed.

Firstly, as to choice of materials. I have already said, more than once, that it makes no difference to your roses where their nitrogen (or phosphorus, or potassium) comes from; nitrogen is nitrogen all the world over, and you cannot get a "higher quality" by paying a higher price. Obviously, then, the cheapest source is the best, provided it has no snags to it. In Fig. 13 I have listed the more important substances, showing the proportion of the element they contain, the current price of seven pounds of the substance, and the equivalent price of one pound of the element derived from it. The last, of course, is the figure to keep your eye on. There is no doubt at all that on the prices quoted (which I have taken from the catalogue of one of the largest garden suppliers in this country), ammonium sulphate, superphosphate and potassium sulphate are the cheapest sources; and since none of them suffers from any serious disadvantages, the best. I have included iron sulphate in this table, for comparison purposes, although I do not recommend its inclusion in a mixed fertiliser. On an alkaline soil it is not likely to be effective, while an acid soil usually contains more than adequate supplies of iron.

Pretty well all the authorities are agreed that in mixing fertilisers the aim should be to obtain a "balanced" mixture. In so far as that expression means anything at all, it is presumably right; the question is, what constitutes a balanced mixture? One might suppose that the best solution to the problem would be to analyse a rose and ascertain the proportions of the various elements which are present in the growing plant. Unfortunately, if one does so, one finds that the proportions differ between different parts of the plant; they differ on different soils; and they differ in different weather conditions. Could one perhaps take an average figure? No. After all, what matters to the rose is the proportion of elements available to its roots in the soil, and this obviously depends not only

Source	Cost per seven pounds	Percentage of element	Cost per pound of element
NITROGEN			
Ammonium sulphate	27½p	20	20p
Nitro-chalk	29p	15·5	26½p
Potash nitrate	31p	15	30p
Dried blood	59p	13	65p
Hoof and horn meal	52½p	14	52½p
PHOSPHORUS			
Superhosphate	24p	18	18½p
Basic slag	22½p	13	25p
Bone meal	35p	20	25p
POTASSIUM			
Potassium sulphate	29p	48·5	8½p
Potash nitrate	31p	10·4	43p
MAGNESIUM			
Magnesium sulphate	32½p	20	23½p
IRON			
Iron sulphate	27½p	37	11p

Fig. 13   Availability and cost of nutrient elements.

upon what you add to the soil, but upon what is already there—an essential point that the manufacturers of general fertilisers conveniently overlook when they claim that their particular mixture is the one perfectly balanced one. There are other snags, too. We have no right to take it for granted that a rose takes in its nutrient elements in exactly the same proportion as they exist in the soil; it may (and almost certainly does) take in some more readily than others, and the ease of intake is governed by a number of factors, as witness the difficulty in absorbing iron and manganese when the soil is alkaline.

It might be argued that, no matter what the conditions in the soil may be, the nutrient elements ought to be replaced in just the same proportions as they are taken out of the soil by the rose—that is, in the average proportions given by the plant analysis. But this is a fallacy. In the first place, this would in theory restore the soil to the same state that it was in when the rose was first planted—and there are no grounds for assuming that this was necessarily the best possible state for growing roses. And in the second place, in practice this result would not be achieved, since it leaves out of consideration the many other factors operating to alter the state of the soil: the elements absorbed by weeds, and by soil bacteria, the elements lost by leaching in heavy rain, the elements gained by the action of bacteria on animal and vegetable matter in the soil. The blunt fact is that nobody knows what are the ideal proportions, either in the soil or in the fertiliser to be added to it.

This fact is made only too clear by a glance at Fig. 14, where I give the analyses of a score or so of fertilisers, every one of which, it is safe to say, has given complete satisfaction for many years to thousands of users. It is true that only some of these are intended specifically for roses, but after all, roses have been grown for centuries on an exclusive diet of farmyard manure; it is a pity, to say the least, that none of the special rose mixtures shows any resemblance to the proportions found in the latter. (I should add that the analysis given represents a very good sample of manure; it varies very greatly, and is likely to contain less than the proportions given—sometimes very much less.) But the rose mixtures themselves show no consistency whatever. The three R.N.R.S. mixtures all show a great preponderance of potassium over the other elements, up to nearly five times the quantity of nitrogen; Messrs. Fison's formulation, on the other hand, shows less potassium than either of the other two elements. What is one to conclude?

My own conclusion, I am afraid, is that all this talk about correct balance is so much eyewash, and that the actual proportions are not critically important. It is a curious coincidence (though nothing more, I assure you) that if one takes an average of all the entries in the table one gets a formula of 5·6 N, 6·0 P and 6·8 K, which is remarkably close to the proportions in National Growmore. This last mixture deserves a word of comment; it is not a proprietary product, but a formula sponsored by the Government in the Second World War, when we were all digging for victory and the authorities were anxious for us to produce as much as possible. As one can see from the last column of the table, it is by far the best value for money of all the fertilisers quoted. I have no hesitation in recommending it strongly.

Description	N	P*	K*	Cost	Rel. cost
Farmyard manure	1	0·5	1	?	?
Meat and Bone meal	6	(14)	—	65p	13·8
Hoof and Horn meal	14	—	—	92½p	12·4
I.C.I. Rose Plus	6·5	6·0	5·0	82½p	2·1
John Innes Base Fertiliser	5·1	7·2	9·6	75p	1·8
P.B.I. Toprose	5·0	5·2	12·0	77½p	2·1
R.N.R.S. (1952)	4·2	6·5	14·5	—	—
R.N.R.S. I (1963)	4·25	8·1	19·1	—	—
R.N.R.S. II (1963)	4·6	6·5	13	—	—
National Growmore	7	6	7	51p	1·3
Fish Manure (Eclipse)	6	4·5	6	70p	2·0
Clay's Fertiliser	4·43	(8)	0·21	67½p	15·6
Tonks' Rose Manure	4·16	5·02	11·6	72½p	2·0
Hop Manure (Adcompost)	3·25	4	1·1	49p	2·3
Hop Manure (Fison's)	2	2·75	2	55p	3·6
Hop Manure (Wakeley's)	0·8	1	1	?	?
Fison's Rose Fertiliser	6·5	6	5	82½p	2·1
Welgro	15	30	15	£3·67½	2·7

* As P_2O_5 and K_2O respectively.

Fig. 14 Analyses of some popular fertilisers.

Notes. (i) The cost given is the retail price of fourteen pounds of fertiliser.

(ii) The "relative cost" shows how much more expensive the fertiliser is than a mixture of ammonium sulphate, superphosphate and potassium sulphate containing the same quantities of nutrients.

(iii) The phosphorus in Meat and Bone meal and in Clay's Fertiliser is in the insoluble form and therefore not available to plants.

(iv) The R.N.R.S. formulae are to be mixed by the gardener himself, and are not sold ready-mixed.

(v) Wakeley's Hop Manure is sold in bags of unspecified weight.

On the other hand, you will get your fertilisers even cheaper still if you choose to mix your own. There is no lack of recommended mixtures in the literature; but their authors will forget that you are compelled to buy most of these materials in seven-pound lots, or multiples of seven pounds, so that "five parts of this" and "four parts of that" and "twelve parts of the other" are extremely awkward to make up, and almost inevitably leave you with odd quantities of the ingredients left over. None of the three ingredients I have recommended will deteriorate in storage, in the sense that they will lose their nourishing properties, but they are liable to cake into a solid mass which is very difficult to reduce to powder again; and they are liable to corrode any metals they come in contact with. Here, then, is my own recommendation, which surely cannot be attacked on the score of undue complexity: seven pounds of ammonium sulphate; seven pounds of superphosphate; and seven pounds of potassium sulphate. This will give you twenty-one pounds of fertiliser with an analysis of 6·7 : 6·0 : 16, at a cost of eighty new pence, or slightly less than the same weight of Growmore, and will be enough to treat about 200 roses. (About two ounces per plant or per square yard is a fair rate of application.) If you want to guard against a possible magnesium deficiency, add one pound of magnesium sulphate for each seven pounds of ammonium sulphate; this will add roughly one per cent of magnesium to your analysis, and the cost will be small enough, even if your sundries-man refuses to "break bulk" and you are forced to buy it at the chemist's.

The rate of application of this or any other mixture can be computed by reckoning that each rose bush or each square yard of soil needs about a quarter of an ounce of nitrogen a year—or at least, that is the quantity they get from the majority of fertilisers at the recommended rates of application. Both Growmore and the mixture recommended in the previous paragraph contain about seven per cent of nitrogen; that is, seven ounces of nitrogen are yielded by one hundred ounces of fertiliser—therefore one ounce will be yielded by $100/7$ ounces—therefore $1/4$ ounce will be yielded by $100/7 \times 1/4 =$ about four ounces. Two applications a year will suffice: say, half this quantity in April, when the leaves begin to unfold, and the other half in July, when the first flush of flowers is going over. For the average man, a handful is about two ounces; but if you depend on guesswork for your distribution, make sure that you give too little rather than too much; a few ounces left over when you have fed all your roses can be added to the compost heap with advantage, but if you run short before you have finished it can be awkward. Dry fertiliser lying on the top of a sun-baked bed is doing no good at all to your roses, so try to time your application when the soil is moist—and if you can complete it just before a shower of rain, so much the better. Otherwise it ought to be watered into the soil with the hose as soon as possible after application.

I have included no liquid fertilisers in Fig. 14, since as these are not sold by weight no comparison with the solid mixtures is possible. You will find that they exhibit just the same sort of variation in their analyses as the others; the chief difference is that the manufacturers almost invariably recommend the use of a very dilute solution, which has to be applied at intervals of a week or ten days. No doubt this is in theory the most efficient way to apply fertiliser, but it is doubtful if roses benefit significantly from this sort of baby-feeding, as compared with a richer diet at longer intervals. It is true that this "little and often" system allows the manufacturer to claim that sixpennyworth of his product makes a tremendous number of gallons of fertiliser, while naturally omitting to stress the fact that the dose has to be repeated so often; on the other hand, the manufacturer knows best what he puts in his mixture, and I certainly do not suggest that you should try to use it at ten times the normal strength and at ten times longer intervals. One reason for keeping liquid fertilisers very dilute is that many mineral salts tend to burn the foliage if they remain in contact with it for any length of time. And although a liquid feed, at the maker's recommended strength, is usually too weak to do any harm, it is just as well to avoid drenching the foliage excessively, unless you are practising "foliar feeding" with a fertiliser guaranteed to be suitable for the purpose.

*   *   *

Beside the common way and road of reception by the root, there may be a refection and imbibition from without . . .

Sir Thomas Browne (1658)

As may be seen from the above quotation, the idea that plants may be fed through the leaves as well as through the roots is by no means a new one. A few years ago, however, the idea of foliar feeding was revived in the United States, and the enthusiasm of the pioneers raised hopes that by this means we should be able to grow roses of a size and quality surpassing all that nature could do unaided. These hopes were not fulfilled; what does seem to have been established is that it is possible to produce just as good results by this mode of feeding as by the more natural one, but no better; so that there is no advantage in it unless one is cursed with a soil which cannot conveniently be brought into a good condition for growing roses. A garden on the slope of a chalk down may present this sort of difficulty, where the top-soil is thin and the water draining down the slope has picked up an undesirable excess of calcium from the chalk. Or a very dry, sandy soil, with a minimum of clay and humus and rapid drainage, may have such difficulty in retaining any nutrients that roses grown on it are permanently in a state of semi-starvation. In such circumstances one may be justified in letting the soil go hang and concentrating on getting the necessary nourishment into the roses by other channels.

For foliar feeding, the solution should not contain more than about one ounce of fertiliser in five gallons of water, to avoid any risk of burning the leaves. Moreover, there is a limit to the quantity of solution that will be retained on the leaves, since beyond this point the surplus will simply drain off. Hence it is desirable to use the richest possible sources of the elements, whose extra cost is offset by the small quantities used; one gallon of solution is enough for about twenty-five rose plants. It will be seen from Fig. 14 that Welgro is a very rich formulation of this sort, containing over fifty per cent of available nutrients. If you prefer to make up your own mixtures, four ounces each of urea, potassium phosphate and potassium nitrate (the true salt, not the Chilean variety), two ounces of magnesium sulphate and one ounce of iron sulphate will give an analysis of sixteen per cent nitrogen, sixteen per cent phosphorus, twenty-four per cent potassium, 2·7 per cent magnesium and 2·5 per cent iron. This quantity will make seventy-five gallons of solution, enough to give one feed to nearly 2,000 rose bushes. The mixed powders will keep reasonably well if stored dry in a sealed container such as a Kilner jar. It will be necessary to add a wetting agent or "sticker" to the solution, in accordance with the instructions of the maker of the particular brand you can obtain from your local sundriesman or chemist, to cause the solution to spread over the whole surface of the leaves instead of forming into droplets and running off, which is its natural tendency. I cannot quote a price for such a mixture, since these ingredients are not widely sold, and much must depend upon where you buy them. On the whole, you would probably be wiser to select a proprietary brand ready-mixed.

The fertiliser solution should be sprayed on your roses at fortnightly intervals throughout the growing season—say from first leaf to early September, in the south of England. One advantage of this method of feeding is that it is possible to incorporate most of one's ordinary sprays with the feed; Lindane (benzene hexachloride) for greenfly and other insect pests, Captan for black spot, Karathane for mildew, Zineb for rust, can all be safely incorporated with the fertiliser—provided, of course, that you obtain them in a water-miscible form. As for the more old-fashioned remedies, nicotine, sulphur, copper-white-oil emulsions, etc., you would be wiser to hold your hand; I have seen no reports of tests in the literature, and you might run into unfortunate incompatibilities. Also, it is just as true of a foliar feed as it is of other sprays, that a shower of rain is quite capable of undoing your work if it should come shortly after your spraying is completed. The fact that your feed is absorbed by the leaves, whereas the pesticides and fungicides are merely deposited on the surface, is little protection, alas; the rain-water can leach these chemicals out of the leaves even after they have been absorbed, so if you suffer a heavy down-pour within twenty-four hours of one feed it will be as well to bring the next feed forward a week.

Contrary to general belief, foliar feeding, though undoubtedly tedious, is not expensive. In theory, the whole of the nutrients which are applied to the leaves should be absorbed into the plant, and although this is of course never achieved in practice, the efficiency of this method of absorption is much higher than when the chemicals are mixed with the soil in the hope that part of them will enter the roots. At the rates of application which I have recommended above, the total amount of nitrogen supplied in a year is only about one-sixteenth of what one would add to the soil, a fact which offsets the apparently high price of commercial formulations such as Welgro. Generally speaking, there is little to choose between the two systems on the score of cost—unless one includes the value of the time spent in feeding the roses.

*   *   *

A note on farmyard manures will not be out of place here. It is commonly supposed that these consist primarily of animal dung, but this is not so; the most important constituents are the litter—chopped-up vegetable matter—in which the beasts are stalled, and the urine which it absorbs; hence if the manure is stored for any length of time on an absorbent ground, much of its richest component drains away and is lost. The composition of manure varies widely, according to the manner of its collection and storage, and also, of course, according to the nature of the beasts from which it comes, though there is really very little to choose between horse, cow and pig manure; their chief differences lie in their consistency and smell. Poultry manure, however, is definitely richer than the others and may contain as much as 1·5 per cent of nitrogen and phosphorus. Fresh manure is liable to cause damage to growing plants if it comes into contact with them, so it should always be well rotted before it is applied; but a manure heap which is left exposed to the weather for many months is likely to lose most of its nutrient value, though its value as a source of humus is little impaired. It also heats up considerably during the rotting process, which should be borne in mind. Horse manure was used for making hot-beds long before electrical soil heating was thought of.

Manure must be applied in large quantities if its full advantages are to be obtained, and applications of up to ten pounds per square yard are not excessive, except in the case of the chemically-enriched hop manures, for which the rate of application should be reduced in proportion. Garden compost when well made according to the conventional methods has much the same properties as farmyard manure and can be used in the same way; but a rose garden yields little that can be of value to the compost enthusiast. Manure itself can be composted, thus overcoming any objections that may be taken to its appearance or smell. The composted manures not infrequently advertised in the gardening press are no doubt excellent materials, but to offset the high price the sellers usually advise a rate of application which is so low that however useful it may be as a soil conditioner, its nutritional value must often be almost negligible. One enterprising merchant in the United States has recently been offering composted horse manure which is not only guaranteed to come from none but pedigree racehorses, but is also sweetly perfumed. It seems a pity that he cannot offer it in one's choice of old school colours.

*　　　*　　　*

Since I have been at pains to emphasise that water is an essential plant food, I ought to say something about its application to the rose garden. We do not often have cause to complain of the excessive dryness of our climate, nevertheless, recent research has suggested that even in a normal English summer the average garden receives rather less than the ideal amount of water. Allowing for the higher rate of evaporation from the soil in the hotter months, something like the equivalent of one inch of rain per week is what the experts recommend. This is equal to four gallons

*A mirror of past elegance, **Polly** (Hybrid Tea). Raiser: George Beckwith and Sons Ltd., Hoddesdon, Herts., England. Introduced 1927. Parentage: Ophelia seedling × Madame Martinet. Ochre bud, opening cream, central petals suffused pink, tinted with orange. Medium-sized blooms of perfect helix formation with sweet fragrance. Free flowering on long firm stems. Deep olive-green foliage. Moderately vigorous, branching habit. Has been described as the nearest approach to the Tea Roses. Photograph: J. L. Norton, A.R.P.S.*

Lal *(Hybrid Tea). Raiser: Walter Easlea and Sons, Eastwood, Leigh on Sea, Essex, England. Introduced* 1933. *Parentage: Commonwealth (H.T.)* × *Florence L. Izzard. Medium to large high-centred blooms in pink, suffused yellow, reverse deep pink, giving it a bi-colour effect. Very fragrant. Very free flowering. Deep green foliage on vigorous, branching growth. A very good pot rose for forcing. R.N.R.S. Certificate of Merit* 1934. *Photograph: J. L. Norton, A.R.P.S.*

of water per square yard. If your garden is on the dry side, therefore, it will be a good thing to apply this quantity every week in dry weather, if you can spare the time. No high degree of accuracy in measurement is called for, but it is always a good thing to know the rate of delivery of your garden hose. Measure two gallons of water into a bucket, and mark the level of the surface; then throw it out and refill the bucket to the same mark through your hose, and note how many seconds it takes, when a simple calculation will tell you how many gallons a minute it is delivering. (If you use more than one rose or nozzle on the hose, you will of course have to make a separate calculation for each one; and altering the length of the hose will make a considerable difference in the rate of delivery.)

It is an unfortunate instance of the natural cussedness of things that an official ban on the use of domestic water for one's garden always comes just at the time when the need for watering the garden is greatest. If, however, you have been following the routine of "four gallons per square yard at the end of every week in which no appreciable rain has fallen", you will at least have the satisfaction of knowing that your soil is in the best possible condition to withstand a drought when the ban is imposed. Thereafter you will do best to abide by the ban and hope for the best; the plants in your garden have their own means of adapting their internal economy to dry conditions, and it is often surprising how well roses will come through quite a severe drought. There is a lot of truth in the old saying that once you start watering you must go on watering. Soil dries out from the surface downwards, so that in time of drought the roots tend to penetrate deeper into the subsoil in search of moisture; water applied to the surface tends to reverse this process and bring the roots upwards, where they will suffer if the dry conditions return. (I must frankly admit that I do not know if this explanation is true for roses— perhaps their roots do not react to the changed conditions as quickly as this—but at any rate, it does sound reasonable to me.) And even the magic "four gallons per square yard" does not penetrate very deeply in a thoroughly dry soil, as one can easily judge for oneself, and the amount lost by evaporation is very great.

I do not know what the law is on the subject of syphoning out one's bath-water on to the rose beds when domestic supplies are being conserved; I will content myself with saying that if you try this, see that the water does not contain any great quantities of soap or bath-salts, which are both strongly alkaline.

N

Chapter Eleven

SOIL

The earth was made so various . . .
Wm. Cowper (1731-1800)

Little drops of water and little grains of sand may make a pleasant land, but it takes a good deal more than those two to make a fruitful soil. The sand, indeed, is one of the least important constituents, and nothing at all would grow in a soil consisting of sand alone, however well it might be watered; on the other hand, a soil entirely devoid of sand would be almost equally useless. It takes many different substances, animal, vegetable and mineral—and microbiological—to make up a soil fit for roses to grow in.

It is perfectly possible to grow plants—including roses—in chemical solutions, without the aid of anything at all that we should call soil in the normal way. But the ordinary gardener finds no advantage in these methods and builds his garden on a foundation of soil—such soil as providence has endowed him with, with such improvements as he is able to effect. Fifty years or so ago it was an article of faith with rose growers that "Roses prefer clay". Today it is the fashion to contradict this and say that roses prefer a "greasy loam". As usual in such cases, both statements are right and both are wrong. Neither roses nor any other plant will grow in a soil consisting of pure clay and nothing else (such soils are rarely encountered, anyway); but the garden rose being a moderately tall plant, with shallow roots, it needs a fairly firm soil to prevent its being blown out of the ground by the winter gales, which implies a soil containing a fairly high proportion of clay—which is what is meant by a "greasy loam". But before we go any farther it would be as well to make sure that we understand what we mean by these sands and clays.

Their chemical constitution does not greatly matter. They are formed from small particles weathered from the rocks and are therefore insoluble in water, otherwise they would all have been washed away millions of years ago; and as plants cannot make use of any materials that are not dissolved in water, they are indifferent to the chemical nature of any materials which do not dissolve. What is important is the size of their particles, and the names we use for the different rocky components of the soil have reference almost exclusively to this character. They may be roughly summarised as follows:

Stones:	1 inch and upwards
Gravel:	Between 1″ and 1/10″
Coarse sand:	Between 1/10″ and 1/100″
Fine sand:	Between 1/100″ and 1/1000″
Silt:	Between 1/1000″ and 1/10000″
Clay:	Below 1/10000″

A "loam", it should be explained, has no precise meaning, but merely implies a soil containing a well-balanced mixture of all the necessary constituents.

Now the effect of differences in the size of the particles is twofold. In the first place, the larger the particles, the larger the spaces between them when they are piled together. On the other hand, the larger the particles, the smaller the total amount of surface area exposed in any given weight of soil. If this latter statement is not easy to grasp at first, consider what happens when you break a stone in two. None of its original surface is lost in the process, but a new surface is created at the break on both halves. In point of fact, the increase of surface area is directly proportional to the reduction of size, so that, for example, a pound of silt will have a hundred times as much surface area as a pound of coarse sand.

Let us deal first with the spaces between the particles—the pore-spaces as they are called. Clearly the larger the pores, the more easily can water enter into them—and the more easily it can run out, too. So that a soil with a high proportion of sand in it will take in water freely, and will also drain freely; often too freely. No soil ever consists of all sand or all clay; what we call a sandy soil will still contain as much as twenty-five per cent or even thirty per cent of clay, while a clay soil may contain up to forty per cent of sand. (We may disregard silt, which has no peculiar properties of its own.) A sandy soil will hold something like fifteen per cent of its own weight of water. A clay soil may contain as much as fifty per cent of its own weight of water. Thus the amount of water available to plants will be three and a half times as much in a clay soil as in a sandy one.

Water, however, is not the only thing that roots need to thrive; they also need air. When water drains from a water-logged soil it leaves spaces behind it, which are filled with air drawn down from above; hence a sandy soil is well aerated, while a slow-draining clay tends to be badly aerated. A good soil, then—a loam—should contain very roughly equal proportions of both sand and clay, sand to promote good drainage and aeration, and clay for water retention.

There is another property of clay that I have not mentioned hitherto, but which is of enormous importance to the soil. It not only clings tenaciously to water, but also, and quite independently, to certain mineral substances which are dissolved in the "soil solution", as the water in the soil is called, and which form many of the essential foods of a growing plant. Hence when these substances are present in the soil solution, either naturally or through having been added in the form of fertilisers, an appreciable part of them is held in temporary combination with the clay; so that its important mineral constituents are not lost or leached out but are retained in temporary attachment to the clay particles, from which they can be recovered in due course by the plant roots. Clay in the soil acts as a very valuable insurance against the loss of plant foods by leaching. An important exception to this is the class of salts known as nitrates, which do not attach themselves to the clay particles and so can be leached out and lost. There are, however, other means whereby the soil can be enriched with nitrates, which will be discussed later, apart from the obvious but tedious one of adding them in the form of fertiliser every time a shower of rain removes them from your rose beds.

So much for those constituents of the soil which are derived from the weathering of the rocks and which we might regard as its mineral skeleton. In addition to these, however, a fertile soil also contains a high proportion of living matter, and of dead matter which was once living, of which the most important is the class of microscopic growing cells that we call bacteria. There are several thousand million of these in every teaspoonful of soil; it has been computed that the weight of all the bacteria in a stretch of pasture-land is just about equal to the weight of grazing cattle that it will support. As each bacterium is much too small to be seen with the naked eye, it will be understood that this implies quite a number of them. In addition to the bacteria there are millions of fungi, which in their simplest forms consist of minute specks of living matter little larger than the bacteria, but which are capable of growing long threads of *mycelium*, sometimes many yards in length, and of putting up fruiting bodies—toadstools and mushrooms—of considerable size.

All these subterranean microbes derive their food from the remains of the higher plants and animals that have grown on the surface (and also below it) and subsequently died. The process which we call rotting is simply the destruction of the remains by the bacteria and fungi that feed on them. In the process they break down the dead vegetable and animal matter into simpler substances, some of which they absorb themselves, and some of which escape into the soil to dissolve in the soil solution and form a source of food for more of the higher plants.

Bacteria, like all other living things, need nitrogen for growth, and there are some bacteria in the soil which can obtain the nitrogen they need from the air (of which it forms four-fifths by volume), converting it into the material of their own bodies; others, which live in the nodules which form on the roots of many members of the pea family, obtain it from the same source and make it available to their plant hosts as well as to themselves. (That is why vetches and clovers are such valuable "green manures" when they are ploughed under.) When these bacteria die, their remains are attacked by another class of bacteria which convert their complex nitrogen compounds into the simpler form of nitrates, thus continually making up for the loss of nitrates from the soil by leaching. The loss is not so great as it might seem. All the nitrate-bearing soil solution which runs out of the soil in your garden must go somewhere else, and the fact that spring water in general does not contain large quantities of dissolved nitrates shows that wherever it goes, the nitrates are extracted and put to use in some way.

The importance to the soil of this microbe population can hardly be exaggerated. When you add farmyard manure or "organic" fertiliser to your beds the amount of actual plant food that you make available to your roses is almost negligible. What you are actually doing is to provide food for the bacteria and fungi, which alone can flourish on such a diet, and it is they that provide the food for your plants in due course. The same process goes on in your compost heap, which starts out as a heap of dead vegetation and ends up as plant food.

The dead matter on which the bacteria feed is also of great importance to the soil in another way. As the process of decay continues, the green vegetation passes through the stage of peat and finally ends up as a dark brown, almost black, treacly substance which is known as humus—a word which is often wrongly applied to almost any former living material. (Dead leaves, peat, etc., do not contain humus, but they will eventually form humus when their rotting has proceeded to its final stage.) Humus possesses two very valuable properties. Being sticky, it helps to bind the soil particles together into a good "crumb" structure, but unlike clay, it never becomes compacted into a completely impervious material in any circumstances, and it does not bake into a brick-like hardness however dry the weather. It also contains a quantity of matter in a very fine state of division, as fine as that of the finest clay, and these minute particles share with those of clay the ability to hold on to the nutrient substances in the soil solution and prevent them from being lost by leaching. In fact, humus has all the advantages of clay with none of its disadvantages. It has little or no food value in itself, but it is an invaluable constituent of the soil. It is the concentration of humus which gives the dark colour and good tilth to any soil which has been cultivated for a long time.

Lastly, we must not forget that the soil contains an extensive fauna. The larger members of this, such as moles and mice, are an almost unmitigated nuisance, yet even they have their uses in helping to drain and aerate the soil, and even to improve its structure. If you are plagued with a heavy clay soil you cannot fail to note with envy the beautiful texture of the heap of earth thrown up by a mole, however infuriating it is when the mole-hill appears in the middle of your lawn. And moles and mice are only mortal; they die in due course, and their remains go to swell the supply of plant foods and humus. The next in order of size, the earthworms, can be bracketed with the moles, except that the good they do is greater and the damage less. For the rest, they range from slugs and snails and beetles down to insects so small that you need a magnifying glass to see them; they go to and fro about their lawful occasions, disturbing and aerating the soil, manuring it with their excrement, and with their own bodies after death; some of them preying on our precious plants, and some preying on them; but in the aggregate doing very little harm and a great deal of good. Their numbers are enormous; not so astronomical as those of the microbes, naturally, but they outweigh even them. It is estimated that there are a million spiders on every acre of grassland in this country, which is roughly two to every square inch, and the other beasties outnumber the spiders by at least ten to one.

*   *   *

So far I have spoken of the soil as it is, rather than as you would like it to be. Suppose you are making plans for a new rose garden and suspect that the soil may not be as good as you wish, what ought you to do about it?

The first thing to do is to stick a spade into the ground and see for yourself what it is like. Much depends upon what use it has had before. If it is virgin grassland the probability is that you will have nothing at all to complain of (except perhaps a superfluity of weeds); in the course of years the grass will have laid down a layer of topsoil, plentifully supplied with humus and beautifully broken up by the countless grass roots which have penetrated it and died. Such a soil is one of the richest you can find and will give you a very good start with your roses, though you will have to feed it from time to time as the years pass. But if the top layer of soil is only an inch or two thick and below it you strike what looks like pure sand, and you will do well to make such improvements as you can during your initial preparation of the beds.

It is as well to make sure first of all how deep the sand goes. Take out a hole a couple of feet deep, and see if it is sand all the way down, and do this in several positions in your future garden. With the advent of the bulldozer our surface soils have been so thoroughly mixed up in some parts of the country, especially in built-up areas, that you never know what you may encounter. If you should come upon a layer of hard clay within a foot or so of the surface, dig down into it for six or eight inches and then fill the holes with water; if it has disappeared within twenty-four hours you may judge that the drainage is satisfactory in spite of the apparently impermeable subsoil. But assuming that your soil is all sand, although you will do well to improve the top layer, your digging will be a simple matter, since there will be no need of "double digging" to break up the subsoil. The rose is a shallow-rooted subject and few of the roots of a dwarf plant go down more than about eighteen inches below the surface; what is below that, they do not care, so long as it allows excess water to drain away. Your beds will only need to be dug one spit deep, but you will want to take the opportunity of incorporating something to help in the retention of water, which is likely to be inadequate in such a sandy soil. Should this be the clay which is lacking from your natural soil?

Preferably not. Clay is the most impossible stuff to work, and the job of mixing it thoroughly with your sandy soil, either by hand or with the help of one of the mechanical cultivators available today, is virtually an impossible one. The answer to your problem is humus; and since you cannot buy humus in bottles or cans, you will have to add organic matter to the sand in order that the humus may be formed on the spot where it is wanted. The best stuff to add is granulated peat, since this is vegetable matter which has already undergone a quite extensive process of decay, and it is itself very retentive of water. It will help to hold the water in your soil from the outset, while when the soil bacteria have got to work on it and converted it into humus, it will retain plant foods also, beside having a binding effect on your too-loose soil. After your beds have been planted, it will pay you, for the first few years at least, to add a mulch of peat each spring, which will help to prevent the soil from drying out in hot spells, and can be worked into the soil at the end of each season to add further supplies of humus. On such a soil you should feed your plants with farmyard manure (if you can get it) or home-made compost. But you must be on your guard against one thing. Sandy soils are often acid soils, and peat—more particularly moss peat, as opposed to sedge peat—is liable to be extremely acid. A soil has to be very acid before it is wholly unsuitable for growing roses; but if the sand, or the peat, or both, are acid enough on test to make you feel doubtful about them, set your mind at rest by adding lime at the same time. Only don't overdo the lime; it is better to be too acid than too alkaline.

Now let us suppose that in your preliminary excavation you find not sand but a stiff clay. As before, dig a few holes in various parts of your plot, but only about a foot deep, and fill them with water to test the drainage—which you will probably find to be inadequate. If it is unsatisfactory, take out your holes another foot in depth and see what you find. You will sometimes encounter quite a thin layer of clay which has compacted into a "hard pan", which will allow the water to drain away if it is broken up. If it is not more than about eighteen inches below the surface you will just have to double dig the whole of your beds (and the rest of the plot too, if you have the time and energy for the task) and see that the hard pan is thoroughly broken up. But if the hard pan is too deep or not there at all, you will just have to face the fact that your drainage is poor—unless, on a suitable site, you care to go to the trouble and expense of draining it artificially. My own experience has led me to believe that the importance of good drainage can be exaggerated. The best roses I have ever grown were in a small garden on the bank of a river whose margins had had to be banked up because throughout the winter the level of the water was above that of the surrounding land. My beds were less than twenty feet from the water's edge, and it was lucky for me that the soil was an impervious clay, otherwise they would have been submerged for several months in the year. On one or two occasions of exceptionally high water they actually were submerged for a week or two on end, yet I never lost a plant from this cause. Artificial drains were obviously out of the question, as instead of letting the water out they would have let it in and drowned my garden. As there was no way of lowering the water-level in my soil, I adopted the only possible alternative and raised the soil above the water. There was no point in double digging, as I struck water six inches below the surface, so I contented myself with breaking up the top soil on my beds and then added more until I had raised their level by eight or ten inches. Two narrow beds, little more than two feet wide, had containing walls round them, built of concrete slabs about two feet by eight inches by four simply laid in position with adequate gaps between them; the wider beds had nothing to retain the surplus soil, which was simply banked at the sides, with adequate channels between them and the grass surround to catch the standing water which made its appearance every winter. I kept that garden for eight years, racking my brains every winter to devise some better means of draining it; yet I might have spared myself the mental strain, as my roses throve mightily. If any of my readers, similarly placed, should have difficulty in laying hands on sufficient soil to build the beds up in this way, it is worth remembering that the same effect can be obtained by taking out the whole of the top spit and replacing it with gravel, stones, clinkers, almost any rubbish—though if the soil is alkaline one should steer clear of limestone or builders' rubble, which is likely to aggravate the condition —and then replacing the top soil above it. Indeed, such preparation will have the effect of improving such drainage as there may be; but one should take care to see that the roses have at least nine inches of decent soil for their roots to inhabit. And it will do nothing but good if when replacing the top soil, you take the opportunity to incorporate with it as much sand, peat, vegetable rubbish, crumpled newspapers, coal dust, fine ashes—almost anything, in fact, which will rot down, or is fairly finely divided and harmless to plant life. You will not be able to mix it thoroughly with the clay, but at least it will serve to separate one lump of clay from another and prevent it from re-compacting into a solid mass. This work should preferably be done in the autumn, so that the frosts of the coming winter may help to break down the distressing great slabs of clay which constitute your "soil". For this reason only I would recommend that your plants should not be planted until the spring. Normally, I prefer to put them in as early in the autumn as I can get them from the grower.

In the last analysis, the answer to a heavy clay soil is cultivation—cultivation in both its senses. Certainly the hoe should be kept busy, breaking up all the hard lumps which form as the soil dries out in the warmer weather—only don't disturb the roots of your rose trees, which don't appreciate it. Even more important is cultivation in the sense of encouraging plants to grow in the soil. Your initial preparation will have done a lot to aerate the soil and prevent waterlogging, thus encouraging the soil fauna and flora to multiply and flourish, which is also helped by adequate feeding. For the first year or two, you will probably curse the intractability of your soil; then you will forget about it; and then one day you will realise that the heart-breaking clay that you started with has turned into a rich, dark, crumbly soil, as greasy a loam as the most critical gardener could hope for. In the meantime, you will have been spared the search for farmyard manure, which is so much more often seen in gardening books than in gardens, since on your clay soil the chemical fertilisers are just as effective, besides being a good deal cheaper; and your roses will have repaid your labours a hundredfold.

*   *   *

A question which often crops up in discussion on soil—more often than its importance really deserves, probably—is what is called the "soil reaction": its degree of acidity or alkalinity. This is expressed by the symbol pH (which is pronounced "roe aitch"—the first letter is not a small p but the Greek letter rho), which is the accepted symbol for hydrogen ion concentration, the chemical measure of the degree of acidity of a solution. For most of us it will be enough to know that a pH of seven represents neutrality, a figure of less than this standing for an acid reaction, while greater than seven indicates alkalinity. It is, however, important to know that every whole number above seven indicates not twice but ten times greater alkalinity, while every whole number below seven shows ten times higher acidity. In Great Britain the great majority of garden soils have a reaction lying somewhere between pH 4·5 and pH eight; and obviously the first question to arise is, what is the ideal value for growing roses? Nobody knows. There probably isn't one. Roses as a crop are not of sufficient importance in the world for extensive, and expensive, experiments to be made to determine the facts. It is stated in one American textbook of soil chemistry that the acceptable range for roses is from 4·5 to 7·5, which is certainly in accord with general experience, and is almost certainly based on that, and not on controlled experiment. One not infrequently sees a figure of 6·5 quoted as the ideal, but there is little doubt that this originated as a haphazard guess on someone's part, which has been copied and recopied until it has become accepted as an established truth—which it is not.

A point which is often overlooked in these discussions is that a knowledge of his soil reaction tells the ordinary gardener very little beyond the fact that a high figure for the pH is associated with a high proportion of lime in the soil—or more precisely, of the element calcium, which is an essential constituent of the various substances which we refer to as lime. It tells him practically nothing about the other components of the soil. A soil with a pH of 6·5 may be anything from an impossible heavy clay to the lightest sand, and its suitability for roses depends upon many other factors beside the pH. Broadly it may be said that so long as all other conditions are favourable, roses will do well in any soil whose reaction ranges from about 4·5 to seven; it is when the figure rises above seven, i.e., when the soil is alkaline, that difficulties are encountered.

The effect of an alkaline soil on your roses, which is manifested in iron or manganese starvation, has already been described in Chapter Ten. I said there that the best cure for these conditions is to acidify the soil, but I must admit that this is easier said than done. When rose beds consist of a foot of soil lying on a layer of chalk five hundred feet thick, it is plain to see that the cards are stacked against you from the start. But things are not as desperate as they might seem. The old belief that much of the water in the soil was raised to the surface by capillary action is no longer accepted; the passages between the soil particles do not form effective capillary tubes. Hence although the soil solution in contact with the chalk is likely to be very alkaline, it has no great tendency to move upwards into your top-soil, and if you can reduce the pH of that to a figure of seven or less, it will remain acid or neutral for much longer than one would expect. The best way of effecting the initial adjustment is to incorporate as much acid moss peat in the soil of your beds as you conveniently can; thereafter an annual dressing of the same material, which can conveniently be added as a mulch, may be all that you require to keep things comfortable for your roses. You should use ammonium sulphate as the source of nitrogen in your fertiliser, since this substance has the effect of removing approximately its own weight of lime from the soil. You should avoid nitro-chalk, which contains a large proportion of added lime; but you need not be afraid of the calcium in superphosphate, which is present in the form of calcium sulphate or gypsum which does not add to the alkalinity of the soil. Such acidifying devices as the addition of powdered sulphur to the soil, or even watering with dilute sulphuric acid, are probably best left alone.

If your garden is on the top of a chalk down, these measures should prove effective. If, however, it is situated lower down the slope and subjected to a constant flow of water draining from the chalk, even these may not suffice to remove the symptoms of lime-induced chlorosis from your roses, and you will have to adopt one or other of the special feeding methods described in the last chapter.

While we are discussing alkaline soils, let me utter a word of warning. Never add lime to an alkaline clay in the hope that it will make it easier to work. It won't; it will only make your alkaline soil more alkaline still, with no advantage to offset this grave disadvantage.

So much for the problems of an alkaline soil. An acid soil is unlikely to cause you any headaches, unless the reaction is below pH five, in which case your roses may suffer from a deficiency of calcium in their diet; a very acid soil can also cause deficiencies of magnesium and phosphorus. The addition of lime to the soil will provide all the calcium your plants need for food, and the consequent raising of the pH will also serve to "unlock" the available supplies of magnesium and phosphorus, so the remedy is simple. Clay soils need twice as much lime as sandy soils to produce the same effect; on the other hand, sandy soils need to have their lime replenished more frequently. For roses, however, you do not need to bring the soil up to the neutral state (and certainly not above it) but simply to raise the pH above the danger point. With a pH of five or less, a pound of lime to the square yard every year will be quite enough on sand. Clay should in theory receive something like three pounds per square yard every three or four years, but a pound a year will almost certainly do all you need in this case also. Above a pH of five it is doubtful if your roses will really need any extra lime at all, especially if you feed them with nitro-chalk or basic slag; anything over half a pound per square yard on sand imposes a risk of putting the pH up beyond seven (though it will not stay up there for very many months), but it will be safe enough on a clay. Always remember the golden rule: never add anything to your soil unless you know it is needed.

I have not yet said anything of how the gardener is to find out for himself whether his soil is acid or alkaline. If you would like to know about this you will have to buy or order a soil indicator kit. This is a coloured liquid which behaves in a similar way to litmus when a few drops are added to any solution, but with greater versatility. If it turns blue, the pH is 7·5 or over; green, neutral; yellow-green, 6·5; yellow, six; orange, 5·5; and red, five or less. To avoid complicating this more delicate test by the influence of your tap-water, put a teaspoonful of your soil mixture on a white saucer (it should be collected at a time when it is neither very dry nor very damp) and add the indicator drop by drop until it begins to ooze from the edge of the heap, when its colour may be judged against the white background. When employed with the proper precautions, and in conjunction with a prepared colour-chart, such a multiple indicator is capable of yielding results of a high degree of accuracy, but no such accuracy is needed in your garden. Your samples of soil may or may not be truly representative, and in any case what you will find is only an average figure for a quantity which actually varies from place to place and from day to day. It is not a bad thing to repeat the test from time to time, particularly on any occasion when you are contemplating liming your soil.

*   *   *

If your soil is liable to dry out in hot weather, you are usually advised to treat it with a mulch—that is, a non-conducting layer applied to the surface to insulate it from the sun's rays and so keep it cool and prevent excessive evaporation. Whether the average mulch is much better as an insulator than the top inch or two of the soil itself is a question which I have never seen discussed, let alone answered; but even if its cooling effect is negligible, a mulch can still be of value as a potential source of humus. The use of lawn-mowings for the purpose is often advocated, and indeed they can do nothing but good—provided that the lawn has not been treated with a weed-killer shortly before cutting—but the actual amount of good that they can do is pretty slight, unless your rose garden contains an unusually high proportion of grassed area. They look quite attractive when first applied; less so when they are dead and brown; less still when a high wind has blown them all over the garden.

Elimination of weeds is always a good thing, both as an end in itself, and as a means of conserving water. Every growing plant constitutes as it were a natural pump, drawing in water by the roots and raising it to the leaves, where most of it is lost by evaporation; the effect of weeds in robbing your soil of water is far more important than their demands on plant foods. Never allow yourself to be fooled into adopting a "living mulch" by underplanting your roses with small carpeting plants, however enthusiastically your adviser may draw your attention to the cool moisture of the soil beneath their leaves. That cool moisture has all been drawn up from the deeper layers of the soil, and if you want to conserve water you would do far better to leave it there. Not that there is any serious objection to carpeting your rose beds with violas, alyssum or such-like small flowering plants, provided that you realise that by doing so you are increasing the drain on your water supplies, not easing it. If you like the look of them, by all means plant them; they do at least help to smother weeds, even though they make it increasingly difficult to deal with those weeds which succeed in penetrating the cover. Remember, too, that your rose soil is, or ought to be, a rich one, and your carpeting plants may develop a greater vigour in their growth than you are accustomed to see. They may smother the weeds, but don't let them smother the roses too. Above all, remember that a bed carpeted in this way will need more water in dry weather, not less.

Sawdust makes a good mulch, apart from its tendency to blow away if a high wind should arise before it has packed down firmly. But sawdust, like other woody substances such as chopped straw or shredded bark, contains comparatively little nitrogen, so that the bacteria which rot it down, needing nitrogen for their own growth, are forced to take their supplies from the soil beneath, so that a mulch of this kind may cause a temporary shortage of nitrogen in the top few inches of soil. The nitrogen is not lost, but only locked up in the bodies of the bacteria (if such minute single-celled organisms may be said to have bodies) and the condition will cure itself in a short while, but it is not a bad idea to damp down such a mulch after application with a solution of an ounce of ammonium sulphate to five gallons of water. Compost and farmyard manure are often applied as nominal mulches, but their value as insulators is less than as plan food and soil conditioners; if one must be technical, one would say that they are top-dressings rather than mulches.

For obvious reasons, a mulch should be applied at a time when the soil is wet; to wait until a drought is established before mulching would be a perfect instance of locking the stable door after the horse has been stolen. On the other hand, you must not mulch too early in the year; not in fact until the danger of hard night frosts has passed. The effect of a night frost in April or May is largely mitigated by the heat which is given out by the earth which has been warmed up during the daytime; if you interpose an insulating layer between the earth and the air, this ground heat is intercepted and the temperature of the air will fall to a lower figure than it otherwise would. Roses generally can stand quite a lot of frost, but there is no point in subjecting them to it needlessly, especially when the new growth is young and tender. At the other end of the season the problem is not so acute, as by that time the mulch has packed down and rotted and become much less effective, while the roses are in a better state to withstand the cold. Nevertheless it is well to see that the remains of the mulch are broken up and hoed into the soil by the end of October or thereabouts.

However, taking it all round, there is seldom any real need for a mulch in this country. On those rare occasions when the sun beats down and the rain holds off for weeks on end, one's sorrow for one's thirsty roses is lost in one's pleasure in the enjoyment of a really fine summer.

Part Three

REPRODUCTIVE

Chapter Twelve

VEGETATIVE
PROPAGATION

Be fruitful, and multiply, and replenish the earth.
Genesis 1:28

In the vegetable kingdom the faculty of regeneration is so common-place that we take it for granted; yet even the most unimaginative of us must sometimes be struck by the extremes to which it is carried. Not only can a begonia grow a new leaf to replace one which has been cut off, but the old leaf can itself put out roots and grow into a new plant.

This form of reproduction, without the interposition of the sexual principle which we are prone to regard as the normal mode, is called vegetative propagation. The new plant, being actually formed from a part of the old one, grows into an exact duplicate—in so far as exact duplication is possible among plants—of its vegetative parent, and for this reason it is extensively resorted to in horticulture. Our usual method of growing roses from cuttings is to take sections about nine inches long and stick them vertically in the ground, the lower ends firmly embedded, preferably in sandy soil, which permits of good drainage and good aeration, while the upper ends are left exposed to the air. The results obtained from cuttings treated in this way are very variable. It is commonly said, and apparently with good reason, that the yellow Hybrid Teas are particularly reluctant to "strike" successfully. Three factors are constantly at work to rob us of success. In the first place, although it is the normal practice to remove all the leaves from the cutting, yet the green outer layers of the stem themselves act as leaves, and in particular they constantly pass out water vapour into the air, which has to be replaced by water drawn up from below; and as for a long period the cutting has no roots, it has great difficulty in taking in water. Secondly, the cutting, with an open wound at its exposed end, is at the mercy of any wandering spores of disease, and in its necessarily enfeebled state, hovering on the verge between life and death, it is in no position to put up a fight against intruders. And thirdly, the exposed cutting is in the most favourable position possible to suffer from any frosts which may come along.

In this country, the professional rose grower does not propagate his roses from cuttings, except for the very tough and vigorous sorts—mostly forms of R. *canina*, the Dog Rose—used as understocks, which strike easily and are cheap enough to make a small percentage of failures a matter of indifference. But the advantages of growing roses "on their own roots" are not negligible, and means have been designed to help the amateur to overcome the difficulties. In the U.S.A., though not here, I think, he can buy small covers, rather like igloos of transparent plastic a few feet across, inside which a constantly moist atmosphere can be maintained by a fine "mist" spray; since the air is kept saturated with moisture, the danger of the cuttings drying out is avoided, and the risk of infection is also reduced to some extent. (Mist propagation of other plants, which are regularly propagated from cuttings, has been adopted by most nurserymen in this country, but it is not an economic procedure for roses, except miniatures which are customarily grown from cuttings.) If he possesses a greenhouse he can adopt the same procedure by erecting a polythene-covered tent around his cuttings, with the additional advantage of avoiding the risk of frost. But most of us, who recognise, or are anxious to test, the advantages of "own-root" roses, are content to stick the cuttings in the ground and hope for the best. In special cases we can help things by covering each cutting or group of cuttings with a wide-mouthed glass jar, such as a large Kilner jar, over the top, with its mouth well pressed down into the soil. Cloches are of very little use, since they are not air-tight and do little to conserve moisture. Conveniently, cuttings are inserted in autumn, when the cooler weather helps to prevent drying out, but the time of year is not critical; one may conveniently do it at the same time that the roses are pruned, when, if the cuttings are inserted in the immediate vicinity of their parent plants, they will not even require labelling.

The advantages of growing roses on their own roots are twofold. In the first place, it will not necessarily prevent them from sending up suckers from the roots, but any such suckers which do appear will be of the same variety as the plant itself, so that they need not be removed unless they appear in the wrong place. Secondly, such roses are less liable to frost damage; the entire top growth may be killed off by frost, but if the roots survive the plant may yet recover, whereas a rose growing on an understock would be lost entirely in such circumstances, the only surviving part being the stock.

You will often hear it said that roses do not do so well on their own roots as when budded on to an understock, but if you were to challenge the speaker to produce evidence to justify his statement he would be hard put to it to find any. I only know of one trial, made in the United States some fifteen or twenty years ago, when a number of different varieties were tested on different understocks and also on their own roots. The roses were rated by measuring the actual weight of flowers that they produced in a single season, and it is perfectly true that those on their own roots gave inferior results; but the difference between the best and the worst was so slight that it was only on the border of significance, and the ordinary rose grower could quite safely ignore it. There is no reason to doubt that every rose in the catalogues can do well on its own roots. After all, apart from sports, every rose started life as a seedling which was necessarily on its own roots, and it must then have exhibited enough health and vigour to survive the very severe weeding-out process that the breeder's seedlings undergo. But it does not follow that every rose is easy to obtain in own-root form; some of them are very reluctant to strike as cuttings.

For some years now it has been possible to buy chemicals—so-called "plant hormones"—intended to assist the rooting of cuttings. They are reasonably cheap, and easy to use, and since there is ample evidence in the literature that they are effective, their use can be confidently recommended, especially in difficult cases. But they are not infallible, and one must not expect that every treated cutting is bound to succeed.

Another way of helping things on is to make use of the practice of "layering". It is never employed commercially by rose growers, since it is only suitable in the ordinary way for plants which have fairly long and flexible canes, and in the rose world these will usually strike readily enough from cuttings; in any case, there is no market in this country for own-root roses at present. The cane to be layered is bent down so that it touches the ground at a point some little way back from the growing tip;

at this point the cane is wounded, either by cutting half-way through it, or by cutting away a portion of the bark—the practice varies with different plants and different practitioners—and the damaged part is covered with soil, the cane being pegged down so that it cannot move. (Here again the application of a rooting hormone can be helpful.) Since the tip of the cane is not wholly disconnected from the roots it will continue to grow, but at the same time new roots will be put out from the "callus" which grows over the wound; in effect, the tip of the cane becomes a cutting which is kept alive by a sort of artificial respiration while the roots are forming. After about a year one may cut through the original cane below the new roots and grow on the detached portion as a new plant.

If a particular variety of rose refuses to put out roots of its own, either from a cutting or by layering—or if one is anxious to obtain a new plant with the minimum of delay—there is no choice but to graft it on to a ready-made set of roots supplied by an understock. The form of grafting universally employed in the rose world is the simplest possible, in which the scion, as the part of the plant to be propagated is called, is reduced to the smallest possible dimensions, being no more than a fragment of bark containing a single dormant bud. Hence the process is known as budding. The technique is as follows.

A T-shaped cut is made in the bark of the stock, the longer vertical cut being about an inch long and the shorter cross-stroke half an inch or less; the actual size is determined by the size of the bud to be inserted, and a few minutes' practice will show the beginner what is needed better than any description. The cuts must go right through the bark down to the wood, so that the two side flaps of bark so formed may be lifted up and separated from the wood. This is most conveniently done with a special budding-knife, which has a sharp blade at one end, while the other is drawn out into a sort of rounded chisel-edge, usually made of horn, ivory or plastic, which will lift the bark without any risk of cutting it. The bud to be inserted is then taken, preferably from a healthy stem which has just finished flowering. The cut is made downwards, starting about a quarter of an inch above the bud (which, it will be remembered, is always found in the axil—the "armpit", so to speak—of a leaf) and emerging about half an inch below it; it should go just deep enough to take a very fine sliver of wood as it passes below the bud. You will now have a slip of bark shaped like a narrow shield (the process is known in France as "shield-grafting"—*greffe-en-écusson*), with a leaf growing from the broader end. This leaf should be cut off, leaving half an inch or so of stalk to act as a handle. The narrow end is now inserted into the T-cut of the stock and slid down under the raised bark as far as it will go; if a small portion still overlaps the upper cross-cut it should be cut off level. Next bind the graft firmly with a strip of raffia, which will be much more easily handled if it is wetted before use, taking care to cover the whole of the cut and just leaving a tiny gap for the bud to grow through; and that is all.

The practised budder usually takes the trouble to remove the small sliver of wood from the inside of the bud before inserting it into the stock; but this can be a tricky business, and the inexpert can very easily remove the actual bud itself with the wood, so that on the whole the beginner is better advised to let it alone. Provided that only a thin sliver of wood is left with the bud, its removal is not necessary, and the bud will take perfectly well with it still in place—whereas if the bud is damaged it will not take at all.

Budding is usually performed in the months of July and early August, when the stocks are in the most easily workable state. However, the amateur, who is not faced as the professional is with the task of budding acres of ground containing hundreds of thousands of stocks, need not worry about the speed which comes of combining acquired skill with the easiest possible conditions, and can make his attempts at any time when the plants are growing strongly, so that the damaged surfaces heal as quickly as may be. One must wait about three weeks to make sure whether the bud has taken or not. If it still appears green, all is well, but if it is brown and dry it is dead. It sometimes happens that the bud will shoot and grow on in the same season that it is inserted. This is undesirable, as the graft is still in an immature state, and a knock or the force of the wind on the new shoot may detach it entirely from the stock; if it is a specially precious one, both the stock and the new shoot may be firmly but carefully staked, to prevent any movement. Ideally, the bud should pass the winter in its dormant state and shoot in the following spring, by which time it should have grown firmly into the stock. A bud which shoots prematurely is best pruned back as soon as growth begins to slow down, leaving only a couple of eyes on the new growth; this will help to avoid the risk of damage from wind. For the same reason the stock itself should be pruned back to a point about an inch above the bud, but it is better to leave this until the whole plant is completely dormant, in January or February, according to the weather; the longer the plant is in a state of active growth, the more firmly will the bud and the stock grow together. In any case, the stock *must* be cut back as soon as the bud shoots in spring, so that it may have no competition for the nutrients and water supplied by the roots. An eye should be kept on the raffia tie, which ought to rot and fall away during the winter; if it does not do so, it must be cut away to prevent it from strangling the new shoot. In May, the growing tip of the bud should be pinched out to induce it to make more basal growth.

For a good many years, practically all bush roses in this country have been budded on various forms of the Dog Rose, which are marketed under such euphonious names as "Brög's Canina", "Schmid's Ideal", etc. Such advantages as one may have over another are chiefly of interest to the professional grower; Brög's form, for instance, is almost thornless, which is clearly helpful to the budder. As regards performance in the amateur's garden there is really very little to choose between them. It is significant that while each nurseryman usually sticks to his preferred variety, no nurseryman has any monopoly of prizes at shows, and no nurseryman is able to offer plants which are so obviously superior to those of his competitors that he steals their trade. Our grandfathers were often content to collect their Dog Roses from the hedges, growing them on from cuttings, which struck reliably. Since, however, the publication of Rowley's preliminary report on the trials carried out at the John Innes Horticultural Institution a few years ago, which showed (a) that roses budded on the so-called *R. laxa* (which is actually *R. coriifolia froebelii*, a close relative of the Dog Rose) were consistently inferior to all others, even though only in a very minor degree; and (b) that roses budded on *R. multiflora* stocks were consistently superior to all others; we may expect to see the use of multiflora increase. The latter has for many years been used extensively in France and the U.S.A. Whether the greater vigour of plants grown on multiflora is really an advantage is something of a moot point. We have become accustomed to dealing with rose bushes of a certain average size, and if they are to be bigger in the future we shall just be forced to grow fewer of them in any given space. Part at least of the increased vigour of roses budded on multiflora manifests itself in the production of branching stems carrying a number of flowers, as compared with the less vigorous plants on other stocks which were more prone to produce solitary flowers, more suitable (other things being equal) for the show-bench. It has been stated that roses budded on multiflora are not so long-lived as those on other understocks, but this has not been put to any thorough test. The one unquestionable advantage of the multiflora stock is the fact that it is less prone to throw up suckers than any of the others, with the exception of laxa. For the amateur, then, the choice really boils down to two; if he wants large, floriferous plants, relatively free from suckers, he should choose multiflora stocks; if he prefers his flowers to come singly on smaller plants, any of the rest will be suitable. It is not essential for an understock to be a true species; the old variety, Gloire des Rosamanes, produced by Vibert in 1825, has long since fallen out of our catalogues, but it is extensively grown in California under the name of Ragged Robin for use as a stock. Probably most of our garden ramblers would be quite suitable. There is always the possibility that the variety to be budded would be incompatible with the variety selected as a stock, but such cases are so slight and so rare that none has yet been clearly established.

Bush roses are always budded as low down on the stock as possible. For this reason, the understock should not be planted too deeply and the soil should be earthed up. The latter should be scraped away from the base of the plant before setting to work. Climbers are treated in the same way. Standards have become "standardised" in this country at a height of three and a half feet from the ground to the bud, while "half-standards" are budded at a height of two and a half feet. The so-called "Rugosa" stock is now almost universally employed for standards, for reasons of cheapness. This is actually a hybrid which was formerly called by the (invalid) name of *R. rugosa hollandica*, and which has a habit of throwing up straight, vertical canes of suitable height for standards. In other respects, however, it leaves much to be desired; it has a tendency to throw suckers and its stems are not nearly strong enough to support the head of a mature standard, so that it needs very firm staking. Until quite recently, a few growers would offer standards on canina stock at increased prices; perhaps they still do; in any case, the amateur can find his own canes in the hedgerow and strike them as cuttings. A rugosa stock for a standard is budded in exactly the same way as a bush rose, except that in the interests of symmetry it is usual to insert two or even three buds at equal intervals round the stem. A canina stock offers rather more difficulty, since by the time it has grown sufficiently to make a good standard its bark is usually in no state to allow budding in the ordinary way, so that it is customary to insert the buds in the bases of lateral shoots (on the upper side, naturally), which means that the two or three buds are separated by some little distance vertically. However, this is no longer apparent when the plant is well grown. A good canina stock four or five years old will be stout enough to support its head without any staking—though a stake must always be provided, if only to guard against the effect of winds. A rugosa stock should be fastened to its stake at two or three points down its length, otherwise it is liable to sag under the weight of its head.

It is a good thing that the heights of standards should be fixed by convention; some uniformity in height is desirable in a row of standards. But it must be remembered that it is not enough to decide the height at which the buds are inserted; the final appearance of the plant depends equally on the habit of growth of the scion. This was brought home to me some years ago when I wanted a pair of standards, one red and one white, and decided upon two new varieties (as they were then), Soraya and Message. I remembered when ordering to insist that they should be a matched pair as regards height, and so they were; but while Message formed a nice rounded head, Soraya's long stems insisted on growing straight upwards, thus in effect adding just about a cubit to its stature. The final result was, from my point of view, deplorable. (I was reminded of the remark of a famous French rosarian of the last century, who disliked standards, which he described as "bouquets on broomsticks".) If you want a uniform row of standards, you must take care that they all adopt the same habit of growth, either all sprawlers or all of upright growth. Sprawling is a wicked vice in a bush rose, to which many otherwise good roses are subject; but in a standard I am rather of the opinion that the sprawler makes the best head. Certainly the upright growers, like Soraya, Betty Uprichard and McGredy's Yellow, do tend to look like besoms. In any case, it is a waste of time to worry about an inch more or less in height; though you need not take too literally the advice which used to be given by a famous grower in his catalogue, to the effect that standards must always be planted at *exactly* the same depth as they were grown in the nursery, as shown by the soil-mark on the stem, and that if any attempt were made to achieve uniformity by planting an extra tall one a few inches deeper than its neighbours it would infallibly die. It will not; but there is nothing to be gained by proving this for yourself.

The amateur is not bound by any conventions and is free to bud his standards at any height that suits his own convenience. The so-called "weeping standards" are formed by budding one of the laxer-growing ramblers at a height of about six feet, and allowing the flexible canes to droop towards the ground. They can indeed be bought from many of the larger rose nurseries, but they are usually sold with a warning that few of them will really weep, the stiffer-growing varieties needing to be trained over a sort of umbrella frame mounted on the top of the stake and then persuaded to grow downwards with more or less success—usually less. They never achieve the graceful effect of a true weeping tree, and although they make a fine display when in flower, they are none the more beautiful for growing upside down. I have never seen an example budded from *R. wichuraiana*, whose canes are perhaps less rigid than those of any other rose; it might succeed where too many others fail. The so-called *R. paulii* (which is actually a hybrid, not a species), in its pink and white forms, is another rose which tends to creep along the ground rather than to reach for the sky, and might also be persuaded to weep. At the other end of the scale, I have often wondered why the amateur does not sometimes bud his bush roses on to "standard" stems of no more than about six inches high, thus providing them with a footstalk like a gooseberry bush. It would at least simplify the identification and removal of suckers, and there seems no reason why the bushes should be any less shapely than the head of a normal standard. It would also simplify the weeding of our rose beds; nothing is more infuriating than the tuft of grass which grows up in the middle of the basal canes of a bush rose, so that each individual stem has to be approached from a different angle, and which invariably leaves some roots in place even after the last stem has been plucked out. At the moment of writing this, my entire rose garden consists of three plants in pots on the window-sill of a London flat four stories up, but if I ever come to plant a new rose garden I shall be very tempted to adopt this plan.

From time to time there has arisen a vogue for what one may call trick-budding, though it has been out of fashion now for a good many years. There is little to be said for a standard with a head composed of two different varieties, especially if they have different habits of growth; but the multiple standard, with two or even three heads budded on to the same central stock a foot or two apart might be attractive. I have never seen one, and I do not know. One can find instructions for producing them in old books, but whether the drawings which illustrated them showed what they really looked like, or what the writer hoped they would look like, I cannot say. Presumably they were at any rate feasible, or a later generation of writers would have warned the reader against attempting anything of the sort. On the other hand, so many comparatively modern writers are at pains to stress the need for preventing one's climbers from growing bare at the base that there would seem to be something to be said for budding both a bush rose and its climbing sport on the same stock—if only, in the true spirit of research, to see what happened. On the face of it, one might expect the bush rose to display an enhanced vigour, being supported by a much greater growth of roots than it would normally acquire on its own; but if in fact it lingered and died, one would be no worse off.

Chapter Thirteen

PROPAGATION FROM SEED

Male and female created He them.

Genesis 1 : 27

As I said earlier, it was the English naturalist Nehemiah Grew who first announced to the western world that the reproduction of plants was a sexual process similar to that of the animals. On the 9th of November, 1676, he lectured to the Royal Society, and in the course of his lecture he made the following statement: "In discourse hereof with our Learned Savilian Professor, Sir Thomas Millington, he told me, he conceived, That the Attire [the stamens] doth serve as the Male for the generation of the Seed. I immediately reply'd, That I was of the same Opinion." Grew's lecture was not printed, and the manuscript draft in the Royal Society's archives does not contain the statement quoted; but it appears in his *Anatomy of Plants* which was published six years later, and there is no good reason to doubt that he and his friend Millington deserve the credit for this important discovery. Millington, a physician and founder-member of the Royal Society, was Sedleian (not Savilian—that was a slip) Professor of Natural Philosophy at Oxford.

Sex manifests itself in the vegetable kingdom in three different ways. Some plants are what is called dioecious (the "oe" is properly a diphthong, so that the "o" is not pronounced), the male and female flowers being borne on separate plants. Others are monoecious, the male and female flowers being distinct but borne together on the same plant. The third class, which includes the rose, are hermaphrodite and every flower possesses both male organs (stamens) and female (pistils or styles). It is interesting to note that sex differences in the Date Palm (which is dioecious) had been known and appreciated for thousands of years—which is not surprising when one considers that it furnished such an important article of diet in the early civilisations which flourished in the Middle East. A thousand years before the present era, it was well known that no crop of dates was to be looked for unless one male palm was grown in each clump of fruit-bearing trees, and the analogy of the ram in a flock of sheep was too obvious to be missed. In the British Museum one may see the tablets of Asser-nasir-pal (about 850 B.C.) which depict the collection of the date pollen and its application to the female flowers by the priests in what was clearly an important religious ceremony. But the date palm was regarded as a unique phenomenon, and 2,500 years were to pass before what was true of the date was found to be equally true of all plants.

The sexual process is the same in both plants and animals. Two different sorts of reproductive cells—we may as well call them by their scientific name of *gametes*, since this is a reasonably short and simple one—are produced by the appropriate generative organs, of which the female gametes are sedentary and remain in or near their place of formation; the male gametes, on the other hand, are highly mobile, and by various means they are enabled to travel—many miles, in the case of some plants—until they encounter a female gamete of the same species. When they come into contact, the male gamete penetrates the female gamete and discharges its contents into it. This is the essential act of fertilisation, and when it is complete the fertilised cell, which now contains the elements derived from both parents, is called a *zygote*; it divides into two —these divide again—and the process continues until the single cell has grown through all its embryo stages into the mature individual, be it plant or animal.

The number of variations on this theme is legion, but from now on we shall confine our attention to the roses. In these, the female gametes or *ova* are formed deep down within the receptacle which forms the base of the flower. Above them are the pistils or styles, a bunch of very fine tubes which stand up vertically in the centre of the flower; in one class of roses, the *synstylae*, they are all fused together into a single column. The styles terminate in a small thickening, analogous to the head of a pin, which is called the stigma, and which forms a trap for the pollen. The male gametes or pollen cells are formed inside the rather larger knobs, known as anthers, which terminate the stamens, and which grow in a ring surrounding the styles. When the time is ripe, which is usually when the flower is about half open, the pollen grains emerge from the anthers, forming the familiar yellow dust that we all know—though in some roses it is almost white—some of which falls on to the stigmas (the correct plural of stigma is stigmata, but we needn't bother with too much pedantry) in the centre. Shortly after the anthers begin to shed their pollen, the stigmas produce a minute quantity of sweetish, sticky secretion, which both holds the pollen grains in place and stimulates them to further activity. The pollen grain puts out a long, fine growth which passes down the tube in the centre of the style until it reaches the ovum, which it penetrates. The nucleus of the pollen cell then moves down this growth, which is itself tubular, and enters the ovum, thus fertilising it and converting it into a zygote. The zygote begins to subdivide, and growth continues until it has formed the embryo plant, which at this stage consists of little but a minute speck of matter with two appendages which will later form the cotyledons or seed leaves which are the first to unfold when the seedling appears above ground, and whose function is to act as a storehouse of food substances needed for the growth of the young plant until it is capable of taking in food for itself. The embryo is surrounded by a hard, woody shell technically known as the *testa* and the whole constitutes the seed. At this point growth virtually ceases, and the ripe seed lies dormant for some time. It is worth noting that a seed is not by any means the original starting point from which a new plant develops; the true origin is the zygote, which has to undergo considerable growth and development before it assumes the form of a seed.

The seeds of a rose are found inside the hips, embedded in a sort of silky down; they vary in number according to the species. *R. rugosa*'s big tomato-like hips may contain sixty or seventy or more, while our comparatively infertile garden hybrids may have only one—or even none. Unlike many fruiting plants, the rose is capable of forming hips even when it has not been effectively fertilised, though the empty ones are usually small and mis-shapen. The seeds are very irregular in size and shape, and may be any colour from white to dark brown or almost black; the white ones are not necessarily unripe, nor the dark ones diseased. It not infrequently happens that the outer shell of the seed develops normally but the embryo inside does not; such defective seeds can be detected by shaking them up in water, when they will float, while the sound ones will sink. They are also very erratic in their germination. Unless specially treated, they will normally lie dormant in the soil for at least a year, and they may delay their emergence for several years. The reason for this long period of dormancy and erratic rate of germination has recently been discovered. They are caused by the presence in the testa, or seed case, of a plant hormone known as abscisic acid in relatively large quantities. Research into a possible way of neutralising the effects of this hormone is now being undertaken and the scientific literature on the subject is increasing.

The seeds should be gathered as soon as the hips are ripe, which is, generally speaking, as soon as they have lost their green coloration. I cannot say, as soon as they are red all over, because the hips of some species such as *R. spinosissima* do not turn red, but dark brown; others among our garden varieties turn a sort of russet colour when they ripen. Rowley's experiments with the Dog Rose at Bayfordbury showed that if the hips are left until they begin to soften, the seeds are slower to germinate. In nature, of course, most of the hips do not fall to the ground until they are dry and shrivelled; but then in nature the delayed germination which this seems to induce may often be advantageous, however much of a nuisance it may be to the rose grower. In this country the rose-seed harvest is not usually prolonged after about the middle of November; if the hips have not ripened by then they are unlikely to ripen at all, but it may be worth while to gather them all the same. Henry Bennett, the father of the Hybrid Teas, recorded that in his experience immature seeds germinated sooner than fully ripe ones—though he admitted that they usually yielded feeble plants.

The seeds should be removed from the hips as soon as they are gathered; there is no advantage to be gained from keeping the hips unopened. Many attempts have been made to devise some means of speeding up germination, but the only success which has been achieved so far has been from a form of heat treatment which is rather ineptly known as "stratification". This entails burying the seeds in moistened sand, vermiculite or any other convenient medium from which they can be sifted out in due course; they are then stored for two months in a warm place such as a greenhouse, after which they are transferred to a refrigerator and kept at a temperature of about 32° F for another two months. After this

A spectacular striped rose, **Ferdinand Pichard** *(Hybrid Perpetual). Introduced by R. Tanne, France, 1921. Evidently a sport, but parentage not disclosed. Medium-sized, full, cupped blooms, solitary and in clusters of 2–5, pale pink streaked and splashed scarlet, ageing to crimson. Very fragrant. Profuse summer flowering, repeated in autumn when established. Plentiful mid-green foliage on very thorny, tall growth to 7 ft. Very vigorous. Like all Hybrid Perpetuals of tall habit, best results are obtained by pegging down. Photograph: J. L. Norton, A.R.P.S.*

Deepest of the blue roses, **Baby Faurax** *(Polyantha). Raiser: Leonard Lille, Lyon-Villeurbane, France. Introduced 1924. Parentage not stated, but suggested as possibly a dwarf segregate from Veilchenblau (Multiflora Rambler). Small, cupped blooms in trusses of 6–12 on short stems in a uniform deep violet, white at base of petals. Fragrant. Pale green foliage and wood. Vigorous, very dwarf growth rarely exceeding 1 ft. Free flowering with most intense colour in autumn. Now receiving the attention of hybridists. Photograph: J. L. Norton, A.R.P.S.*

the seeds are recovered and sown, when a large proportion of them may be expected to germinate within a few weeks. These conditions are not critical; the one essential is exposure to low temperature for a fairly long period before the temperature is raised to induce germination. One obvious simplification that the amateur can introduce is to sow his seeds in John Innes seed compost as soon as they are harvested and then to apply the cold treatment to the seed boxes. Early germination is not so important to the amateur as it is to the professional hybridist, and the former may well find it sufficient to leave his seed boxes outside where they are exposed to the normal winter weather (taking due precautions to see that they do not dry out and are not attacked by mice, which are very partial to rose seeds) before bringing them into a greenhouse—or a living-room—towards the end of March. Working in Norfolk, I have found that the first seedlings usually appear in the first half of April, heralding a germination season which lasts for about six weeks; there is sometimes a small recurrence in September, and the occasional seedling may appear at almost any time of the year.

There is nothing very distinctive about a rose seedling at its first appearance. The cotyledons or seed-leaves are roughly oval in shape, and do not differ markedly from those of many other weeds which may come up beside them, though they tend to be somewhat larger than those of their common competitors. The first true leaf is often single and lobed, or else consists of three leaflets springing from the same point on the stem, but the normal rose character is usually established in the second, with three or five leaflets, the number increasing up to the normal whatever it may be as the plant grows. The amateur working on a small scale, whether he is trying his hand at hybridising or only sowing the seeds produced by his garden roses by open pollination, will usually find that he seldom has more than fifteen or twenty seeds of a particular kind, and I have found it convenient to divide my seed-boxes by transverse partitions of thin wood into a number of strips a couple of inches wide or so, each strip being devoted to one kind of seed. (The partitions need not be fixed in place; it is sufficient to force them down into the compost.) It is of great importance that the risk of mixing up the seeds should be reduced to a minimum. I always remember seeing the foreman at a justly famous rose nursery wandering through half an acre of assorted varieties, sticking his finger into one flower after another in the endeavour to find a good source of pollen for a particular cross he contemplated

P

making. He eventually found what he wanted and went back to the hybridising house with it; and I have often wondered which of the dozen or more varieties whose pollen he must have mixed was credited with the parentage of that cross, if it ever came to anything. Every seed has its origin in a single grain of pollen too small to be seen with the naked eye.

One is often advised to pot up the seedlings when the first true leaf appears, but in my own experience they can be moved with perfect safety at any time. In theory at least there is something to be said for potting them as soon as they appear above ground, since at this stage they are still drawing much of their nourishment from the cotyledons, and so are less dependent on external conditions. Certainly the later they are transferred the greater the danger of damaging the roots in the process. It sometimes happens that a seedling will emerge with the tips of its cotyledons clasped together by the remains of the seed-husk; this would hardly interest the professional hybridiser who raises 100,000 seedlings a year, but the amateur who cherishes every single one of the few that he produces will usually try to detach this strangling incubus, and may sometimes succeed only in breaking the plant in two. In such a case, the lower portion consisting of the root and a short length of leafless stem may survive for several months, but I have never known it to make any further growth; whereas the upper part, consisting of the rest of the stem and its cotyledons, may sometimes be induced to put out fresh roots and continue to grow if it is planted as a "cutting", and the soil kept well moistened. I do not put this forward to justify carelessness in handling precious seedlings, but it is a tip worth knowing. The baby seedlings are most conveniently potted into small peat pots placed in shallow trays and grown on in a greenhouse. The necessary water is poured into the trays, whence it is rapidly absorbed by the peat pots. (At a pinch, an inch of water in the trays may suffice for a week or more, if they have to be left unattended for any reason; but it is not a practice that I would recommend for normal use.) Under glass rose seedlings are found to be rather susceptible to the form of fungus attack known as "damping-off", which can be controlled by watering with Cheshunt Compound or other fungicides.

A Hybrid Tea, floribunda or polyantha seedling will usually put out its first flower bud when it is about eight to ten weeks old, by which time it will have grown to about four inches high or perhaps more. The flower produced at this age will bear little resemblance to those which will come at maturity; it will be an inch or so across, and is unlikely to have more than about twenty petals at most. With double flowers the number of petals tends to increase as the plant matures, sometimes to the point where the number is quite excessive, so that the flower is unable to open properly. On the other hand, even from the most many-petalled parents the flowers are quite likely to come and to remain single; doubleness is not a simple quality to be inherited with any certainty. It is, after all, an abnormal condition; it is perhaps more surprising that it can be inherited at all. The colour of the first flower gives a very fair indication of what is to be expected in the future, though even that is not to be wholly depended upon, I have had a polyantha seedling which yielded four successive flowers in its first year from seed, all of which were of quite different shades of pink, although when mature its colour was quite uniform. If the first flower is scented, it is very likely that all subsequent ones will be, too, but the opposite is not necessarily true. Let me give an example from a Hybrid Tea which I raised some years ago. It was a self-seedling from Lady Sylvia, and in its first year its flowers were a pale blush-pink and flat, with about a dozen petals. In the following year it had about twenty petals, of which the outer ones lay flat while the inner ones were curled upwards, giving it rather an attractive cup-and-saucer shape. A friend having seen it and expressed a liking for it, I arranged with my good friend Mr. Morse to have half a dozen plants budded from it (I am rather clumsy with the knife myself), which was lucky, as I lost the original plant from some accidental cause shortly afterwards; I was unable to visit his nursery the next year, so never saw the first budded flowers, but in the following year, its fourth (and a season in which all my roses were exceptionally vigorous), the flowers had about a hundred petals or more, and never opened properly. In its fifth year it settled down to produce flowers with forty or fifty petals, and for the first time yielded a strong fragrance. Since then it has remained the same; its colour remained unchanged through all these variations in shape. The expert, after years of experience, develops an ability to judge the possibilities inherent in the first-year flower. He has to, since he cannot possibly grow on all the seedlings he raises. Even so, it is certain that many a gold-medal winner must be thrown away with those that he rejects. It doesn't matter —there are too many first-class rose varieties in the world as it is, so that most of us must go to our graves without having seen half of them, and there are far too many indifferent ones.

It is not only in the flowers that maturity brings changes; one must also be prepared for surprises in the habit of growth, especially if the seedling is a cross between two very different types of rose. A cross which I once raised between R. *pisocarpa*, which is a graceful, upright shrub seven or eight feet high, and a dwarf polyantha, showed such moderate growth that I nearly threw it away; by the end of the first year it was still no more than two inches high, a matchstick with four leaves. But in the following year it went off with a bang, putting out four or five separate canes which reached a length of eighteen inches or two feet. Eventually it developed into a large bush, three feet high and nearly six across. Personally, I get much pleasure from watching these changes, but if you are impatient to see what the final result will be, you can short-circuit much of the development process by budding on to a small understock at an early age. This can be done even in the first year, but it needs a steady hand to deal with such minute buds. This is of particular value in the case of the climbers and once-blooming shrub roses, which often take three or four years or more before putting out their first flowers. But I always like to keep the original seedling by me, if only because I prefer to grow my roses on their own roots.

When the seedlings are eight or ten weeks old, they are ready to be planted out in a nursery bed. For the normal crop this will be by about the beginning of July, and if you choose a warm period, no "hardening-off" will be needed. They can go into the ground, pots and all, if the pots are of peat, and will need no further special treatment; they are perfectly hardy, and will stand the winter as well as any other rose.

By the late nineteenth century, a large number of important new roses had been introduced into cultivation, the great majority of which were hybrids, and the natural variation of hybrid seedlings is of an entirely different order from that of the species. It was sufficient, in fact, to yield eight or ten thousand new cultivated varieties of rose, all obtained from seed, and nearly all without any conscious attempt at hybridisation. Each of the nineteenth-century "classes" of garden roses consisted of no more than the descendants—or putative descendants—of one single rose which gave its name to the class, as with the Bourbon and Noisette Roses, or else of two or more varieties which were assumed to be closely related, as with the Tea Roses and Hybrid Perpetuals.

This method of raising new varieties is just as valid today as it was a hundred years ago. Almost every new rose raised today comes from a deliberate cross between two varieties, but it must be admitted that most of this crossing is a pure waste of time. The conscientious breeder who makes a deep study of the science of genetics gains very little from it—unless of course he enjoys the study for its own sake—since we simply do not know enough of the genetics of the rose to enable us to forecast with any serious hope of accuracy what will be the outcome of any particular cross. It has been truly said that "a knowledge of genetics does not bring success in plant breeding—it only helps to explain one's failures". The professional raiser of new roses will cheerfully tell you that he rejects a thousand seedlings for every one that he brings into commerce; it may be unkind but it is true to point out that this means that whatever theories may have induced him to make those particular crosses have proved to be wrong a thousand times for every once that they give the right answer. Indeed, the proportion is less than this, since the one rose that he puts on the market out of a thousand failures may be, and often is, something entirely different from what he was hoping for. Practically speaking, the only real object in making a cross between two Hybrid Teas, say, in our present state of ignorance, is to ensure that the offspring is something different from the parents; and as this result is virtually inevitable even with self-seedlings, the crossing is wasted effort, except when something entirely new arises by pure chance. The number of really important and fruitful crosses that have been deliberately made in the past hundred years can almost be counted on the fingers of one hand. Henry Bennett inaugurated the Hybrid Tea class by crossing Teas with various other sorts; Lord Penzance crossed the Sweet Brier with garden hybrids to give us the "Penzance Briers"; Pernet-Ducher's cross between a Hybrid Perpetual and the Persian Yellow laid the foundations of the once-termed "Pernetiana" class which ultimately extended the colour range of the Hybrid Teas; the Ramblers were produced by several workers, crossing *R. multiflora* and *R. wichuraiana* (and in Barbier's hands, perhaps, *R. luciae*) with various garden roses; Pemberton produced his ill-named "Hybrid Musks" from crosses between Hybrid Teas and the perpetual climber Trier; and Poulsen launched the Floribunda class by his crossing of dwarf polyanthas with Hybrid Teas. For the rest, a cross between two roses of the same established class does no more than to give a fresh stir to a pudding which is already completely mixed. The amateur who takes to raising roses from seed in the hope of producing some new medal-winner among the H.T.s or floribundas need not trouble himself with hybridisation; he may collect his seeds where he finds them in his rose garden, in the certainty that they will produce new varieties which are just as likely (or unlikely) to win medals as those produced by a McGredy or a Le Grice. But he must raise them in very large numbers if he hopes to emulate the success of those gentlemen.

Chapter Fourteen

PRACTICAL
HYBRIDISING

*Nature is made better by no mean
But nature makes that mean . . .*
The Winter's Tale

If you want to take up hybridising as a hobby, well and good; it is a very fascinating one, very simple, and calls for no special skill. Practically every rose in your garden is already a very complex hybrid, and the seeds that it sets by open pollination will yield an infinite variety of new roses. Let us do a little exercise in proportion. The professionals tell us that in raising H.T.s they expect to find one seedling in every thousand which is good enough to develop and put upon the market as a new variety. A diploid hybrid of relatively uncomplicated pedigree can yield over a hundred million different seedlings when selfed. Therefore, if one in a thousand is up to commercial standards, one may expect to find something like a hundred thousand marketable new varieties in the progeny of a single hybrid, without recourse to any crossing.

There are no grounds whatever for supposing that self-seedlings are in any way inferior to those produced by crossing. Pay no attention to the pundit who warns you against the evil effects of in-breeding; in-breeding is the rose's natural mode of reproduction, and the great majority of wild roses have been in-bred for thousands of years without suffering any deterioration. Almost the entire class of Hybrid Perpetuals was produced by in-breeding. Indeed, one of the most popular fallacies of the present day is the oft-quoted statement that the degeneration from which a few varieties have suffered over the years is due to the complexity of their hybrid ancestry—or in other words, to the fact that they have not been in-bred enough! It is obvious that such contradictory beliefs cannot both be true; but they can both be false, and in fact they are. So much nonsense is talked nowadays about the "triumphs of the rose breeder" that the ordinary man cannot help feeling that there must be something in it; that what Ruskin called "the victorious beauty of the rose" must be due in some measure to the skill and judgment of the hybridiser. Human nature being what it is, the beginner who has raised a few score, or a few hundreds, of rose seedlings without once ringing the bell begins to lose heart and seizes upon the practice of hybridising as the obvious cure for his non-success. The first prize that he wins with a rose derived from his own crossing confirms him in his belief, and from then on he is a persistent pandar to his breeding stock. But it is an almost complete waste of time. The only true skill and judgment that the professional breeder exercises is in the selection of the good from the bad amongst a heterogeneous collection of seedlings that are on the whole no better and no worse than if he had left their conception to the unaided forces of nature.

Here is another useful tip. If you want to produce marketable varieties, concentrate on the floribundas. A Hybrid Tea has practically no chance of a gold medal unless it possesses not less than about twenty-four petals, which must also be arranged to form a flower of the currently fashionable shape—which is roughly the fashion set by the variety Ophelia sixty years ago; whereas a floribunda may have flowers of any shape and with any number of petals from the five of the single flower upwards. Even the so-called "Floribunda-Hybrid Tea types" often display faults—ragged or distorted petals, split centres, etc.—which would condemn a Hybrid Tea out of hand. No doubt the standards will be tightened up as time goes on, but at present they are low enough to allow you to pick out three or four promising floribunda seedlings for every good H.T.

However, this book is not written for the professional, but for the amateur who indulges in hybridising for the mere pleasure of it, and for the fun of seeing what turns up—and even, conceivably, in the hope of making some new discovery about the genetics of the rose. But I should be wrong to hold out any great hopes in the latter direction. It is true that the rose, for good reasons, has played little or no part in pure genetical research; none the less, there are one or two skilled geneticists associated with the work of the largest rose breeding establishments in the United

States, and with their relatively enormous facilities they are not likely to overlook new facts that may reveal themselves to the back-garden amateur. However, don't let that discourage you; you can get a great deal of interest from the pursuit, even if your name is not engrossed on the roll of fame beside those of Kölreuter and Mendel.

The first thing to decide is whether you intend to pursue some fixed objective, or whether you will prefer to work at random and see what Nature provides. There is much to be said for both attitudes towards your work. For the committed hybridiser, there are plenty of gaps in our rose catalogues waiting to be filled, and there are other types of roses whose classes deserve to be extended. The old Blush Noisette, for instance, is almost unique; a five-foot shrub which bears clusters of small, double flowers as luxuriant as those on a rambler, but is fully perpetual. The later Noisettes, although descended from this, bear very little resemblance to it. It is pale blush in colour, and similar roses in other tints would be very welcome. Cécile Brunner and Perle d'Or are a charming pair of roses whose dainty grace puts most of our modern floribundas to shame. Mrs. Ratcliffe added a third to this "class" (they are in fact classed indiscriminately with the Chinas, polyanthas and the floribundas) when she crossed Cécile Brunner with Fashion to produce Jenny Wren, which takes strongly after the former, but nothing further has been done. And, of course, there is always the search for a true blue rose and for roses which are immune to black spot and mildew.

On the whole, however, my advice would be to forswear the pursuit of a definite aim, which so often proves a will-o'-the-wisp and leads to frustration and discouragement, and to amuse oneself by making haphazard crosses between the most dissimilar parents. Get hold of half a dozen species as far removed as possible from the small group which is represented in our garden hybrids, and cross them with each other and everything else in sight. We are often urged to bring new species into our garden hybrids; there is, we are told, a wealth of untapped possibilities in the scores of wild species which have so far played no part in furnishing our rose gardens. Personally, I have doubts whether any of the so far untried species have anything really important to offer, but I could easily be wrong. Fortune favours the bold and we have before us the examples of Mermaid and Nevada. Both are sterile "mules" but anyone who raised a rose of equally outstanding merit would consider his efforts very well rewarded indeed.

As for the species you choose to breed from, that is up to you. I would strongly recommend *R. moyesii* as one of them, not so much for its potential as breeding material as for its own unsurpassable beauty, with its blood-red single flowers and enormous urn-shaped hips, borne in profusion. Get the form Geranium, which is more vivid in colour than the normal form and less vigorous in growth. *R. moyesii* is a hexaploid with forty-two chromosomes, and is unlikely to give fertile hybrids unless it is crossed with a diploid, such as a China, Polyantha pompon, or a Tea. The latter may be hard to find and that most generally available, Lady Hillingdon, is a triploid and sterile but the breeding potential of the Teas is well worthy of investigation.

R. rugosa is very easy to work with as a seed parent, since its hips ripen early and the seeds germinate with commendable regularity in the first spring after sowing, but being a diploid, it will call for diploid pollen if the seedlings are to be fertile. The chief drawback with *R. rugosa* is that the first crosses always take strongly after their rugosa parent, as did all of the f_2 seedlings that I ever raised. Another species worth considering is *R. pisocarpa*, whose slender canes stand straighter than those of any other rose I know and reach a height of seven to eight feet. The flowers are a mauvy-pink, about an inch across, borne profusely in small clusters; after the first burst, they tend to come one or two at a time until the end of the season. Two other attractive members of the same Cinnamomae section are *R. davidii* and *R. multibracteata*, which are both tetraploids and so offer greater possibilities for crossing with the H.T.s and floribundas, which share the same chromosome pattern.

Whilst on the subject of species, it is perhaps worth mentioning that Messrs. Hilliers of Winchester and Murrells of Shrewsbury offer a selection of rose species not generally available from other firms of rose specialists.

Like most of us, you will probably want to breed roses which are both double and perpetual in character, whereas all the species I have mentioned with the exception of *RR. rugosa* and *pisocarpa* (which repeat sparingly but quite reliably) are once-flowering and single. Double forms of some of them do exist, but I hesitate to recommend them as there may be doubts about their fertility. I am afraid that you will have to judge for yourself the fertility of any double forms of species you encounter by seeing if they set hips. As for the perpetual habit, this can only be introduced by a cross with a China or a China derivative if you are using a diploid species, or any H.T.s or floribundas with the few tetraploid species that are available. As we have seen earlier, remontant seedlings will only occur in the second (f_2) generation and then only in a small proportion of them.

*   *   *

The actual process of making a cross is simplicity itself, and calls for nothing more in the way of apparatus than a sharp knife or a pair of nail-scissors, a quantity of tissue paper, and a supply of small tie-on labels—the sort used as price-tags in shops is excellent. A powerful magnifying glass, or better, one of the small hand-microscopes of the "fountain-pen" type, is a very useful accessory. The need for this modest tool-kit is dictated by the fact that when a rose receives two sorts of pollen, its own and a strange variety, the former is "prepotent" and the latter always ineffective—yet another of the observations that we owe to Kölreuter; so that when we have decided on the rose which is to act as seed parent in our proposed cross, our first care must be to remove all its stamens before they have had a chance to shed any pollen.

A rose—and more especially a double rose—will often commence to shed its pollen before the petals have opened even enough to allow the stamens to be seen, so that the proper stage at which to prepare the seed parent for pollination must be a matter of judgment. In single flowers I have found that the best time is when the sepals have separated and begun to bend back from the petals, but before the latter have unfolded at all; with double flowers the external development may be allowed to proceed a little further. But the only practical way to learn is to wander round your garden and dissect flowers here and there until you are familiar with their internal appearance at various stages of development. You will find that in the immature flower—below the age of puberty, so to speak—the stamens are packed close together against the styles in the centre; later they straighten up and stand clear of the styles, and very shortly after this the first grains of pollen make their appearance on the anthers. It is here that your magnifying glass comes in useful; if it reveals so much as one grain of pollen, then you are too late and it is not safe to proceed with that flower. It does not matter much if you are a day or so too soon.

In preparing the flower for pollination, first, as a matter of convenience, pull or cut off all the sepals and petals, taking care not to damage any other parts of the flower in the process. Next, with your knife or the nail-scissors, remove all the stamens, taking great care not to leave a single one in place—or out of place, either; you may often find one with its anther tucked down into the groove which surrounds the styles, and this must be carefully picked out also; even after the stamens have been severed they may survive long enough to shed their pollen some hours later. When you have done this, the seed parent is ready for pollination.

One is sometimes advised to defer the application of the pollen until the seed parent is ready to receive it, a state which is indicated by the glistening appearance of the sticky secretion which is exuded on the stigma; but I cannot endorse this advice. Even if it were easy to detect this secretion—which it isn't—I would still prefer to have my seed parent well secured from outside interference at this stage. As every sufferer from hay-fever knows to his cost, the summer air is laden with grains of pollen of every sort and kind, and if one or more of these from a rose of the wrong sort should happen to reach the stigma of your seed-parent before you have finished the job, all your work may go for naught. It is preferable to prepare the pollen parents at the same time as their prospective mates, and then to leave them together in peace to consummate the match undisturbed. The pollen parent should be at about the same state of development as the seed parent or if anything a little later; the important thing is that the pollen should be in contact with the stigma when it comes into its receptive state. The selected flower must be cut off with an inch or so of stalk, and the sepals and petals removed as before; the stamens of course must be left in place. Next take a piece of tissue-paper two or three inches square, depending upon the size of the flowers one is dealing with, and roll it up into a tube with the pollen parent inside it, its head near the middle of its length, and then crumble the paper around the stalk to secure it; it is a wise precaution to tie it with a scrap of thread or raffia. Then slip the open end of the tube over the seed parent and slide it down until the two flowers are in contact. Take one of your labels with its little loop of cotton and double the latter back on itself to form a running loop; slip this over the paper tube, and draw it tight around the stem of the seed parent, thus sealing it off from the outside world and also holding the pollen-parent firmly in position. Next take a soft pencil and write on the label the code letter or number by which you mean to record the cross; and then, before you do anything else (it is astonishing how easy it is to forget), take out a note-book and enter up the record: "1/71—

R. thingumajig × *R. whatyoumaycallit.*" If you are a careful person—and even more if you are not—you may find it useful to write your labels with crayons (waterproof, of course) of four different colours, using them on successive days, so that all the crosses made on one day may be recognised at a glance. It will usually suffice to leave the couples together for two or three days, or four at the most if the weather has been exceptionally cold and dull; after that, everything may be removed except the label, which must remain until the time comes to harvest the hips.

As one of the difficulties you will encounter in hybridising in the open in this country is the long time required for the hips to ripen, it will always pay you to make your crosses as early in the season as possible. But here you are likely to strike another snag, as not all roses come into flower at the same time, and some of the earliest may be over before others have opened their first flowers. However, the difficulty is not insurmountable. Pollen can be stored for many weeks without losing its potency, provided that it is kept absolutely dry. The simplest way to hold back pollen for later use is to prepare the pollen-parent in the usual way—though with a rather longer stalk—and then to put it in water like any other cut flower. In a few hours, or perhaps a day or so, depending upon the stage at which it was prepared, the pollen will make its appearance, and can be shaken off the anthers on to a piece of paper. When enough has been collected, the paper must be carefully folded to enclose the pollen and then placed in a wide-mouthed jar with a lid capable of being hermetically sealed—a Kilner jar will do at a pinch—which contains at the bottom a layer of an inch or two of fused calcium chloride (which any chemist can get for you, though he may not have it in stock). This is a white, rocky substance, looking rather like chips of pumice stone, which has a tremendous affinity for water, so that it will extract all the moisture from the air in the jar, so long as the latter is kept sealed. To avoid contamination, the calcium chloride should be covered with a layer of cotton wool or a few sheets of paper, to make sure that it cannot come into contact with the pollen. After a while the calcium chloride will absorb enough water to become moist, when it should be discarded and the jar thoroughly cleaned and dried before renewing the drying agent. The calcium chloride can be restored to its effective form by prolonged heating, but this is hardly worth the trouble; it is not expensive.

The advantages of doing your hybridising under glass are obvious, especially as regards ripening of the hips. But the one great disadvantage is also obvious; you have to possess—or purchase—a greenhouse, and one large enough to house all your potential seed parents. I honestly don't think it is worth the expense for the amateur; working in the open air imposes so few restrictions that one could easily spend a lifetime at it and never feel the want of better conditions. If you have ample space under glass, by all means use it, but if you haven't, don't give it a thought.

Finally, a word as to the records you will keep. Every man has his own methods, but whether you use the backs of old envelopes or an extensive card index system it is pretty certain that a day will come when you wish, for one reason or another, that you had kept more complete notes. On the other hand, it cannot be denied that the more complicated your system is, the greater is the temptation to scamp the job when you are hurried or feeling lazy. You could manage with no more than three books. The first is a rough notebook for recording the crosses as they are made; it must be small enough to go easily into the pocket, and in fact the smaller it is the better, since it fairly often gets trodden underfoot or left out in the rain, so that it is liable to begin to disintegrate long before it is filled—when it is tucked away at the back of a drawer and a new one is brought into use. The entries in this consist of no more than the date, followed by the code numbers and particulars of each cross made at that particular session. The second book is brought into use when starting to gather the ripe hips; this is the "seed register", a more permanent affair, about quarto size—a stiff-covered exercise book does admirably. Each entry in this book records the sowing of one particular lot of seeds, headed by the code number and particulars of the cross, taken from the rough notebook, thus:

"63/60. R. gallica versicolor × High Noon"—and on the next line, add further details to date, e.g. "crossed 6/7/60. Five seeds sown, 12/10/60." Under that leave enough blank space to allow one line to each seedling if and when it appears, before making the next entry. The example given here is an actual extract from my register; the full entry now reads, below the two lines quoted:

1. 10/4/61. P.25/4/61. B.11/6/61. T.20/2/62.
2. 7/11/61. P.12/2/62.
3. 11/11/61. P.12/2/62. B.6/4/62.

The letter P stands for "potted up"; B for "bedded out"; and T for "transplanted"—that is, from the nursery bed into the rose garden proper. (Perpetual roses usually earn an additional entry with the letter F, for "first flower", which comes before B.) The first seedling has now earned its right to an independent existence, under the code designation of 63/60/1; the second and third both succumbed, the second to natural causes and the third to cats, which are also natural causes of a sort. (It is interesting to note, by the way, that Nos. 2 and 3 made their first appearance in November, and remained out of doors until they were potted up in the following February.)

Self-seeds from my other garden roses are also entered in this register in just the same way, being allotted code numbers as they come to hand which follow on from the code number of the last cross made in the same year. Thus this book contains a complete list of all my seedlings, both actual and potential, after weeding out the crosses which failed; but it is awkward as a reference book, since the entries are made in chronological order of sowing, which has no particular significance. So I also keep a register in a loose-leaf book, in which a separate page is allotted to each seedling which reaches the stage of being transplanted; the relevant information from the seed register is copied into this book, which also serves to record any further interesting events in the history of the rose. This last book constitutes a list, in numerical order of code numbers for easy reference, of all the roses of my own raising which I think worth growing on permanently. What the show judges might think of them I neither know nor care; they are my own darlings.

Chapter Fifteen

PESTS AND DISEASES

Timor mortis conturbat me.
William Dunbar (1465?-1530?)

The true meaning of the word pest is disease—as witness such still current usages as pestilent, pest-house, fowl-pest, etc.— but as often happens the meaning broadened out over the years to include any sort of plague or calamity; later it shrank again, so that today, in the garden at least, it is used to denote almost anything, other than disease, which attacks our plants. We reserve the word disease for those troubles which arise from the attacks of bacteria, fungi and viruses. The distinction is not clear-cut; one might put it, that if you can see what is causing the trouble, then that is a pest; if you cannot, then it is a disease.

GREENFLY

The best-known and best-hated of all the pests of our rose gardens is the aphis or greenfly. A single greenfly is a fairly harmless visitor; it is guilty of nothing worse than sucking the sap from the softer parts of the plant and excreting a sweetish, sticky substance called "honeydew", which attracts ants and encourages the growth of sooty mould; the trouble lies in the fact that it remains single for such a short time. The importance of the greenfly is due almost entirely to its remarkable breeding habits. The eggs, which may be laid on the rose itself or on other host plants, according to the species—there are several different species of aphis which attack our roses—hatch in spring, the insects which emerge being all females. These, however, do not lay eggs in their turn; instead, and without the assistance of the male greenfly, they give birth to living young

A class apart, often grouped with the China Roses, but more strictly Tea-Polyantha, (left) **Jenny Wren.** *Raiser: Mrs. Ratcliffe, Chilton, Berks., England. Introduced 1957. Parentage: Cécile Brunner × Fashion. Pink outer petals, apricot centre, darker pink reverse. (Centre and top right)* **Cécile Brunner.** *Raiser: Veuve Ducher, Lyons, France. Introduced 1881. Parentage: a Polyantha × Madame de Tartas (Tea). Pale pink. (Lower right)* **Perle d'Or.** *Raiser: Joseph Rambaux, Lyons, France. 1884. Parentage: a Polyantha × Madame Falcot (Tea). Apricot, fading to deep cream. All are very fragrant, scaled-down Tea Roses in large sprays (8–20) on long, wiry stems, borne continuously. Vigorous, branching habit from 4–5 ft. Very healthy, but resent hard pruning; best grown as small specimen shrubs. Photograph: J. L. Norton, A.R.P.S.*

Rosa moyesii. Native of western China, first European introduction 1894. Large (2½–3 in.), single blooms, solitary or in pairs in bright crimson with a conspicuous circlet of yellow stamens and anthers. Free flowering at midsummer, followed by colourful, large urn-shaped hips. Dark green foliage on tall, upright growth to 10 ft. Not fragrant. The form "Geranium" (R.H.S. Wisley Gardens 1938) has more brilliantly coloured flowers, fewer thorns and a more compact habit to 7 ft. The characteristic hips are also present. Often regarded as the most beautiful of all the rose species in cultivation.

only a few days after they emerge from the eggs, and these in turn do the same, so that enormous colonies of the insects can be built up in a very short time. All these insects are wingless; but sooner or later a winged brood appears—still all females—which take their departure and proceed to build up new colonies on other plants in the neighbourhood. It is not until the end of summer, when the last winged brood makes its appearance, that both males and females are produced; these mate and the females proceed to lay clusters of eggs, which remain dormant over the winter, ready to repeat the whole cycle the next year.

For those of us who are in the happy position of being able to visit our roses every day, greenfly are not a serious problem. They are sluggish, helpless creatures, which are very easily detached from their feeding places by a light tap or a flick with the finger and thumb; the woody parts of the plant close to the ground are immune from their attacks, and once detached they seem to perish without any attempt at a come-back. They are common enough in my part of Norfolk, and my garden is never entirely free from them, but for the past ten years I have never found it necessary to take any more drastic measures than this to keep them in check. For the weekend gardener, however, their monstrous fecundity represents a real menace, and he will often find it necessary to apply an insecticide spray to get rid of them. Almost any of the popular insecticides will be found effective, *except* D.D.T.; this will do little harm to the greenfly, but on the other hand it is likely to kill off many of their natural enemies such as ladybirds, hover flies, lacewing flies, etc., so that the effect of D.D.T. may in the long run encourage the pests instead of deterring them.

Of recent years a new weapon has appeared in the form of the "systemic" insecticides, which are watered into the ground, taken into the roses by the roots, and poison the greenfly when they absorb the poisoned sap. At first sight this seems an ideal method of dealing with them, and for all I know it may be; but I have never used it myself. Perhaps many others like myself are reluctant to make use of substances which are generally very deadly poisons, to be used with the greatest care and discretion. For obvious reasons they should never be used in or near the vegetable or fruit garden, and they are unpleasant things to have about where children may find them.

Greenfly are not always green in colour; red ones are frequently encountered, but the colour has no sinister significance. There is, however, another species which is dark brown or black, and lives on the roots of our roses, where it may sometimes flourish unsuspected. If your roses are healthy, you need have no qualms about them, but it is always as well to examine any new roses before you plant them; the root aphids are easily removed, if present, by washing the roots before planting; the eggs, which are black and shiny, are laid in clusters on the rose stems near the ground, and may be simply rubbed off if any are found.

LEAF ROLLERS

It is in early summer that one most commonly finds the damage caused by these intruders. If the leaf is fairly lightly rolled and still looks otherwise healthy, the trouble is due to the caterpillars of one of the various species of tortrix moths, which wrap the leaves neatly round themselves and fasten them into position with silk threads; in this way each one makes a comfortable little hermitage for itself, in which it can pupate in peace. The trouble caused by the leaf-rolling sawfly is of a different kind. The female fly punctures the leaf in order to insert her egg, and at the same time injects a chemical substance which causes the leaf to roll up spontaneously; in this case the leaf is very tightly furled and usually looks somewhat wrinkled.

There is little one can do about it in either case; the damage has been done before it is discovered. If the damage is sufficiently extensive to make you feel vindictive about it, you may take pains to pinch each of the rolled leaves, so as to destroy its occupant, or you may pull the leaves off and burn them; in this way you will at least contribute your mite towards the reduction of future generations of the pests. Insecticide sprays are rarely effective, since it is very difficult to get them to penetrate the rolled-up leaves. If you should chance to notice a plague of shiny black flies hovering over and settling on your roses in the month of April or thereabouts, a spray or dusting with B.H.C. will probably kill many of them; but you can hardly lie in wait and keep watch for them, and in any case, the use of insecticide on roses is always liable to kill more friends than foes.

LEAF CUTTERS

There is only one miscreant in this case, the leaf-cutting bee, which cuts out portions of the blades of the leaves with a neat circular sweep and takes them away to line her nest. The damage caused is quite unmistakable, but it is seldom of any great importance. If you should encounter it in your garden, my advice would be to keep watch and try to catch the bee at work—not with the idea of killing it, but for the pleasure of seeing how swiftly and expertly it works. It is about the size of an ordinary honey-bee, but a little fatter and more furry. If they should become so numerous that your admiration turns to exasperation, the best method of control is to follow them home to their nests, which are made in holes and crevices in wood and stonework, and deal with them as one would with a wasps' nest.

LEAF EATERS

There are innumerable caterpillars, maggots, "slug-worms", etc. which have a taste for the foliage of our roses; some of them chew ragged pieces out of the leaves; some—more tidy feeders—eat away the soft tissues of the leaf and leave it skeletonised. Many of them prefer to commit their depredations on the undersides of the leaves, where they are not so conspicuous. They may all be dealt with alike: the finger and thumb for individual cases or small numbers, or a good insecticide spray for large invasions.

There is another leaf eater which is rather more difficult to deal with than these, and that is the red spider mite, a minute eight-legged creature (six-legged in its earlier stage of development) which makes its home on the undersides of the leaves, which it rapidly covers with a mat of silk threads which forms a most effective protection against the penetration of insecticide sprays. Our climate is the best safeguard against these pests in the garden, and it is only in exceptionally hot, dry summers that they are likely to be a nuisance. They are susceptible to a Derris spray, but it will have to be very forcibly applied to the undersides of the leaves, and should be repeated three or four times at intervals of a few days, as the generations overlap and the eggs are not affected by the spray. Under glass, where the mites flourish more easily, they can be effectively dealt with by Azobenzene smokes, used in accordance with the makers' instructions.

LEAF BORERS

The caterpillars of the rose leaf miner moth spend their lives actually within the substance of the leaves, where they drive little tunnels which wander about in all directions. The harm they do is negligible—which is just as well, since being completely enclosed within the leaf they cannot be reached by any spray (though a systemic insecticide might deal with them).

If you resent the disfigurement of the foliage, you can at least take your revenge by pulling off the invaded leaves and burning them.

FLOWER EATERS

The most important of these is the thrips, also known as the thunder fly. (Please note that there is an s on the end of thrips in the singular as well as in the plural. There is no such thing as a "thrip".) These little black flies lay their eggs in the rose petals when the flowers commence to open (and also in the young leaves), and the immature insects spend their time concealed in the crevices between the petals, where, unfortunately, the ordinary insecticide sprays cannot reach them. The effect of thrips infestation is seen in a distortion of the petals, often combined with discoloration, and in the garden there is little one can do about it beyond removing and burning any flowers seen to be affected. Under glass they can be effectively dealt with by fumigants such as Azo-benzene.

The various caterpillars which devour the rose leaves also transfer their attentions to the flowers from time to time; they are, however, easy to deal with. More difficult are the dor-beetles or chafers—the garden chafer, which flies at midday, and the cockchafer, rose chafer and summer chafer, which are more often seen in the dusk. These sometimes swarm in large numbers in late May or June, and if a swarm descends on the rose garden they can do much damage to the flowers and buds in a short time. Their eggs are laid in the soil, and the grubs, which include the notorious "Joe Bassett", which is the larva of the cockchafer, spend from two to four years underground, where they may do much damage to roots and underground stems of the roses. They prefer a light, sandy soil, and when digging a bed in a soil of this nature it is always worth while keeping a look-out for large numbers of the grubs; a serious infestation may be dealt with by fumigating the soil, but before undertaking this you will do well to consult your local Agricultural Advisory Committee. The beetles themselves are susceptible to persistent insecticides like Lindane, but it is a question whether it is worthwhile to maintain a poison barrage for weeks on end to forestall an attack which may never materialise, especially when one considers the harm that one may do to friendly insects. Admittedly it is heartbreaking to find that a bud which one has been grooming for stardom at the local flower-show has been chewed to rags in the night; on the other hand, the judges are unlikely to award a prize to a bloom which is smothered in insecticide.

One may sometimes find the centre of a rose when full-blown occupied by a swarm of tiny beetles, no more than a tenth of an inch long, greenish-blue in colour with a metallic sheen; these are pollen beetles, and as their name implies, they will be busily engaged in making a meal of the anthers of the flower. In my experience, once they have devoured all trace of the stamens they disappear as mysteriously as they came; but in this I may have been lucky, as they are also accused of eating holes in the petals when their favourite food is exhausted. The raspberry beetle, that well-known plague of the kitchen-garden, will also sometimes transfer its attention to our roses. A flick of the finger will disperse them; a Derris spray will effectually put an end to their activities.

HOPPERS

There are two sorts of jumping insects which are found in the rose garden, the roseleaf-hopper, and the frog-hopper or cuckoo-spit insect. In both cases the adult insects do little harm; it is the larvae which suck the sap and cause, in the case of the first-named, a mottling of the leaves, and in the case of the second, a weakening of the shoots. The former conceals itself by remaining on the undersides of the leaves throughout its life; the latter surrounds itself with the familiar mass of foamy "spittle", which acts as a protection from birds—and from insecticide sprays. A thorough application of insecticide to the undersides of the leaves will deal effectively with the former; to cope with the latter the spray must be directed with sufficient force to wash away the spittle and expose the insect; in the event of a serious invasion it must pay you to wash them first with the garden hose and then to go round with the spray.

The greyish, semi-transparent "ghost fly" which is found standing inert on the undersides of rose leaves is not an insect at all, but the cast skin of the roseleaf-hopper, and so is of no importance—except in so far as it betrays the presence of its former occupant.

SCALE INSECTS

There are two or three different species of these, but they all spend an inactive existence, clustered in hundreds or thousands on the stems, like barnacles on a rock. They look more like a lichenous growth than a swarm of insects; but besides being unsightly they also weaken the plant on which they cluster. A winter wash of tar oil or one of the more modern substitutes is probably the most effective means of getting rid of them.

GALLS

There are other insects beside the leaf-rolling sawfly which inject poisons into the plant substance which give rise to distorted growth. The pea galls, small lumps on the underside of the leaf, are rare in gardens and of no importance; they are caused by two species of gall-wasps. A third species is responsible for the best-known and most wonderful of all these abnormal growths, the robin's pincushion, sometimes called the bedeguar—a word more often seen in print than heard in speech. It is common on wild roses, particularly the Sweet Brier, not so common on our garden hybrids where, if it is found, it may as well be allowed to remain, since it does no particular harm, and most people find it attractive. Crown gall of roses is not caused by an insect, but by a bacterium, and so calls for discussion with the other diseases.

*   *   *

The more important diseases of the rose are caused by the attacks of parasitic fungi. Three of these are chiefly manifested in the leaves, these being mildew, black spot and rust; a fourth, stem canker, affects the stems. They are all incurable, in the sense that the part of the rose which is invaded by the parasite is injured past hope of recovery; they can, however, be kept within bounds by two forms of treatment: the diseased parts can be cut out, thus preventing the further spread of the disease to other parts of the plant, and the plants can be protected by means of a fungicide spray which kills the fungus spores before they have a chance to develop and so prevents further infection in new sites.

MILDEW

This is perhaps the most widespread of all rose diseases. It firsts manifests itself in the form of whitish-grey patches, usually on the youngest leaves, which spread rapidly until the whole of the leaf surface is covered with microscopic white threads, often having a powdery appearance. The young leaves are weakened and distorted, and all the leaves affected will eventually die and drop away, thus seriously affecting the health of the whole plant. Although the fungus is rooted in the substance of the leaves, its growth is almost wholly external, so that the mildew can easily be rubbed off with the finger. This should in fact always be done as soon as the first symptoms of an attack are discovered, but it is not in itself a practical way of preventing an outbreak; a careful watch should be kept on the affected plants (and others) and if further outbreaks are seen the infected plants—and their neighbours—should be thoroughly sprayed with whatever your local supplier recommends for the purpose. At the time of writing, Karathane is the most fashionable specific against mildew, but it must be understood that there is no one chemical which is absolutely certain in its effect. If your supplier is also a nurseryman, he is likely to recommend whatever he himself has found to be most effective, and his advice is probably good; but there are many different strains of these disease fungi, and some are more resistant than others, so it is not necessarily his fault if what he sells you is not as effective as you hope. The spread of these fungus diseases is greatly influenced by the temperature and humidity in your garden, a fact which makes it very difficult for the ordinary gardener to assess the effectiveness of any given chemical spray.

As with all fungus diseases, the effect of an anti-mildew spray is entirely preventive; it does not cure the disease, but simply prevents its spread by covering the leaves with a poisonous layer which kills the fungus spores before they have a chance of becoming established in the substance of the leaf. It is, therefore, essential that a spray should be applied generously enough to ensure that the whole of both surfaces of all leaves is covered with the spray; and since the coating is far from permanent, the spraying is best repeated at weekly intervals until the disease disappears. There is obviously no point in applying a spray while it is actually raining, or indeed shortly after—or before—a shower of rain. I hope that those of my readers who are weekend gardeners, and who spray when they can, not when they would, will forgive me for rubbing in this exasperating fact; but it is a fact, none the less. They can, however, take some comfort from the thought that a smart shower does wash off an enormous number of spores from the leaves before they have a chance to germinate. Indeed, Mr. Roy Hay has shown that an automatic device which applies a spray of plain water for one minute out of every hour throughout the twenty-four will keep a bed of roses entirely free from fungus infections.

A systemic mildew fungicide which has been developed in the United States is currently under test and will probably be marketed by the time these words are published. If it fulfils its early promise, the chore of spraying against mildew will become a thing of the past.

BLACK SPOT

This seems to be the most dreaded of all rose diseases. As its name implies, it manifests itself by the appearance of black spots on the leaves, roughly circular in shape and with rather ragged edges, looking like ink blots. These spots multiply, expand and coalesce, until when they have covered a certain proportion of the surface, the leaf shrivels up and falls. *R. foetida*, the Austrian Brier, is particularly susceptible to it, and all its hybrids, including, of course, all our modern Hybrid Teas and floribundas, share this susceptibility. It is, however, quite wrong to accuse this species of having introduced the disease to our gardens, since it also attacks many of the older roses which were introduced many years before the "Pernetianas". Gloire de Dijon can be a martyr to it; the Rosier de Meaux and the so-called *R. dupontii*, which is probably identical with Gerard's Blush Rose, are also attacked. I know of no hybrid rose at all which is actually immune from the disease.

So far as can be seen, the damage caused by this disease is entirely due to the weakening brought about by the loss of effective leaf surface. This, however, can be very serious, and a victim which is totally neglected may well die off altogether in a couple of years. It is true that a plant which has been totally defoliated will put out a new crop of leaves to replace those lost; but it must be remembered that the first leaves to appear in the spring are built up out of the food reserves which have over-wintered in the stems and roots of the plant, and as soon as they have expanded they commence to manufacture more food to support further growth, whereas a plant which loses all its leaves in mid-season has no winter stores to draw on; even though it may appear to have recovered by the end of the season, it may fail to survive until the following spring. It ought to be well fed and watered and generally cosseted during the recovery period, and it may also be a good thing to prune it back a bit, to avoid too much dispersion of effort. It is, of course, very important to guard against a second attack.

As with all fungus diseases, no "cure" is possible once the leaf is invaded. At the first sign of infection, all affected leaves should be picked off and burnt. Do *not* put them on the compost heap. A few years ago, I hardened my heart and took no control measures at all throughout the whole of the flowering season, with the object of seeing what would happen. Three or four plants were infected early in July, and as the season progressed the disease spread to their neighbours, but when I came to sum up at the end of the year, I found that only six plants out of over two hundred had suffered complete defoliation, and that the infection had not spread laterally more than six feet from any one centre of infection, while none of the "patients" failed to survive and flourish the next year. This suggests that there is no compelling need to spray the whole of your rose garden when you discover an isolated case of the disease—though this is a wise precaution if you can spare the time.

The effectiveness of sulphur as a fungicide is clearly demonstrated by the fact that black spot is rare in large towns and industrial areas, where the foliage is constantly contaminated by sulphurous deposits from domestic and factory chimneys. Reports from smokeless zones in large towns which were previously free from the disease seem to indicate that this happy state of affairs no longer holds. In general, however, Captan seems to be the most popular chemical for use against black spot. The extensive trials which have been carried out in the U.S.A. for some years past have clearly shown that it is effective; unfortunately they have also shown that Captan, like its rivals Zineb, Maneb, etc., varies somewhat in efficacy from year to year and from place to place, so that it is impossible to say with any certainty that it, or any other chemical, is undoubtedly the best. The spraying technique is just the same as for mildew: a fine spray, directed to under and upper sides of the leaves, and renewed weekly so long as the disease remains active. Don't be tempted to make up the spray at a greater strength than that recommended by the makers; it will serve no useful purpose, and may cause damage to the plants.

Black spot shows a tendency to reappear in the same places in successive years, though there is difference of opinion as to how it succeeds in over-wintering, some maintaining that the organism survives in infections in the stems, others that fallen leaves act as a reservoir, and yet others that the infection is maintained in the soil. That all fallen leaves should be collected and burnt, together with prunings from infected plants, is the merest common sense; but whether it is worthwhile to apply a spray to one's plants, or to the soil of one's rose beds, in spring must be a matter of opinion. Such a practice is unlikely to do any harm, at least; though as a matter of principle it is perhaps as well not to apply any more poisons to one's garden than one is compelled to.

RUST

The effect of rust is very similar to that of black spot—weakening of the plant through destruction of the leaves—but in appearance it is very different. It takes the form of a rash of bright orange-coloured pimples on the undersides of the leaves, changing colour with the passage of time to dark brown or black. A very similar disease is often found on other plants, such as antirrhinums and hollyhocks, and also on decaying wood, such as pergola-supports and the like, but the rosarian can safely ignore these, which will not spread to his roses. Indeed, the rust which is not infrequently seen on *R. canina* and the understock *R. laxa* is also a strain which does not attack our garden roses. The true enemy is, in fact, comparatively rare; but although not so frequently encountered as black spot it is more to be dreaded, for two reasons. In the first place, since in its earlier stages it is confined to the undersides of the leaves, it is much more likely to escape observation until it is well established; and in the second, being less common than black spot, it has attracted less research, so that few if any of the newer chemical fungicides which have come on to the market in the past twenty years are effective against it. As against that I must confess that I read in an American publication a few years ago that a well-known authority had declared that rust could be effectively controlled by Zineb, and by nothing else; but it was *vox et praeterea nihil.* The method of application is the same as before; there is no need in this case to stress the importance of ensuring that the undersides of the leaves are adequately covered, since the location of the disease makes this obvious.

STEM CANKER

This is perhaps the commonest, though probably the least important, of the major fungus diseases. It reveals itself by the presence of a discoloured band round the stem, brownish or purple in colour, which spreads lengthwise as the fungus encroaches and leads at a later stage to a wrinkling of the outer skin. There is nothing one can do for a stem so attacked but to prune it back to an eye below the infected area. The infected wood cut away should be burnt, as all diseased material should; but this is not an urgent need, as the disease is not nearly so infectious as the other three that we have considered. This is because the spores of the fungus are unable to penetrate the outer skin of the plant except at points where it has already been damaged, perhaps by rubbing against a thorn on another stem or, of course, by a pruning cut. Even so, it is not every wound which becomes infected, by any means; the vast majority of them heal up without complications. There is litttle that one can do to prevent stem canker, and indeed little need for preventive measures. A carelessly-made pruning cut, some distance above an eye, will leave a "snag" projecting which will be, so to speak, "short-circuited" by the new growth springing from the eye, and will weaken and die off, giving an admirable opportunity for the entry of the fungus, which may well spread down past the eye, thus "short-circuiting" the new growth in its turn, with fatal results; but the good rosarian will never prune so carelessly. If the incidence of stem canker should threaten to rise to the proportions of an epidemic, one may take the precaution of sealing off all pruning cuts with shellac, or one of the special dopes offered by the sundriesman for the purpose; but I am happy to say that I have never encountered such a necessity. The good rosarian will keep the blades of his secateurs scrupulously clean at all times, for reasons of self-respect as well as hygiene; it goes without saying that they should be cleaned immediately after cutting through any diseased wood.

One not infrequently hears the name "die-back" applied to this disease; but die-back is not strictly a disease at all, but a loose expression applied to almost any form of gradual dissolution which works its way backwards towards the roots, as the majority of mortal ailments do, whatever the immediate cause.

OTHER DISEASES

There are plenty of other invasive fungi which attack our roses, giving rise to a host of diseases, some of which have been given colloquial names, such as leaf scorch, anthracnose, downy mildew (if you have any contacts with France it is worth remembering that to a French rosarian "le mildiou" is the downy mildew which sometimes attacks our roses under glass, and not the powdery mildew already described), brand canker, etc., while others are only familiar to the mycologist under their jaw-breaking Latin names. They seldom if ever constitute a serious threat in the rose garden, and since there is little or nothing that one can do about them, either in the way of prevention or cure, they are best ignored by anyone but the plant-pathologist. At least one disease—crown gall, a sort of cancerous growth most commonly found at the base of the main stem—is known to be caused by a bacterium; but that knowledge is of small use to the rose grower. If the growth should be situated in such a position that it can safely be cut out (and burnt) that should be done; but if, as is often the case, the whole crown is involved, one should either ignore it and hope for the best, or else dig up and burn the whole plant. It will usually be possible to take a cutting from it if it happens to be specially precious; the bacteria are normally confined to the actual neighbourhood of the gall.

Virus diseases, on the other hand, are in quite a different category. They have been known and studied in other plants for many years, and the fact that they are of considerable importance in such close relatives of the rose as raspberries and strawberries suggests that they may also be found in the rose garden. The study of rose viruses is still in its infancy, but more than one modern authority has hazarded the opinion that the great majority of our roses are probably infected, although many of them display no obvious symptoms. I need hardly point out that our normal pruning practice is ideally designed to spread such an infection once it gains entry to the rose garden. Where visible signs of infection are displayed in a rose, they usually take the form of a general loss of vigour, without any specific lesions on leaves or elsewhere; it is pretty generally accepted nowadays that those older varieties which in the past have been accused of deteriorating through age are simply those more susceptible ones which are suffering from a transmitted virus infection. (This does at least hold out the hope that they can be re-established, as the Lloyd George raspberry and the Royal Sovereign strawberry have been, by a search for virus-free specimens from which a new strain can be propagated under sterile conditions.) In the present state of our knowledge there is nothing that the gardener can do to help or hinder matters; we must leave it all to the experts. But at least we can say this: that since the viruses have had things all their own way hither-to, there are grounds for hoping that future announcements may contain good news rather than bad.

The remaining ailments from which a rose may suffer can all be ascribed in one way or another to defects in environment. These may take the form of a shortage or an excess of some element in the soil, in which case a cure is not only possible, it is simple—the difficulty lies in identifying the particular element which is responsible for the trouble. I shall not enlarge here on what I have already said in Chapter Ten on this subject; it is enough to remind the reader that so long as his roses are intelligently fed they will remain free from these diseases of malnutrition. Water being a plant food, the effects of drought may also be regarded as a case of mal-nutrition; in this case the cause is only too plain; the remedy has also been discussed in Chapter Ten. There is, however, one rose trouble—it cannot be called a disease since its cause is at present unknown—which should be mentioned as it often puzzles rosarians. It is called "rose topple" or *pedi-cel necrosis*. The signs are the appearance of a blackish discoloration on the footstalk of the bud, usually when it is just showing colour; development of the bud ceases, and within a day or so, it wilts as if it has become top-heavy. It seems to affect crimson and red roses more than any other colour and occurs more frequently in a wet summer. It is suspected that it is a deficiency disease, lack of potash being the probable cause. A dressing of sulphate of potash at the rate of three ounces to the square yard when the trouble is noticed, and again the following spring usually prevents a recurrence.

We in this country are blessed with a climate which seldom if ever exceeds what our roses can put up with in the way of heat, while extremes of cold sufficient to do serious damage are also very rare. A rose can easily survive prolonged exposure to fifteen or twenty degrees of frost; frostbite, when it does occur, is more often caused by rapid alternation between cold and warmth. It is quite incurable, but it is not progressive like the fungus disease, so that no great harm will result if you fail to locate and cut out the frosted stems on your rose plants; sooner or later they will fail and die off (or "die back"), but you will have the consolation of knowing that the injury was beyond your control, and that your neglect has not aggravated it. (Nevertheless, a cane which has been weakened by frostbite may well prove more susceptible to fungus diseases, so it is always good practice to cut it out as soon as it is known.) The other common effect of cold is seen in the browning and shrivelling of the edges of the young leaves under the influence of the cold, dry east winds which sometimes persist in April and May, especially in the more eastern districts. There is nothing you can do about this; though as the effect seems to be largely due to the drying effect of these winds, I have often meant to try whether a daily spraying with plain water might not be of good effect. I recommend the experiment to the reader.

Glossary

The majority of these words have already been explained in the text, but the explanations are repeated here for the convenience of the reader. Only those names of colours that are consistently misused in rose descriptions are included.

Abscission layer
A layer of corky cells which grows across a stem and effectively cuts it off from the source of nourishment, thus causing the death and consequent detachment of the part beyond the layer. It is by this means that plants shed their leaves in the autumn.

Anther
The swelling at the tip of a stamen, within which the pollen grains are formed and from which they are shed.

Balling
Of a rose bud, failing to open, so that it dies and rots on the stem; due either to a constitutional weakness or to damage by rain.

Bedegard, Bedeguar
A word of Arabic derivation meaning "wind-brought"; applied by Albertus Magnus to a wild rose, but today to the robin's pincushion.

Blind
A blind shoot is one which does not bear a flower.

Bract
The leafy growth which takes the place of a true leaf at the node immediately below a flower.

Bronze
In ordinary speech this implies a brown colour which is never found in a (healthy) rose; when applied to roses, as it sometimes is, it may mean almost anything.

Budding

The form of grafting in which the scion consists of no more than a single bud, with a small portion of surrounding bark.

Callus

The scar-tissue which grows over a healing wound in a plant.

Carbohydrates

An important class of substances, comprising the sugars, starches and cellulose, made up of carbon, hydrogen and oxygen in such proportions that they might (in theory) be formed from equal parts of carbon and water.

Carmine

Is not the name of a colour but of a pigment, which is prepared from cochineal; its actual colour is a light crimson.

Carnation

The common word for "pink", before the latter word had entered the language.

Carpel

The stigma, style and ovary. The archaic word, pointel is sometimes seen.

Chimaera

A single plant composed of two distinct sorts of tissues.

Chlorophyll

The green pigment which gives its characteristic colour to all plants, and which possesses the power to absorb the energy of sunlight and transform it into chemical energy.

Chlorosis

Strictly speaking, this is a medical term, describing a green tinge in the complexion; but it has been borrowed by the plant world to describe the exact opposite, a lack of green where green ought to be.

Chromosome

One of a number of microscopic bodies in the nucleus of a cell which carry the genes, or units of inheritance.

Cinnabar

Not a colour, but an ore of mercury, of a characteristic scarlet hue.

Cochineal

Not a colour, but an extract from the kermes insect, used for tinting foodstuffs. Its colour is crimson.

Colloids

Substances in an exceptionally fine state of division, from which they derive certain characteristic properties.

Compound, chemical

A substance composed of two or more chemical elements in a state of combination.

Copper

As the name of a colour in roses, this may mean anything from scarlet through orange to salmon-pink.

Cotyledon

An organ which supplies an embryo plant with the reserve supplies of food required for its initial growth. In some plants the cotyledons remain underground, but in roses they appear as the first pair of "seed-leaves" when the seedling emerges.

Crimson lake

Not the name of a colour but of a pigment, prepared from cochineal. Its colour is, of course, crimson. See also *Lake*.

Cutting

A piece of stem, usually six to nine inches in length, which is stuck into the ground in the hope that it will put out roots and grow into a new plant.

Cyanidin

A chemical compound, very variable in colour, which is responsible for the red, purple and blue colours of many plants, including roses.

Cytology

The study of living cells.

Damask

Originally meaning "of the city of Damascus", by Shakespeare's day the word had come to mean "of the colour of a Damask Rose", i.e., pink.

Dioecious

Bearing male and female flowers on separate plants.

R

Diploid

Of chromosomes, twice the basic number, which in roses is seven; hence a diploid rose possesses fourteen chromosomes in its body cells.

Double

Of roses, possessing more than the five petals of the natural flower, the extra petals being formed at the expense of stamens. Between six and about twenty-four petals is sometimes described as semi-double. Fully double implies the possession of the maximum possible number of petals—150 or more—and no stamens at all.

Element, chemical

One of the hundred-odd different substances of which the whole material world is made up. An element is a simple, homogeneous substance, but few of them are commonly found in this form; more usually two or more are combined together to form compounds. Gold, sulphur, oxygen and nitrogen are examples of elements found in the pure, uncombined state; water, salt and chalk are compounds.

Fauna

The whole animal population of a region.

Fertilise

Strictly, "to make fruitful"; hence one may fertilise the soil by adding plant foods, or one may fertilise a flower by applying pollen and so causing the development of the seed.

Fixed

Applied to a colour or climbing mutation which remains stable.

Gamete

A reproductive cell, either male or female.

Gene

A unit of inheritance; that part of a chromosome which is responsible for the presence of a single heritable character. (In practice a single gene may well be responsible for more than one; alternatively, a single character may be due to the presence of a combination of genes.)

Genetics

The study of heredity.

Gold, Golden

As a colour, yellow with a strong admixture of red in its make-up; rarely found in roses.

Guard Petals

The outer petals enclosing a flower bud.

Haploid

Of chromosomes, the number of unpaired chromosomes formed in the gamete (q.v.).

Heptaploid

Of chromosomes, seven times the basic number; in roses, forty-nine.

Hermaphrodite

Bearing flowers each of which possesses both male and female reproductive organs.

Hexaploid

Of chromosomes, six times the basic number; in roses, forty-two.

Hormone

A substance secreted by one organ which causes changes in other parts of the organism.

Hue

The quality which distinguishes one pure colour from another. Every hue gives rise to a whole range of colours, according as it is pure or diluted with white or black or both.

Ion

An electrically-charged particle arising from the dissociation of a molecule in solution.

Inorganic

See *Organic*.

Lake

A lake is a pigment formed by dyeing the otherwise colourless particles of some finely-divided substance. The word has nothing to do with the colour of the pigment so formed.

Lavender

Properly a bluish-mauve, a colour never seen in roses; but the word is commonly applied to any pink rose with a mauve or grey tinge.

Layering

A form of vegetative propagation in which the scion remains attached to the parent plant until it has formed its own roots and can safely be detached.

Leaching

Removing by washing with an excess of water.

Lemon yellow

Properly a yellow hue tending towards green, but used to describe any yellow rose whose colour is very pale.

Lilac

Pinkish-mauve; the most correct description for most modern "blue" roses.

Lime

Properly either quicklime, which is calcium oxide, or slaked lime, which is calcium hydroxide. The former is never used in gardens; the latter may be, but is needlessly expensive; the ordinary lime of gardens is calcium carbonate, in the form of ground chalk or limestone. The word is also used loosely to designate the element calcium in any form.

Maiden

A rose plant in its first year after budding; thereafter it becomes a "cut-back". The distinction is of no importance.

Meiosis

The reducing division whereby the number of chromosomes is halved in the formation of gametes.

Mitosis

The normal mode of cell-division whereby the daughter cells are provided with identical sets of chromosomes to those in the parent cell.

Molecule

The smallest particle of a chemical compound which can exist independently. It consists of two or more atoms semi-permanently bound together in a characteristic pattern.

Monoecious
Having male and female flowers on the same plant.

Mulch
An insulating layer applied to the soil to prevent loss of water by evaporation.

Mutation
A spontaneous inherited change in a gene or chromosome set altering the particular character controlled by that gene or chromosome pattern. In roses, this is usually the petal colour or habit of growth.

Mycology
The study of fungi.

Node
The point in a stem from which a leaf, and subsequently a bud, springs.

Octoploid
Of chromosomes, eight times the basic number; in roses, fifty-six.

Orange
Commonly used to describe the colour scarlet in roses.

Orange-scarlet
Used as an admission that the word orange alone is a quite false description of a scarlet rose.

Organic
Of fertilisers, derived from living substance. Organic fertilisers, however, require to be reduced to an inorganic form before the plant can make use of them.

Ovule
The female gamete, which develops into a seed after fertilisation by a male gamete or pollen cell.

Pentaploid
Of chromosomes, five times the basic number; in roses, thirty-five.

Periclinal
Of chimaeras, one in which one form of tissue forms the whole outer layer of the plant, enclosing the other. In a perfect periclinal chimaera the outer tissue wholly determines the appearance of the plant.

Pillar rose

A moderate climber, suited for training up a pillar.

Pistil

The style or female reproductive organ in the centre of a flower.

Pollen

The fine yellow or whitish dust secreted by the anthers. Each grain of pollen contains a pollen cell, the male gamete.

Pollination

The application of pollen to the stigma of a flower, thereby effecting fertilisation. When left to the unaided forces of Nature it is called "open" pollination, and normally (though not invariably) results in "selfing".

Potash

Properly, potassium carbonate, originally derived from wood-ashes; but the word is loosely used to denote the element potassium in any form.

Propagation

The multiplication of plants by various means. See *Vegetative*.

Proteins

A class of very complex chemical compounds, characteristic of all living matter.

Purple

Commonly used to describe any colour intermediate between red and blue. But the original Tyrian purple dye, which produced the imperial purple of the Roman emperors, was actually red.

Remontance

The property of yielding more than one crop of flowers—perpetual flowering.

Reversion

A return to any former state; generally applied to a mutation or sport; often loosely termed "sporting back".

Rose

As a colour, this word always meant red, like a red rose. In most European languages except English, *rose* or *rosa* means pink. The word rose-pink is quite a newcomer to the English language.

Rubbing-out
Removing unwanted buds by breaking them off with the fingers.

Scarlet
A bright red colour inclining towards orange, but entirely distinct from it.

Scion
A part of a plant which gives rise to a new one by vegetative propagation.

Seedling
A plant grown from seed. The expression "a seedling of" (or "from") "such-and-such a variety" is very loosely used to mean (a) a self-seedling, i.e., one in which the same variety acted as both seed and pollen parent; (b) a seedling obtained by open pollination, which may be a self-seedling or may not; and (c) a seedling raised from a seed of that variety irrespective of the source of pollen.

Selfing
Fertilising a flower with its own pollen.

Semi-climber
A climber of moderate growth.

Semi-double
See *Double*.

Sepals
Leaf-like extensions to the calyx and enclosing the flower bud; in roses they are five in number.

Sessile
Of flowers, having so short a stalk that it appears to sit directly on the stem from which it springs.

Silver
A meaningless word implying some light shade of pink.

Single
Of flowers, having only one row of petals, comprising five in all rose species except *R. sericea*, which has only four.

Solitary
Of flowers, borne one to a stem.

Somatic

Of plant cells, those comprising the body of the plant, i.e., all except the reproductive cells or gametes.

Spit

The earth raised by one stroke of a spade. As a measure of depth in digging it is usually reckoned at about nine inches.

Sport

The popular term in gardening for a mutation (q.v.).

Stamen

The male reproductive organ of a flower, surrounding the style or female organ.

Stigma

The swelling at the tip of a style, which receives the pollen.

Stipule

The leafy process which grows along the side of a leaf-stalk at the point where it joins the parent stem.

Stock

See *Understock*.

Strike

Of cuttings, to form roots and grow.

Take

In budding, a bud which survives and develops is said to "take".

Taxonomy

The science of classification.

Tetraploid

Of chromosomes, four times the basic number; in roses, twenty-eight.

Triploid

Of chromosomes, three times the basic number; in roses, twenty-one.

Understock

A vigorous and easily-propagated variety of rose on to which other varieties are grafted or budded. The term, rootstock, is synonymous.

Vegetative propagation

The multiplication of plants by the removal of small parts of them, which are induced to grow independently by various means.

Velvet

In rose descriptions, usually implies a deep colour.

Vermiculite

A granular mineral used as a soil conditioner, owing to its great ability to retain moisture.

Vermilion

Not a colour, but an artist's pigment prepared from cinnabar. Its colour is scarlet.

Wilting Point

The state of a soil at which no further water can be made available to the plants growing in it.

Xanthophyll

The natural pigment responsible for the yellow colours in roses and autumn leaves.

Zygote

A reproductive cell after fertilisation, containing the full chromosome complement from both the ovum and pollen cell.

INDEX

INDEX

Rose species are listed under *Rosa*; varietal names under Rose varieties

Principal rose raisers and hybridists cited in the text

Nineteenth century

Béluze, Jean; Lyons, France
Bennett, Henry; Shepperton, England
Bonnet, Gustave; Nantes, France
Bruant, Georges; Poitiers, France
Cochet-Cochet, Charles; Coubert, France
Cranston, John; Hereford, England
Descemet, M.; Saint-Denis, France
Desportes, Narcisse; Paris, France
Desprez; Yèbles, France
*Dickson, Alex. and Sons; Newtownards, Northern Ireland
*Ducher, Veuve (Widow); Lyons, France
Guillot *fils* (Jean-Baptiste); Monplaisir, Lyons, France
Hardy, M.; Luxembourg Gardens, Paris, France
Jacques, A. A.; Neuilly, France
Lacharme, François; Lyons, France
Laffay, M.; Auteuil and Bellevue, France
Margottin, Jules; Bourg-la-Reine, France
Nabonnand, Gilbert; Golfe Juan, France
Parmentier, Louis; Enghien, Belgium
Paul, George and Son; Cheshunt, England
Paul, William and Son Ltd.; Waltham Cross, England
Penzance, Lord; Eashing Park, Godalming, England
*Pernet-Ducher, Joseph; Venissieux-les-Lyon, France
Roeser; Crécy-en-Brie, France
Schwartz, Joseph and Widow; Lyons, France
Vibert, Jean Pierre; Angers, France

Twentieth century

Barbier and Co.; Orléans, France
Boerner, Eugene S.; Newark, New York, U.S.A.
*Cant, Benjamin R.; Colchester, England
Dawson, Jackson; Arnold Arboretum, Jamaica Plain, Mass., U.S.A.
*De Ruiter, Geo.; Hazerwoude, Holland
De Vink, Jan; Boskoop, Holland
*Dicksons of Hawlmark; Newtownards, Northern Ireland
*Dot, Pedro; San Feliu de Llobregat, Barcelona, Spain

Easlea, Walter; Leigh on Sea, England
Horvath, Michael; Mentor, Ohio, U.S.A.
*Jackson and Perkins; Newark, New York (now Newport Beach, Calif.), U.S.A.
*Kordes, Wilhelm and Sons; Sparrieshoop, Holstein, Germany
Lambert, Peter; Trier, Germany
*Le Grice, E. B.; North Walsham, England
Levavasseur, Ernest and Sons; Orléans, France
Manda, W. A.; South Orange, New Jersey, U.S.A.
*McGredy, Samuel and Son,; Portadown, Northern Ireland
Meilland, Francis; Tassin-les-Lyon and Cap d'Antibes, France
*Meilland, Louisette and Alain; Cap d'Antibes, France
*Moore, Ralph; Visalia, California, U.S.A.
Müller, Dr. Franz; Weingarten, Germany
Nabonnand, Philippe; Golfe Juan, France
Nonin, Auguste and Sons; Châtillon, near Paris, France
Paul, George and Son (as above)
Paul, William and Son (as above)
Pemberton, Rev. Joseph H.; Havering-atte-Bower, England
*Pernet-Ducher, Joseph; Venissieux-les-Lyon, France
Poulsen, Dines; Kvistgaard, Denmark
*Poulsen, Svend; Copenhagen, Denmark
*Tantau, Mathias; Uetersen, Holstein, Germany
Turbat, E. and Co.; Orléans, France
Van Fleet, Dr. Walter; Glenn Dale, Maryland, U.S.A.
Walsh, M. H.; Woods Hole, Massachusetts, U.S.A.

* Raiser or successors still active.